Impact GRAMMAR

GRAMMAR THROUGH LISTENING

Rod Ellis
Stephen Gaies

Series Editor
Michael Rost

LONGMAN

Published by
Addison Wesley Longman Asia ELT
2nd Floor, Cornwall House
Taikoo Place
979 King's Road
Quarry Bay
Hong Kong
fax: +852 2856 9578
e-mail: aelt@awl.com.hk
website: www.awl-elt.com

and Associated Companies throughout the world.

This book was developed for Addison Wesley Longman Asia ELT by Lateral Communications Ltd., USA.

First published 1999
Produced by Addison Wesley Longman China Ltd., Hong Kong
SWTC/01

Project director: Michael Rost

Project coordinator: Keiko Kimura

Production coordinator: Eric Yau

Text design: Keiko Kimura

Cover design: Lori Margulies, Keiko Kimura

Content editor: Terre Passero

Illustrations: Mark Ziemann

Photographs: Shooting Star, Rubberball Productions, Fox Images, PhotoDisc, Ken Kitamura, Diamar Portfolios

Recording supervisor: David Joslyn

The
publisher's
policy is to use
paper manufactured
from sustainable forests

ACKNOWLEGEMENTS

The editors and authors would like to thank the following individuals for their assistance with the research, development, piloting and reviews of *Impact Grammar*:
Jennifer Altman, Masahiko Anabuki, Luis Barientos, Marvin Greene, Scott Grinthal, Koji Igawa, Kazuko Kudo, Monica Merino, Masako Morita, Masanori Nishi, Yasuko Ohmi, Linda O'Roke, Amy Parker, William Passero, Jackie Pels, Mark Sawyer, Sonia Solís, Tadakuni Tajiri, Masahiro Tanaka, Akemi Tsuji, Shoichi Tsuji, Naoko Tsujioka, Marcel van Amelsvort, and Masako Yamada.

We would also like to thank the staff of Addison Wesley Longman for their support of the project. In particular, we wish to thank: Dugie Cameron, Chris Balderston, Joanne Dresner, Wong Wee Woon, Andrew Yeo, Anne Boynton-Trigg, Kate Lowe, Mieko Otaka, Gregg Schroeder, Sandra Pike, Craig Zettle, and Katsuhiro Kawahara.

ISBN 962 00 1428 6

Impact GRAMMAR

Impact Grammar is an innovative textbook for students who wish to improve their knowledge of English grammar. The book, with its accompanying audio CD, is designed to be used as a classroom text or for self-study.

Impact Grammar consists of 50 units. Each unit focusses on a particular grammatical point that is known to be problematic for second language learners. The 50 units are divided into five levels, reflecting the general difficulty of the grammar points. *Impact Grammar* provides a thorough coverage of the most problematic areas of grammar for second language learners.

Key features:

1 **50 units of key grammar points, organized into five levels of difficulty**
The Table of Contents and the Index will help you identify the units you want to use.

> LEVEL ◇ ◆ ◆ ◆ ◆

2 **2-page units, each containing five carefully sequenced exercises**
The exercises guide students through this sequence: Comprehending (with use of the audio CD), Noticing, Understanding the Grammar Point, Checking, and Trying out the Grammar Point. Each unit requires about 50 minutes of classroom time.

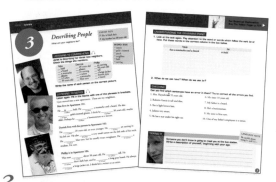

3 **An audio CD that contains the passages for each unit**

These segments, needed for the Comprehending and Noticing sections of each unit, can be cued and repeated as often as needed. (Tracks 1-50 correspond to the units in the book.)

4 **Grammar Explanation**
(the "Yellow Pages") in the back of the book with concise grammar guides, clear examples and common errors of the grammatical point of each unit.

5 **Review Tests for each of the five levels**
These can be used to check students' understanding of the grammar points in context.

6 **A complete Answer Key which contains tape scripts and answers for all exercises**

This section is perforated so that it can be removed.

Students at all levels can use *Impact Grammar* to improve their grammar, and thereby become more confident and effective at communicating in English.

Impact Grammar draws upon current research in second language acquisition:

1 *The need to attend to both meaning and form when learning a second language*
Impact Grammar guides students to process a passage for meaning and then to attend to how a particular grammatical form is used in that text. Thus, both learning needs are addressed. All of the units in *Impact Grammar* provide extended passages (dialogues and monologues) to illustrate the meanings of the grammatical points in context.

2 *The importance of learning grammar through comprehending input*
Learning grammar through listening will help learners process the grammar in real time — which is exactly what they need to do to acquire the grammar. Thus, in addition to teaching grammar, *Impact Grammar* also provides practice in listening. It is a two-in-one textbook.

3 *The role of awareness in helping learners slowly and gradually acquire grammatical features*
Awareness facilitates and triggers learning. *Impact Grammar* acknowledges this by leading students to an awareness of how grammatical features work in real language texts. In *Impact Grammar* learners are treated as active thinkers who can be challenged to work with evidence and formulate rules themselves.

4 *The need for opportunities for personal expression*
Personal expression helps to consolidate learning. Each unit in *Impact Grammar* provides opportunities for personalized output that help to make the learning of grammatical structures more meaningful and more memorable.

TO THE TEACHERS

You can work through the units systematically, or you can use the book remedially by selecting units to address particular grammar problems.

The units are designed to be easy to use, without a teacher's manual. Each unit requires about 50 minutes of classroom time with a typical class, although some sections can be assigned as homework.

Here are the basic procedures for the five main sections:

LISTENING TO COMPREHEND
Go over the warm-up questions to introduce the topic. Then elicit descriptions of the pictures to help set the context for the unit. Check the Word Box to be sure that the students are familiar with this key vocabulary. Play the audio CD or read the passage (the script is in the answer key section). The learners are to listen to a short contextualized passage (about a minute long) and try to understand the general meaning of the text. There is a short comprehension task to help learners understand and check the meaning.

LISTENING TO NOTICE
Learners next listen to the same text again in order to focus attention on how the target grammar point of the unit works in the text. Again there is a focusing task to help learners with this noticing phase. Learners can try to fill in the blanks first and then listen to confirm their answers. You can repeat the audio as often as needed, until the learners can hear the grammatical distinction.

UNDERSTANDING THE GRAMMAR POINT
Learners now provide a short analysis of a grammar contrast in the text. Through this analysis task, learners are guided to see how the grammar point works and to formulate a grammar rule. (It is not essential that the learners can articulate the rules and principles in precise English, as long as they demonstrate an understanding of the grammar point.) Allow time for the learners to go through these questions individually or in pairs. Then go over the questions with the class. Finally, look at the Yellow Pages (Grammar Explanation) in the back of the book to introduce further examples and to review common errors.

CHECKING

Learners check their understanding of the grammar rule by completing a short exercise with a new set of sentences or short texts. Again, learners can work individually or in pairs. Answers should be checked with the whole class. (You may wish to have the learners remove the perforated Answer Key pages from the book to prevent them from looking at the answers in advance.)

TRYING IT

In this final part of the unit, learners have an opportunity to try out the grammatical rule with sentences of their own. This short communicative activity will allow you to see whether the learners can use the grammar point correctly.

TO THE STUDENT

You can use this book by yourself or in class with other students. Here are some ideas to help you when you use it by yourself:

(1) Look in the Table of Contents to find a grammar point you want to practice.
(2) Look at the Error Box at the beginning of each unit. Can you correct the errors? If you have trouble finding the errors, try that unit.

After you choose a unit, try each section in order.

LISTENING TO COMPREHEND

This exercise introduces you to the topic. In this section, just focus on getting the meaning. Listen to the CD. You will hear a dialogue, an announcement, a letter, a lecture, a news item or a story. Try to get the main idea. Look up the words in the "Word Box" if you need to. Listen to the CD several times, until you can do the activity.

LISTENING TO NOTICE

This exercise focuses on the grammar point of the unit. First, read the text and try to fill in the missing words. Then listen to the text on the CD again. This time, listen for the missing words. Write the correct words in the blanks. Listen again until you can hear the missing words clearly. Check your answers in the Answer Key at the back of the book.

UNDERSTANDING THE GRAMMAR POINT

This section helps you understand the grammar point and build rules about the grammar of English. Read the directions carefully. Usually, you have to look back at the Listening to Notice section to complete the exercise. Check your answers in the Answer Key at the back of the book.

CHECKING

This section helps you find out whether you have understood the grammar point. While you are working, you may check the Grammar Explanation section (the "Yellow Pages") if necessary.

TRYING IT

This section gives you a chance to practice the grammar point using your own ideas.

We hope you will enjoy using Impact Grammar! Remember: Improving your grammar will make you sound more like a native speaker and will improve your confidence and communication ability.

CONTENTS

LEVEL ONE ◇◆◆◆◆

1 Pronouns: *He, She, It*
At Work

2 *There is/There are*
What's in the Room?

3 *Be* vs. *Have*
Describing People

4 Present Continuous and Simple Present Tenses
Holiday Postcards

5 *Do/Does* in *Yes/No* Questions
Married Life

6 Negatives: *No* vs. *Not*
About People

7 Plural Nouns
Islands in Paradise

8 Countable vs. Uncountable Nouns
Summer Sale

9 Determiners with Nouns
A Shopping Trip

10 *Be* in *Yes/No* Questions
At the Zoo

Level 1 Review Tests

LEVEL TWO ◇◇◆◆◆

11 Stative Verbs
A Visit to the Doctor

12 Simple Past Tense
Great Musicians

13 Prepositions in Expressions of Time
Making an Appointment

14 Prepositions of Location and Direction
Weekend Activities

15 Adjectives vs. Adverbs
Newspaper Stories

16 *Yes/No* Questions in the Simple Past Tense
A Terrible Holiday

17 Transitive vs. Intransitive Verbs
A Year in Madison

18 Subject-Verb Agreement with Simple Present Tense
Movie Listings

19 Present Perfect for Indefinite Past
Job Interviews

20 *Wh-* Questions
The Babysitter

Level 2 Review Tests

If you are using the *Impact* Coursebooks, try these units in *Impact Grammar*:

Impact Intro	Impact Grammar	First Impact	Impact Grammar	High Impact	Impact Grammar
1	1 Pronouns: *He, She, It*	1	27 Modals of Possibility	1	45 Pro-forms: *Too, So, Either, Neither*
2	9 Determiners with Nouns	2	41 Adjectives and Nouns Ending in *-y*	2	35 Verb Complements
3	21 Adverb Position	3	12 Simple Past Tense	3	1 Pronouns: *He, She, It*
4	14 Prepositions of Location and Direction	4	23 Comparative and Superlative of Forms of Adjectives	4	4 Present Continuous and Simple Present Ter
5	4 Present Continuous and Simple Present Tenses	5	20 *Wh-* Questions	5	19 Present Perfect for Indefinite Past
6	7 Plural Nouns	6	37 Participial Adjectives	6	41 Adjectives and Nouns Ending in *-y*
7	46 *Too* vs. *Enough*	7	1 Pronouns: *He, She, It*	7	7 Plural Nouns
8	27 Modals of Possibility	8	8 Countable vs. Uncountable Nouns	8	30 Simple Past and Past Continuous
9	12 Simple Past Tense	9	3 *Be* vs. *Have*	9	35 Verb Complements
10	38 Simple Present Tense for Future Time	10	10 *Be* in *Yes/No* Questions	10	18 Subject-Verb Agreement with Simple Present T
11	8 Countable vs. Uncountable Nouns	11	18 Subject-Verb Agreement with Simple Present Tense	11	37 Participial Adjectives
12	20 *Wh-* Questions	12	31 Unique Reference With and Without *The*	12	43 Passive Voice in the Simple Present Tense

LEVEL FOUR ◆

31 Unique Reference With and Without *The*
Famous Modern Buildings

32 The Indefinite Article *A*
True Stories

33 The Definite Article *The*
Fantastic Toys

34 *Other, The Other, Another*
Brothers and Sisters

35 Verb Complements
Valentine's Day Messages

36 *Let* vs. *Make*
Working Relationships

37 Participial Adjectives
A Personal Problem

38 Simple Present Tense for Future Time
Mission in Space

39 Possible vs. Hypothetical Conditionals
Summer Plans

40 Hypothetical vs. Unreal Conditionals
Life Choices

Level 4 Review Tests

LEVEL THREE ◆◆

21 Adverb Position
Hobbies

22 *Few/A Few, Little/A Little*
Weather Forecast

23 Comparative and Superlative Forms of Adjectives
Quiz Show

24 *Like* and *As*
Animal Idioms

25 Comparative Expressions with Prepositions
European Cities

26 *There is* vs. *It is*
Following Directions

27 Modals of Possibility
Alzheimer's Disease

28 Modals of Obligation and Necessity
A Trip to Russia

29 Present Perfect with *For* and *Since*
Letters of Reference

30 Simple Past and Past Continuous
The Sad Story of Miss Leeson

Level 3 Review Tests

LEVEL FIVE ◆

41 Adjectives and Nouns Ending in *-y*
Personal Opinions

42 Past Perfect with *By* and *Already*
Admirable People

43 Passive Voice in the Simple Present Tense
Computer Care

44 Process Verbs
Dreams

45 Pro-forms: *Too, So, Either, Neither*
Where Should We Go?

46 *Too* vs. *Enough*
Moving In

47 Embedded Questions
Travel Club

48 Relative Clauses with *Which* and *That*
Special Dishes

49 Relative Clauses with *Where* and *When*
A Wedding in Paradise

50 Relative Clauses with *Whose*
Book Notices

Level 5 Review Tests

GRAMMAR EXPLANATION YELLOW PAGES — pages 119 - 144

ANSWERS KEYS & INDEX — pages 145 - 172

At Work

Do you have a job?
What do you do?

LISTENING TO COMPREHEND

Mr. Lim is describing the people in his company. Write *Ms.* **or** *Mr.* **before each name. What position does each person have?**

Employee	Position
_____ Leslie Williams	*technical manager*
_____ Sydney Mills	_____
_____ Anil Chaudari	_____
_____ Jun Kim	_____

WORD BOX
* a technical manage
* a senior programm
* an office secretary
* a sales representativ

LISTENING TO NOTICE

Listen again. Fill in the blanks with *he, she,* **or** *it.*

Hello. I'm the president of Soft World. _____*It*_____'s the world's best computer
                                          1
software company. Let me introduce you to the great team of people who
work for Soft World.

Leslie Williams is our technical manager. When there's a problem with new
software, _____ finds a solution. I think _____'s a genius.
              2   3

Sydney Mills is our senior programmer. _____'s a software wiz.
                                              4
_____ 's from New Zealand. That's where she started designing and
      5
writing software programs. Sydney began working here last year; _____
                                                                     6
thinks _____'s the best place she has ever worked.
            7

Anil Chaudari is our sales representative. _____ joined the company
                                                    8
two years ago. We call him "Language Man"; _____ speaks five
                                                9
languages fluently.

Then there's Jun Kim. _____'s the office secretary. _____'s a really
                              10   11
important job. _____ knows everything; his brain is just like a computer.
                  12
We're a great team.

For Grammar Explanation, See The Yellow Pages p.120 ▶

UNDERSTANDING THE GRAMMAR POINT

1. Find the words *he*, *she*, and *it* in Mr. Lim's speech. Write the word or words that *he*, *she*, or *it* replaces.

he replaces:	*she* replaces:	*it* replaces:
		Soft World

2. Complete the following statements about how to use *he*, *she*, and *it*:

- We use _____ to refer to males.
- We use _____ to refer to females.
- We use _____ to refer to things or ideas.

3. Why are these sentences incorrect?

✗ My sister bought a new car two weeks ago, and he has already had an accident.

✗ I took a book out from the library last week, but I have not started reading him.

CHECKING

Which of these sentences contain an error? Correct the errors.

1. My brother is five years younger than me. *He is* ~~Is~~ an engineer.

2. My sister lives in Hong Kong. She is a computer programmer.

3. My father is a journalist. He has done many assignments for foreign newspapers.

4. My friend Carlos is a real estate agent. He owns his own agency. Is located in downtown Los Angeles.

5. His wife is a well-known psychologist. He works mostly with children and teenagers.

6. My neighbor started a catering business in 1994. He has grown a lot in the last several years.

7. My grandfather came to the United States when he was eight years old. By the time he was 20, she was a successful businessman.

8. My daughter is a buyer for a large department store. He spends a lot of time in other countries.

TRYING IT

LANGUAGE NOTE
Use the pronouns he, she, it.

Describe the jobs of the people you work with. OR Describe the jobs of the people in your family.

My father is a _____. He _____.

My mother is a _____. She _____.

My brother is a _____. He likes his job. It _____.

2

What's in the Room?

Do you live in a house or an apartment?
What is in your room?

LISTENING TO COMPREHEND

Listen to Mr. Wolf, Ms. Strain, and Mr. Stone describe rooms in their homes. Check the things they mention.

Mr. Stone	Ms. Strain	Mr. Wolf
✔ some chairs	__ a table	__ a table
__ a sink	__ a computer	__ some chairs
__ a table	__ a violin	__ a pair of gloves
__ sunglasses	__ some dishes	__ a cup
__ some books	__ some water	__ a camera

Which person might be a private investigator? a music professor? a magician?

LISTENING TO NOTICE

Listen again. Fill in the blanks with *there's (there is)* or *there are*.

Mr. Stone: *There are* three chairs around a table. _____ a black cat
on the table. _____ some things on the counter to the right of the sink:
a false beard and a mustache, a bottle of hair coloring, and a pair of sunglasses.
_____ a couple of magazines on the table, and _____ a stuffed rabbit next to them.

Ms. Strain: _____ two chairs but no table. On one of the chairs
_____ a laptop computer; on the other _____ a violin.
_____ a clock over the sink, and _____ dishes piled up in the sink.
Oh, and _____ several books on the counter next to the refrigerator.
And _____ some water on the floor.

Mr. Wolf: In the kitchen _____ a large, heavy wooden table.
_____ six chairs neatly arranged around the table. _____ nothing
at all on the table, but _____ a lot of things on the counter on either side
of the sink: a pair of women's long evening gloves, a small cassette recorder, a
camera, and opera glasses. _____ a toy fire engine on the floor.

UNDERSTANDING THE GRAMMAR POINT

1. Look at the descriptions again. Circle the word or words following *there's* and *there are*. Write those words below.

there's ...	there are ...
a black cat	*three chairs*

2. What kind of noun follows *there's*? What kind of noun follows *there are*?

CHECKING

Linda is describing her bedroom. Fill in the blanks with *there's* or *there are*.

We live in a large old house. ___*There are*___ several rooms I like to spend time in, but my favorite room is my
                                        1

bedroom. Let me describe it for you. When you walk in the room, _____ a dresser along the wall on
                                                                              2

the left. Above the dresser _____ three Chinese silk paintings of birds. Straight ahead is my bed.
                                  3

_____ lots of pillows on it, and _____ a nightstand on either side of the bed. Nearby _____
      4   5   6

an antique coat tree that belonged to my grandfather. _____ always several shirts and other things on it.
                                                              7

_____ a fireplace on the wall on the right. Even though it doesn't work, _____ logs in it, just for
      8   9

decoration. _____ also a couple of upholstered chairs in the room.
                  10

LANGUAGE NOTE
Use there is and
there are.

TRYING IT

**Describe a room in your home or apartment.
What's in it? What's on the walls?**

....

....

....

3 *Describing People*

What are your neighbors like?

WORD BOX
* tattoo
* gold- rimmed
* patch
* neighbor
* bald
* earring

LISTENING TO COMPREHEND

Janet is describing her three new neighbors.
Check the things she mentions.

Max	Derrick	Phillip
__ bald	__ 20 years old	__ an earring
__ a beard	__ glasses	__ 50 years old
__ a mustache	__ an earring	__ tall
__ glasses	__ a tattoo	__ a beige jacket
__ a T-shirt	__ a mustache	__ brown eyes
__ 30 years old	__ blue eyes	__ a beard

Write the name of each person on the correct picture.

LISTENING TO NOTICE

Listen again. Fill in the blanks with one of the phrases in brackets.

I just moved into a new apartment. These are my neighbors.

Max lives in Apartment 101.

He ___*is*___ bald. He _____ a mustache and a beard. He also
        1 (is/has)   2(is/has)
_____ gold-rimmed glasses. I think he _____ 30 years old, maybe
3 (is/has)   4 (is/has)
older. Perhaps he _____ a businessman or a lawyer.
                   5 (is/has)

Derrick lives with his parents in Apartment 103.

He _____ 20 years old, or even younger. He _____ an earring in
   6 (is/has)   7 (is/has)
his left ear. He also _____ a very small tattoo on the left side of his neck.
                      8 (is/has)
He _____ blue eyes, but he usually wears sunglasses. He _____ a
   9 (is/has)   10 (is/has)
student, I'm sure.

Phillip is in Apartment 104.

This man _____ about 50 years old. He _____ tall. He
         11 (is/has)   12 (is/has)
_____ short dark hair, and he _____ a long gray beard. He always
13 (is/has)   14 (is/has)
_____ a beige jacket on. I think he's a writer or an artist.
15 (is/has)

UNDERSTANDING THE GRAMMAR POINT

1. Look at the text again. Pay attention to the word or words which follow the verb *be* or *have*. Put these words in the correct column in the box below.

have	be
has a mustache and a beard	*is bald*

2. When do we use *have*? When do we use *be*?

CHECKING

Can you find which sentences have an error in them? Try to correct all the errors you find.

1. Mrs. Hayashi ~~has~~ *is* 55 years old.

2. Roberto Garcia is tall and thin.

3. She is light brown hair.

4. Juliana very smart.

5. He has a scar under his right ear.

6. My sister 10 years old.

7. My father is a beard.

8. He's a businessman.

9. My sister is blue eyes.

10. One of my father's employees is a tattoo.

TRYING IT

LANGUAGE NOTE
Be careful about using be and have.

Someone you don't know is going to meet you at the bus station. Write a description of yourself, beginning with your age.

....
....
....
....
....

3

Holiday Postcards

Where do you like to go on holiday?
What do you like to do?

LISTENING TO COMPREHEND

Brad and Gloria are on holiday. Listen to them read their postcards.

1. Where is Brad?
   a. at a jazz festival
   b. on an island
   c. in California

2. Where is Gloria?
   a. in Paris
   b. in London
   c. by the sea

WORD BOX
*nightlife
*jealous
*rush
*seafood

LISTENING TO NOTICE

Listen again. Fill in the blanks with a form of the verb in parentheses ( ).

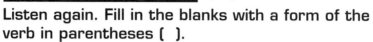

This is the life! Every morning I _____ breakfast by the pool.
1 (have)
Then I _____ for a walk along
2 (go)
the beach or into town. In the afternoon I usually _____ a trip
3 (take)
somewhere on the island. In the
evening I _____ the nightlife.
4 (enjoy)
At the moment I _____ to some
5 (listen)
great jazz. Jealous? You should be!

Brad

Remember George Rush from London? Well, surprise, surprise, he _____ at the same hotel for a
6 (stay)
few days. We _____ a great
7 (have)
time. He _____ me all the best
8 (show)
places in Paris. Well, I must rush now.
We _____ out to this new
9 (go)
seafood restaurant right now. I
_____ you always.
10 (love)

Gloria

**For Grammar Explanation,
See The Yellow Pages p.121** ▶

UNDERSTANDING THE GRAMMAR POINT

1. Look at the postcards again.
   a. Circle all the verbs in the simple present tense.　Ⓘhave
   b. Underline all the verbs in the present continuous tense.　I <u>am listening</u>.

2. Find these adverbials in the postcards.

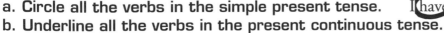

   • every morning　• in the afternoon　•ʼat the moment　• usually
   • for a few days　• in the evening　• always　• now

3. Write the adverbials in the correct column.

Simple Present	Present Continuous
every morning	
usually	

CHECKING

**Can you correct
the errors in this
holiday postcard?**

Dear Daniel,

At the moment I am sitting in a little restaurant in Copacabana. It is late and
the sun ~~just begins~~ *is just beginning* to set. I am watch some teenagers. They playing volleyball on
the beach. A middle-aged man is jogging past my table. Every day I am coming to
the same restaurant. I am eating a light meal — just a salad or some fish — and
drinking a glass of wine. Sometimes I chat with the waiter. He is telling me about
his young boy and I tell him about you. Life is almost perfect, except, of course,
you are not here!

Love always,
Laura

> **LANGUAGE NOTE**
> Use some of the
> adverbials (every
> morning, always,
> now) and the present
> continuous or simple
> present tenses.

TRYING IT

Imagine you are on holiday. Write a postcard to a friend.
Tell your friend what you are doing at the moment and what
you do every day. Try to make the person wish he or she was with you!

....

....

....

5

Married Life

Who should do the housework — husbands or wives?

What kind of housework do you do?

LISTENING TO COMPREHEND

Jill and Beth are talking about their husbands, Jim and Steve. Listen to their conversation. Write *Yes* or *No* in the table.

	JIM	STEVE
... helps with the kids	*Yes*	*No*
... washes the dishes.		
... does the ironing.		
... goes out with his wife for dinner.		
... talks about things with his wife.		

LISTENING TO NOTICE

Listen to the conversation again. Fill in the missing words.

Beth: What's Jim like? __*Does*__ he __*help*__ with the kids?
₁

Jill: All the time. What about Steve? _____ he _____ with the kids?
₂

Beth: Never. He's out with his friends all the time.

Jill: What about around the house? _____ Steve sometimes _____ the dishes?
₃

Beth: Nope. What about Jim?

Jill: Yes, on the weekends. _____ Steve _____ any ironing?
₄

Beth: You must be joking! _____ Jim?
₅

Jill: Well, no. But I don't mind. I find ironing relaxing.

Beth: _____ you sometimes _____ out for dinner together?
₆

Jill: No, never! Jim says he likes my cooking too much.

Beth: We often go out together.

Jill: Lucky you! _____ you _____ about things with Steve a lot?
₇
_____ you _____ about problems and all that?
₈

Beth: Yeah, Steve's a great talker.

Jill: I can hardly get a word out of Jim.

For Grammar Explanation, See The Yellow Pages p.122 ▶

UNDERSTANDING THE GRAMMAR POINT

1. Write *S* next to each statement. Write *Q* next to each question. Write in a question mark (?) at the end of each question. Write in a period (.) at the end of each statement.

_____ 1. Does Jim help with the kids _____
_____ 2. Jim helps with the kids _____
_____ 3. Does Steve wash the dirty plates _____
_____ 4. Steve washes the dirty plates _____
_____ 5. Does Steve do the ironing _____

_____ 6. Steve does not do the ironing _____
_____ 7. Do you sometimes go out to dinner with Jim _____
_____ 8. Jim never goes out to dinner with me _____
_____ 9. Do you sometimes talk about things with Steve _____
_____ 10. Steve and I often talk about things _____

2. **How can you tell which sentence is a statement and which one is a question?**

3. **Which of the questions begin with *does*? Which ones begin with *do*? When should you use *does*? When should you use *do*?**

CHECKING

All of these sentences have errors. Correct the errors.

1. ~~Does~~ *Do* you like watching television with your husband?

2. Do your wife have a job outside the home?

3. You do go on vacation with your husband?

4. Does your wife does the gardening?

5. Do you and your wife cooking together?

6. Does your husband cleans the house?

7. Do your husband wash and iron clothes?

8. Does you and your wife have dinner parties?

9. Does you sometimes cook a special meal?

10. You and your husband does the shopping together?

TRYING IT

1. You are thinking of dating someone.
   Write three questions you would like to ask him/her.

   ....

2. Your friend is engaged to marry someone.
   Ask your friend some questions about his or her husband- or wife-to-be.

   ....

LANGUAGE NOTE
Use Does he . . . ?
Does she . . . ?
Do you . . . ?

About People

What kind of person are you? Are you lazy? busy? amusing?

LISTENING TO COMPREHEND

Listen to the crossword clues about people. Complete the crossword using the words in the box.

WORD BOX

ACROSS:
*lazy   *calm
*boring   *busy
*dead

DOWN:
*happy   *awake
*broke   *amusing
*naughty

LISTENING TO NOTICE

Listen again. Fill in the blanks with *no* or *not*.

Across: 1. He is __*not*__ interesting. He's...

2. She's showing _____ signs of life. She's...

4. He's _____ working. He's...

5. She has _____ free time this week. She's...

9. She is _____ nervous at all. She's...

Down: 1. He's got __*no*__ money. He's...

3. She's got _____ worries at all. She's...

6. He's _____ a dull person. He's...

7. She's _____ a well-behaved child. She's...

8. He's _____ sleeping. He's...

UNDERSTANDING THE GRAMMAR POINT

**1. Circle the word or words following *no* and *not* in the crossword clues.
Write those words in the correct column.**

NOT + adjective	NO + noun
NOT + a + (adjective) + noun	NO + adjective + noun
is + NOT + verb	
not interesting	*no money*

2. These sentences are incorrect. Can you say why?

✗ She is no very rich.

✗ He is not coward.

✗ She is not friend of mine.

✗ She is no talking.

CHECKING

Choose *not* or *no* to complete these sentences.

1. She's got __*no*__ free time this week.

2. He's _____ studying very hard.

3. She's got _____ idea of how to sew a dress.

4. He's _____ anxious to get a job.

5. She's _____ very patient with her friends.

6. He's _____ feeling very well.

7. She's _____ a very thoughtful person.

8. He's _____ very brainy.

9. She's _____ an angel.

10. He's got _____ clean shirts to wear.

TRYING IT

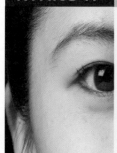

**Think of three people you know well. Write a sentence about
each of them using *no* or *not*.**

....

....

....

IDEA BOX

*personality (kind,
amusing, honest, clever...)

*position (wife, husband,
student, job, money...)

*present activity (working,
studying, dating...)

7 Islands in Paradise

*Would you like to visit an island like Hawaii?
What other places would you like to visit?*

LISTENING TO COMPREHEND

You will hear an advertisement for St. Kitts and Nevis, two islands in the Caribbean. Check (✔) which of the following you can find on these islands.

____ palm trees	____ plantations
____ monkeys	____ discos
____ rain forests	____ a gambling casino
____ a volcano	____ a shipwreck
____ a golf course	____ museums

WORD BOX
*palm trees
*coral reef
*plantation
*to keep someone company
*a shipwreck
*volcano

LISTENING TO NOTICE

Listen again. Fill in the missing words.

Looking for somewhere special for a holiday? I have the answer — the sister

_____ of St. Kitts and Nevis. They have everything — _____ ,
1 (island/islands)   2 (mountain/mountains)

sun, palm _____ .
3 (tree/trees)

This is the place for you! You can keep the _____ company.
4 (monkey/monkeys)

You will enjoy the peace and quiet of the beautiful _____ .
5 (beach/beaches)

On St. Kitts you can walk through rain _____ and visit a _____ .
6 (forest/forests)   7 (volcano/volcanoes)

On Nevis you will find some old sugar _____ .
8 (plantation/plantations)

In the beautiful Caribbean Sea you will see coral _____ and perhaps
9 (reef/reefs)

a _____ or two.
10 (shipwreck/shipwrecks)

Interested? Call 1-800-GET-AWAY.

UNDERSTANDING THE GRAMMAR POINT

1. Look back at the advertisement.
   Write the 10 nouns from the blanks in the correct columns.

Singular	Plural
	islands

2. How do you know if a word is singular or plural?

CHECKING

Find the errors in these sentences. Correct them.

1. In Dominica there are beautiful lake. *lakes*

2. Barbados offers miles of beaches lined with hotel.

3. Enjoy the shop and nightlife of the Bahamas.

4. Antigua welcomes all its visitor with open arms.

5. In Jamaica you will find tropical garden overlooking the sea.

6. Puerto Rico has some good museum.

7. Grenada is a paradise of white beach and tropical rain forests.

8. Dance the night away to the music of steel band in Trinidad and Tobago.

TRYING IT

Are there any tourist attractions in your country?
Write a short advertisement for one.

....

....

....

LANGUAGE NOTE
Use some of these
plural nouns:

hotels	beaches
museums	lakes
clubs	shops
markets	mountains
temples	restaurants
casinos	

7

8

Summer Sale

What are the most popular department stores in your city?

When do they usually have sales?

LISTENING TO COMPREHEND

A department store is having a sale. Place a check next to the departments you hear.

Name of Department

_____ Appliances	_____ Sporting Goods
_____ Men's Clothing	_____ Patio and Garden
✔ Children's Clothing	_____ Jewelry
_____ Luggage	_____ Small Electronics
_____ Appliances	_____ Men's Clothing

WORD BOX

*patio
*clothing
*duffel bags
*furniture
*selections
*advertisement

LISTENING TO NOTICE

Listen again. Choose the correct form of the word in parentheses ( ).

Dillard's, your favorite store, announces its summer sale. You'll find the lowest

____*prices*____ of the year in all our _____ .
  1 (price/prices)   2 (department/departments)

Looking for _____ for the new school year? This weekend, you can
                3 (clothing/clothings)

save up to 25% on shoes, _____ , jackets, and dresses in our
                              4 (shirt/shirts)

children's department.

Are you planning an end-of-the-summer vacation? Then this is the time to

replace your old _____ . We have _____ , duffel bags,
                    5 (luggage/luggages)   6 (suitcase/suitcases)

and backpacks — all on sale.

And remember: There are several more weeks of summer. Our patio and

garden department has everything you need to enjoy the rest of the summer in

style, including a large selection of outdoor _____ .
                                              7 (furniture/furnitures)

Our staff is ready to provide expert _____ . We're open seven
                                        8 (advice/advices)

days a week.

UNDERSTANDING THE GRAMMAR POINT

1. Look at the words you wrote to complete the radio advertisement.
   Write those words in the correct column below.

Singular Noun	Plural Noun
clothing	*prices*

2. Which nouns are countable? Which nouns are uncountable?

3. Complete these statements with *countable* or *uncountable*.
   - _____ nouns can have a plural form (usually *-s*).
   - _____ nouns do not have a plural form.

4. Which of these words cannot be used before an uncountable noun?

   some   many   a   several   one, two, three...

CHECKING

Most of these sentences contain an error. Correct the errors.

1. She buys almost all her sports ~~equipments~~ *equipment* in that store.

2. In this jewelry store they always give good advices about gifts.

3. I couldn't find the small electronics department, so I went to the Informations Desk and asked for directions.

4. Every time he takes a trip he has a different set of luggage!

5. This weekend I am going to buy some new clothings.

6. I think it's time to buy some new silverwares.

7. The secretary ordered more photocopy papers.

8. I'm going to buy some new shoes and socks this weekend.

9. The furniture are on sale for this week only.

10. All the employee are helpful and courteous.

TRYING IT

You have just won a prize! You won two hours of free shopping. Make a list of what you would like to get.

I would like to get ....

....

8

9

A Shopping Trip

Do you go shopping often? What do you like to buy?

LISTENING TO COMPREHEND

1. Maria is talking on the telephone. She is telling her boyfriend Bert about her shopping trip. What did she want to buy?

- _____
- _____
- _____

2. What did Maria end up buying?

WORD BOX

* material
* a roll (of material)
* stale
* a waste of time
* a dish (food)

LISTENING TO NOTICE

Listen to Maria again. Fill in the missing words.

Maria: Hi! Is that you, Bert?

Bert: Yeah, hi.

Maria: Sorry I didn't call before, but I just got back from shopping. There were so ___*many*___ people in the store! I wanted to get a new pair of shoes. I saw _____ pairs I liked but they were all too expensive!

Bert: Oh.

Maria: Then I looked for _____ material to make a dress. I found just the color I wanted but there was only _____ material left on the roll, not enough for a dress.   So I didn't buy _____ material after all.

Bert: Yeah . . .

Maria: Next I headed for the food department. I wanted to buy _____ cookies but they looked stale so I didn't buy _____ . I just bought a loaf of French bread. What a waste of time! Still, at least I didn't spend _____ money.

Bert: Maria . . .

Maria: So where are we going this evening? I know a new Italian restaurant that has _____ great dishes. Why don't you pick me up at eight o'clock?

Bert: Well, . . .

UNDERSTANDING THE GRAMMAR POINT

1. Look at Maria's story again. Write down the determiner you wrote before each of these nouns.

many people	_____ material	_____ cookies
_____ pairs	_____ material	_____ money
_____ material	_____ cookies	_____ dishes

2. Now write the determiners in this table.

Type of Noun	Examples	Determiners
Uncountable (mass) noun	material	*any*
	money	
Plural noun	people	
	pairs	
	cookies	
	dishes	

3. Answer these questions about determiners:

• Which determiners can be used only with mass nouns? _____ _____

• Which determiners can be used only with plural nouns? _____ _____ _____

• Which determiners can be used with both mass and plural nouns? _____ _____

CHECKING

Most of these sentences contain an error. Correct the errors.

1. There were only a little people in the store. *few*

2. I bought some lovely shoes.

3. I bought several wine.

4. I wanted to buy a few material to make a dress.

5. That new Italian restaurant has many great dish.

6. You've brought too much cookies.

7. I ate a few cookies.

8. I also got a little blue cheese.

9. I had several beer in the restaurant.

10. I didn't have many time left so I had to rush.

TRYING IT

Your good friend is coming to dinner. Plan a meal you would like to cook for this friend. Write some sentences about the things you will need to buy.

LANGUAGE NOTE
Be sure to use determiners: some, a little, a few, several...

I'll need to buy ....

Perhaps I'll get ....

10 At the Zoo

Do you like to go to the zoo?
What are your favorite animals?

LISTENING TO COMPREHEND

Nina is at the zoo with her father. Circle the animals she has seen.

LISTENING TO NOTICE

Listen again. Fill in the words you hear.

Nina: Guess what animal I just saw!

Father: ____*Is it*____ a lion?
1

Nina: No, it isn't a lion. You have to ask me questions.

Father: _____ a mammal?
2

Nina: No, it's not a mammal.

Father: _____ a bird?
3

Nina: Yeah, it's a bird.

Father: _____ a tropical bird?
4

Nina: No, it lives in a cold region.

Father: _____ able to fly?
5

Nina: No, it can't.

Father: I think I know.

WORD BOX
* guess
* mammal
* tropical
* region
* striped

Nina: You have to come this way. I didn't know they had these at this zoo!

Father: Are the kangaroos over there?

Nina: No, _____ not kangaroos. Try to guess.
6

Father: Are they from Africa?

Nina: Yes, _____ .
7

Father: Are they dangerous?

Nina: Yes, I think _____ dangerous.
8

Father: Are they striped?

Nina: Yes, they have stripes.

Father: I think I know. They're zebras. _____ right?
9

For Grammar Explanation,
See The Yellow Pages p.124 ▶

UNDERSTANDING THE GRAMMAR POINT

1. Look at the questions in this box. Find the answers in the zoo conversations. Write the answers in the box.

Question	Answer
Is it a lion?	*No, it isn't a lion.*
Is it a mammal?	
Is it a bird?	
Is it a tropical bird?	
Is it able to fly?	
Are the kangaroos over there?	
Are they from Africa?	
Are they dangerous?	
Am I right?	

2. **What part of the sentence comes first in the questions?**
   What part comes first in the answers (after *no* or *yes*)?

CHECKING

Which of these sentences contain an error? Correct the errors.

Is the zoo open today?
1. ~~The zoo is open today, yes?~~

2. Is that an otter? Yes, it is.

3. Are panthers? No, those are leopards.

4. Are dolphins mammals?

5. Is the zoo is near the Museum of Natural History?
   Yes, it's only about a five-minute walk.

6. Are poisonous those snakes? Yes, they're very dangerous.

7. Asleep the lion is? Yes, lions sleep a lot during the day.

8. Is a rhinoceros that? No, that's a hippopotamus.

LANGUAGE NOTE
Write some questions that begin with Is it or Are they.

TRYING IT

Imagine that you are trying to find out what animal someone is thinking of. Write a list of questions to help you guess the animal.

....

....

....

Complete the passage below. Choose from the words and phrases in the box. Use each item one time only. There are some extra items.

many	has	there's	sons	no
do	am playing	does	is	are
not	am	play	a lot of	there
her	son	works	he	she

The Life of a Fashion Model

Marsina Simpson _____*works*_____ as a fashion model. She _____

 1

25 years old. She _____ a husband, Brett. He stays at home with their two

 2

_____ .

 3

"_____ you like your job?" I asked Marsina.

 4

"There _____ some good things about it," Marsina said. "I visit

 5

_____ different places," she told me. "And I earn _____

 6 7

money," she added.

"But _____ I happy?" she asked herself. _____ thought for

 8 9

a moment and then said, "Yes, I am."

"But _____ one bad thing about her job," Brett added. "She has

 10

_____ time to play with the children," he said.

 11

Marsina laughed and said, "I _____ with them now."

 12

Complete the passage below. Choose from the words and phrases in the box. Use each item one time only. There are some extra items.

thousand	runs	a lot of	no	some
not	am	many	has	lives
is running	he	do	she	it
have	are	is	thousands	an

The London Marathon

Rick Larkin _____*lives*_____ in London. He _____ a twin brother, Sam.

1

They _____ 70 years old.

2

Rick _____ 10 miles every day. Every year he enters the London marathon

3

along with _____ of other people.

4

"What about you, Sam?" I asked, "_____ you also run in the marathon?"

5

Sam shook his head. "I've got _____ time for marathons," he said.

6

"You have to do _____ work to get ready for a marathon," Rick said. "Sam

7

does _____ like hard work."

8

"There _____ a lot of cheating," Rick told me. "Last year a woman passed me

9

three times! _____ got a ride on her husband's motorcycle."

10

"Is _____ difficult to run a marathon? Can you give me _____

11   12

advice?" I asked Rick. "Yes. You must run every day," the 70-year-old man said.

11

A Visit to the Doctor

How often do you see a doctor? Do you like visiting the doctor?

LISTENING TO COMPREHEND

Listen to the conversation between a doctor and her patient, Mr. O'Leary. Check (✔) what they discuss.

__✔__ headache   _____ medicine

_____ no appetite   _____ sleeping problems

_____ losing weight   _____ healthy diet

_____ exercise   _____ physical examination

WORD BOX
* prescribe
* lose weight
* appetite
* a physical examinat

LISTENING TO NOTICE

Listen again. Fill in the blanks with a verb in parentheses ( ).

Doctor: Well, Mr. O'Leary, here you are again. I __*notice*__ that this is
1 (notice/am noticing)

your fourth visit this month. You _____ the medicine I prescribed last
2 (take/are taking)

time, aren't you?

Mr. O'Leary: Yes, I _____ it every morning, but I _____ something
3 (take/am taking)   4 (need/am needing)

else. First of all, I _____ a headache. I've had one for almost a week.
5 (have/am having)

And I _____ weight. And my food _____ funny; as soon as I start
6 (lose/am losing)   7 (tastes/is tasting)

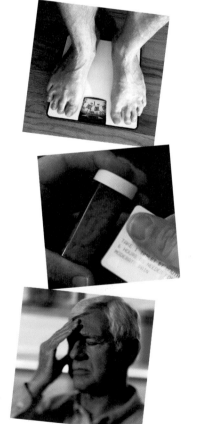

to eat, I _____ my appetite.
8 (lose/am losing)

Doctor: Mr. O'Leary, I _____ you to tell me whether you _____ to
9 (want/am wanting)   10 (try/are trying)

get exercise.

Mr. O'Leary: Yes, I _____ your exact words: "It's important to
11 (remember/am remembering)

exercise, and that _____ walking." And I _____. Some days I
12 (includes/is including)   13 (try/amtrying)

_____ , but when I exercise, I _____ it.
14 (forget/am forgetting)   15 (like/am liking)

Doctor: Well, Mr. O'Leary, it _____ that it's time for you to have
16 (seems/is seeming)

a complete physical examination.

**For Grammar Explanation,
See The Yellow Pages p.125** ▶

UNDERSTANDING THE GRAMMAR POINT

1. Look at the verbs in the conversation. Write each verb in the correct column.
   Sometimes you will fill in both columns.

Verb	Present Simple	Present Continuous	Verb	Present Simple	Present Continuous
notice	*notice*		want		
take		*are taking*	try		
need			remember		
have			include		
lose			forget		
taste			like		
			seem		

2. Most of these verbs are only used in the simple present tense.
   What do they have in common?

3. Which of these verbs are not generally used in the present continuous form?
   cost, arrive, understand, see, sleep, weigh, recognize, work

CHECKING

Complete each sentence by choosing the correct word in parentheses ( ).

1. I (realize/am realizing) now I should get more exercise.
2. A healthy diet (includes/is including) fruits and vegetables.
3. I (try/am trying) to remember when the pain started: maybe three days ago.
4. (Do you remember/Are you remembering) when you first started to feel this pain?
5. She (owns/is owning) a lot of exercise equipment, but she never uses it.
6. He (weighs/is weighing) 83 kilos; that's two kilos more than at the last checkup.
7. The doctor (talks/is talking) to another patient right now; please take a seat and wait.
8. You (need/are needing) to make sure that your cast doesn't get wet.
9. That cut (seems/is seeming) to be healing nicely.
10. I (want/am wanting) you to continue taking your medicine.

LANGUAGE NOTE

Remember to use stative verbs such as feel, remember, want.

TRYING IT

Write a dialogue between you and your doctor. Tell the doctor about your health. Include information about your diet, exercise, weight.

....

....

11

12

Great Musicians

What kind of music do you like?
Who is your favorite musician?

LISTENING TO COMPREHEND

Do you know these musicians: Johnny Cash, Frederic Chopin, Ella Fitzgerald? Write the kind of music each one is famous for?

Johnny Cash ___*country and western*___

Frederic Chopin _____

Ella Fitzgerald _____

WORD BOX
* record
* a contest
* country and western music
* religious
* a biography
* a composer
* popular

LISTENING TO NOTICE

Listen again. Fill in the missing words.

1. *Johnny Cash* ___**wrote**___ his first song when he was 12. In his twenties he
   1 (write)

_____ a number of country and western albums for Sun Records. Later
2 (record)

he _____ with Bob Dylan for Columbia Records. Now, he _____
3 (work)   4 (live)

in the United States with his second wife.

2. *Frederic Chopin* _____ one of the most famous classical composers of
   5 (become)

the early 19th century. He _____ piano concerts all over Europe.
   6 (give)

Unfortunately, he _____ while still young. His *Nocturnes* _____ to
   7 (die)   8 (continue)

be a very popular piano piece.

3. *Ella Fitzgerald* _____ her career in a singing contest in Harlem. She
   9 (begin)

_____ Chick Webb's band and recorded several hits. Later, her *Songbird*
10 (join)

albums _____ her one of the most famous jazz singers of the 20th
   11 (make)

century. Ella was also very kind and religious. People _____ Ella as
                                                        12 (remember)

a person as well as a singer.

For Grammar Explanation, See The Yellow Pages p.125 ▶

UNDERSTANDING THE GRAMMAR POINT

1. Look at the biographies again. Circle the verbs in the past and underline the verbs in the present.

2. Complete this table using the past tense verbs you circled.

Regular past tense	Irregular past tense
recorded	wrote

3. How do you make the simple past tense with regular verbs?

CHECKING

Correct the errors in this biography of Bob Dylan.

Bob Dylan was born in 1941. He ~~teached~~ *taught* himself to play the guitar. In the 1960s he become famous as a folk singer who singed protest songs. He record three famous albums — *The Freewheelin Bob Dylan, Times They Are a-Changin'* and *Another Side of Bob Dylan.* These albums together with *Bringing it Back Home* change rock music forever. They influence bands such as the Beatles and the Rolling Stones. Dylan is the most original pop musician since the '60s. He still tried out new ideas.

Choose a musician you know well. Write a short biography of him or her. Include information about his or her type of music, birthplace, family background, famous songs.

LANGUAGE NOTE
Make sure you include the simple past.

....

....

....

13

Making an Appointment

Have you ever had a job interview?
What happened? Did you get the job?

LISTENING TO COMPREHEND

Listen to Greg and Gloria's conversation. Greg is looking for a job. He had an interview with Mr. Bean. What happened?

    a. Greg never saw Mr. Bean.
    b. Greg saw Mr. Bean but he did not get a job.
    c. Greg saw Mr. Bean and got a job.

WORD BOX

* make an appointment
* cancel
* contact
* reschedule
* a position

LISTENING TO NOTICE

Listen to the conversation again. Fill in the blanks with *at*, *in*, or *on*.

Gloria: Well, have you got a job yet?

Greg: No way, but I've been trying. I made an appointment to see this Mr. Bean guy _____ 3 o'clock _____ a Monday in February. He's the manager of a big company.
                           1   2

Gloria: And did you see him?

Greg: No, his secretary called me _____ the morning to cancel the appointment. Apparently he'd had a car accident.
                                  3

Gloria: What a pity.

Greg: Anyway, I made another appointment to see him _____ the end of February.
                                                 4

Gloria: Great!

Greg: No, not so great. When I got to his office he wasn't there. His secretary told me his wife had died _____ 2 o'clock _____ the morning and he wasn't coming in to work that day.
                             5   6

Gloria: So what did you do?

Greg: Well, his secretary suggested I reschedule for sometime _____ March.
                                                 7

Gloria: And did you?

Greg: Yeah, I made an appointment to see him _____ Monday, March 5th.
                                                 8

Gloria: That was yesterday!

Greg: Yeah, and I actually saw the guy this time.

Gloria: And did he give you a job?

Greg: No, he told me all the positions had been filled _____ February and suggested I contact him again _____ 2010!
                                             9   10

Gloria: Oh, no!

UNDERSTANDING THE GRAMMAR POINT

1. Write the prepositional phrases from the conversation in the table.

AT	IN	ON
at 3 o'clock		

2. When do you use *at*, *in* and *on*?

CHECKING

All of these sentences have errors. Correct the errors.

1. Greg made an appointment to see Mr. Bean ~~at~~ *on* Monday.

2. The appointment was in 3 o'clock on the afternoon.

3. Unfortunately, Mr. Bean had an accident on the morning.

4. Greg made another appointment in the end of February.

5. Mr. Bean's wife died on 2:00 in the morning.

6. Greg eventually saw Mr. Bean at Monday, March 5th.

7. However, all the positions had been filled on February.

8. Mr. Bean suggested Greg contact him again on 2010.

TRYING IT

Do you know when you were born? Write sentences stating:
- *at what time?* • *in the morning, afternoon or night?*
- *on what day?* • *in what month?* • *in what year?*

....

....

....

14

Weekend Activities

What do you like to do on the weekend?

ERROR BOX

✗ The building where I work is at Madison Street.

✗ You can meet us to the entrance to the park.

LISTENING TO COMPREHEND

Listen to the Riverton community event announcements. Draw a line from the event to the location of the event.

Event:	Location:
science fair	56 Third St.
concert	Lake Avenue and Fourth Street
canoe trip	Lincoln Park
dance registration	Lake Avenue Elementary School

WORD BOX
* a science fair
* an announcement
* a canoe
* registration
* a session
* a community event

LISTENING TO NOTICE

Listen again. Fill in the blanks with one of these prepositions:

at   in   on   to

Welcome to the Riverton Youth Community Calendar. Here are some events taking place this weekend:

For future scientists: There will be a science fair __*at*__ Lake Avenue
1
Elementary School. The fair will be held this Friday evening _____ the
2
school gymnasium. For rides _____ the school, call 433-7894.
3

Music lovers: There will be a free concert from 2 to 4 on Saturday afternoon
_____ Lincoln Park. The main entrance to the park is _____ Valley Avenue.
4   5
Come _____ Lincoln Park and enjoy some of the area's best musicians.
6

This next one is for you outdoor types: On Saturday, the Sierra Club is sponsoring a canoe trip _____ Eagle River. Meet _____ the Sierra Club office
7   8
_____ 56 Third Street at noon. Transportation _____ the river will be provided.
9   10

For dance lovers: Saturday afternoon the Riverton Dance Studio is conducting
registration for its next session. The studio is _____ the corner of Lake Avenue
11
and Fourth Street.

**For Grammar Explanation,
See The Yellow Pages p.126** ▶

UNDERSTANDING THE GRAMMAR POINT

1. Circle the prepositional phrases with *in, at, on,* and *to* from the announcement. Write them in the box.

in	at	on	to
the school gymnasium			

2. When do we use *in* to describe a location? When do we use *at*? When do we use *on*?

3. How is the meaning of *to* different from the meaning of *in, at* and *on* ?

CHECKING

Which of the following sentences have an error? Correct the errors.

1. The American Red Cross building is located ~~in~~ *on* the corner of Main Street and Sixth Avenue.

2. The Farmers' Market is held every Saturday morning on the parking lot of the Valley National Bank.

3. The Paramount Theater is located at 320 State Street.

4. Sunrise Day Care is in Washington Avenue.

5. Bus Routes 14 and 16 both stop on the entrance to the park.

6. The Silver Valley Community Center is on Maple Street, near the corner of Walden Avenue.

7. To get to the post office, walk at the next traffic light, then turn right.

8. Our downtown office is on the third floor of the Skyline Building.

TRYING IT

Where do you like to go in your city or town? Describe the location of some of these places. Write directions to go from one place to another.

My town has a recreation center. It is located ...
To go to the post office from my apartment, I walk ...

....

....

....

LANGUAGE NOTE
Try to use the prepositions in, at, on, to

14

15

Newspaper Stories

Do you like to read the newspaper?
Can you remember an interesting newspaper story?

LISTENING TO COMPREHEND

Listen to the newspaper stories.
Choose the correct headline for each story.

_____ Man Tricked with Promise of Marriage
_____ Mother Abandons Children for Hawaiian Holiday
_____ Pachinko Addict Loses Family Fortune
_____ Husband Kills Himself

LISTENING TO NOTICE

Listen again. Write the correct words in parentheses ( ) in the blanks.

WORD BOX
* selfish   * tragic
* foolish   * gamble
* reckless   * threater

Story 1:

Tracy Smith ___selfishly___ left her two
1 (selfish/ selfishly)
children, ages five and eight, in

her Philadelphia apartment while she

went on a five-day holiday to Hawaii

with her boyfriend. "She is a very

_____ woman," a neighbor said.
2 (selfish/selfishly)

Story 2:

Yoko Kitazawa, a _____ Japanese
3 (reckless/recklessly)
housewife, gambled away her family's

savings in the local Pachinko parlor. "I

did not know she could behave so

_____ ," her husband said.
4 (reckless/recklessly)

Story 3:

When Garcia Mundo's wife threatened to
leave him, he _____ shot himself.
5 (tragic/ tragically)
"It's a _____ mistake," she said. "I
6 (tragic/tragically)
just told him that to make him pay more

attention to me."

Story 4:

Hans Schmidt met a woman in a bar and
_____ agreed to marry her. When
7 (foolish/foolishly)
the woman asked for $500 to buy a ring
he gave her the money. The woman took
the money and disappeared. "I guess I
was a really _____ man," Hans told
8 (foolish/ foolishly)
the police.

UNDERSTANDING THE GRAMMAR POINT

1. Complete this table using words from the newspaper stories.

_____ + verb OR verb + _____	_____ + noun
selfishly left	*selfish woman*

2. Complete these sentences:

- Words such as *selfishly* and *recklessly* that end in _____ are called **adverbs**. They modify _____ such as *left* and *agreed*.

- Words such as *selfish* and *reckless* are called **adjectives**. They modify _____ such as *woman* and *mistake*.

**3. Study the position of the adverbs in the newspaper stories.
Where can the adverb *recklessly* go in the sentence below? Put a check (✔) to show where it can go and an ✗ to show where it cannot go.**

_____ Yoko Kitazawa _____ wasted _____ the family savings_____ .

CHECKING

Find the errors in this newspaper story and correct them.

YOUNG BOY DRIVES CAR 100 MILES

Samantha Lawson left ~~thoughtlessly~~ *thoughtlessly*ᵥ her five year-old son in her car when she ran quick into a shop to buy something. When she came out the car mysterious had gone and so had her son.

The boy drove the car safe for 100 miles before the gasoline ran out. "He is a very safe driver but it was very thoughtlessly of me," Lawson said. "I'll never do it again."

TRYING IT

Write a story for this headline:
TEENAGER SETS FIRE TO FAMILY HOME

....

....

....

LANGUAGE NOTE
Use adverbs such as dangerously and adjectives such as dangerous.

15

16 A Terrible Holiday

Would you like to visit London?
What places would you like to visit in London?

LISTENING TO COMPREHEND

Brad just returned from London. Which of these places did he visit?

- [ ] The National Theater
- [ ] Covent Garden
- [ ] Buckingham Palace
- [ ] The British Museum
- [ ] The Tower of London
- [ ] The Houses of Parliament
- [ ] Guy's Hospital
- [ ] Trafalgar Square
- [ ] Tate Art Gallery
- [ ] Hyde Park

LISTENING TO NOTICE

Listen to the conversation again. Fill in the missing words.

Georgia: So you're back from your holiday in London?
Brad: Yeah, I'm back.
Georgia: *Did you have* _____ a great time?
          1
Brad: Well, ...
Georgia: No, don't tell me, let me guess what you did. _____
                            2
Buckingham Palace?
Brad: No.
Georgia: _____ the Tower? The Tower's great.
           3
Brad: No.
Georgia: Oh. _____ into the Houses of Parliament? They're a
           4
laugh.
Brad: The Houses of Parliament? No.
Georgia: _____ around Covent Garden? That's fun.
           5
Brad: No.
Georgia: What about Trafalgar Square? _____ there and see the
                  6
pigeons?
Brad: No. I don't like pigeons.
Georgia: I know. _____ a visit to the Tate Art Gallery? You like
           7
art, don't you?
Brad: Yes, I like art, but I didn't visit the Tate.
Georgia: The National Theater. _____ a play?
           8
Brad: No.
Georgia: Well, I give up. What did you do?
Brad: I fell down some stairs in my hotel and broke my leg on the first day. I
spent the week in Guy's Hospital.
Georgia: Oh, you poor thing!

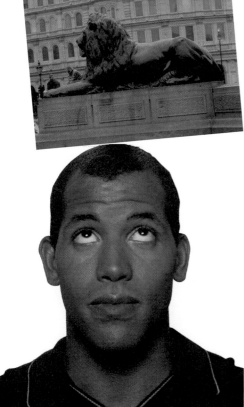

**For Grammar Explanation,
See The Yellow Pages p.127** ▶

UNDERSTANDING THE GRAMMAR POINT

1. Write _S_ next to each statement. Write _Q_ next to each question.

_Q_ Did Brad have a great time?

____ Brad did not have a great time.

____ Did Brad see Buckingham Palace.

____ Brad did not see Buckingham Palace.

____ Did Brad visit the Tower.

____ Brad did not visit the Tower.

____ Did Brad go into the Houses of Parliament.

____ Brad did not go into the Houses of Parliament.

____ Did Brad walk around Covent Garden.

____ Brad did not walk around Covent Garden.

____ Did Brad go to Trafalgar Square.

____ Brad did not go to Trafalgar Square.

____ Did Brad pay a visit to the Tate Art Gallery.

____ Brad did not visit the Tate Art Gallery.

____ Did Brad watch a play.

____ Brad did not watch a play.

____ Brad broke his leg.

2. How can you tell which sentence is a statement and which is a question?

3. Write in the question marks (?) at the end of the questions.

CHECKING

Most of these sentences have an error. Can you correct the errors?

1. Did you ~~climbed~~ *climb* the Eiffel Tower?

2. You did visit Disneyland in Paris?

3. Did you go shopping in the Champs Elysees?

4. Did you saw Notre Dame?

5. You did eat in a restaurant on the Left Bank?

6. Did you walked in the Bois de Boulogne?

7. Did you took a trip to Versailles?

8. Did you go on a boat trip on the Seine?

9. You did spend a day at the Pompidou Center?

10. Did you have a good time?

TRYING IT

Your friend has been on vacation in the United States. Think of five or more famous places in the United States *(the Statue of Liberty, the Grand Canyon)*. Write questions to find out whether your friend went to these places.

LANGUAGE NOTE
Be sure to write the questions in the simple past tense

....

....

17 A Year in Madison

Have you ever been on a homestay?
Where would you like to go for a homestay?

LISTENING TO COMPREHEND

Listen to Yumiko talking to her friend Yoko. Yumiko just returned from a year in the United States. Write True (T) or False (F) for each statement about Yumiko.

_____ Yumiko's family went with her to the United States.

__F__ Yumiko grew up on a farm in Japan.

_____ Yumiko was homesick all the time she lived in Madison.

_____ Yumiko lived on a farm in Wisconsin.

_____ Yumiko kept a journal of her experiences.

WORD BOX
* homesick
* outlook
* dairy
* a journal

LISTENING TO NOTICE

Listen again. Fill in the blanks with the verbs you hear.

Yoko: Welcome back to Japan, Yumiko. Did you ___enjoy___ your year in Wisconsin?
1

Yumiko: I _____ it! But not at first. When I _____ in the United
2   3
States, it was terrible. I _____ every day because I _____ my family,
4   5
and I _____ so many things. After a few weeks, though, my
6
homesickness _____ .
7

Yoko: What _____ ?
8

Yumiko: Well, I made some friends, and my English _____ . Those two
9
things really _____ my outlook.
10

Yoko: Did you _____ Madison?
11

Yumiko: Oh, it's a great place. And it has _____ and _____ a lot
12   13
since you lived there. But I also spent some time on a farm near Madison.

Yoko: A farm?

Yumiko: Yeah, I became friends with a girl whose family had a dairy farm, and
they also _____ corn. That was my first time on a farm — in my whole
14
life! After my first visit, I _____ a journal. When I read it, I know how
15
much this past year has _____ me.
16

UNDERSTANDING THE GRAMMAR POINT

1. Write the verbs from the conversation in the table. If the verb is followed by a direct object, write the verb and the direct object.

Verbs followed by a direct object	Verbs not followed by a direct object	Verbs occurring with or without a direct object
enjoy your year	*arrived*	*improved*

2. Complete each of the following statements:

• Some verbs in English — including *enjoy*, *like*, and *miss* — are always followed by a _____. We call these verbs transitive verbs.

• Intransitive verbs — including *arrive*, *happen* and *cry* — are never followed by a _____.

• Some verbs in English — including *improve*, *change*, *grow*, and *start* — are sometimes followed by a direct object and sometimes not. These verbs can be _____ or intransitive.

CHECKING

Which of these sentences have an error? Correct the errors.

1. ~~Did you enjoy?~~ *Did you enjoy Madison?*

2. How soon did your homesickness disappear you?

3. You've grown!

4. Do you think you've changed?

5. Did you miss your family?

6. When did you arrive Australia?

7. Did your English improve?

8. Do you like?

9. What happened it?

10. I'm happy to hear that you liked Madison.

LANGUAGE NOTE
Try to use some of the verbs you have studied in this unit.

TRYING IT

Write three or four sentences about an experience that changed you. You can write about a trip you took, a person you met, an accident you had.

....

....

18

Movie Listings

Have you seen a movie recently?
What was it about?

LISTENING TO COMPREHEND

Listen to the movie listings. Complete this table.

Film	Type	Subject
1. Grace of My Heart	_____	singing career of Edna Buxton
2. _____	bittersweet comedy	_____
3. Hoop Dreams	documentary	_____
4. The Long Kiss Goodnight	_____	a woman's search for her identity

LISTENING TO NOTICE

Listen again. Choose the correct form of the verb in parentheses ( ).

1. Grace of My Heart

This drama ___*follows*___ the singing career of Edna
    1 (follow/follows)
Buxton as she _____ through the pop music
                2 (move/moves)
world of the late '50s and '60s.

2. Big Night

This bittersweet comedy tells the story of two Italian immigrants who

_____ a restaurant in New Jersey. But their American Dream _____
3 (open/opens)   4 (turn/turns)
sour and things end up badly.

3. Hoop Dreams

This documentary follows four years in the lives of 14-year-olds Arthur Agee
and William Gates, two exceptionally talented basketball players. They

_____ up poor in downtown Chicago and _____ of careers as
5 (grow/grows)   6 (dream/dreams)
highly paid professionals.

4. The Long Kiss Goodnight

This action thriller stars Geena Davis playing a schoolteacher who _____
                                                                    7 (suffer/suffers)
from amnesia. She hires a detective, played by Samuel L. Jackson, and together

they _____ for her past and true identity.
      8 (search/searches)

For Grammar Explanation,
See The Yellow Pages p.128 ▶

UNDERSTANDING THE GRAMMAR POINT

1. Complete this table. Use the information in the movie listings.

Subject	Verb
1. *drama*	*follows*
2. *she*	
3. *who (two Italian immigrants)*	
4.	
5.	
6.	
7.	
8.	

2. Which form of the verb is used with singular subjects?
Which form of the verb is used with plural subjects?

CHECKING

Choose the correct form of the verb to complete these movie listings.

1. The Relic

Penelope Ann Miller and Tom Sizemore ___*star*___ in this thriller. They _____ partners when
                                      1 (star)   2 (become)

a number of murders _____ place in the museum where biologist Margo Green _____ .
                      3 (take)   4 (work)

2. Romeo and Juliet

Leonardo DiCaprio and Clare Danes _____ in this remake of Shakespeare's classic story
                                   5 (star)

of two doomed lovers. The action takes place in a gang-filled Los Angeles neighborhood. A rocking sound-

track _____ the action moving.
       6 (keep)

TRYING IT

LANGUAGE NOTE
Use the simple present tense.

Think of a movie you have seen recently. Write your own listing describing the movie.

....

....

....

18

19

Job Interviews

Have you ever had a job interview?
What kinds of questions did people ask you in the interview?

LISTENING TO COMPREHEND

Listen to Mr. Naraporn and Ms. Adams being interviewed. What jobs are they interviewing for?

Mr. Naraporn	• aerobics instructor
Ms. Adams	• librarian
	• nurse
	• airport baggage handler

WORD BOX

* an interview
* position
* bother
* former

LISTENING TO NOTICE

Listen to the interviews again. Fill in the blanks with the word or words in parentheses ( ).

Interview with Mr. Naraporn:

Interviewer: *Have you done* _____ this kind of job before, Mr. Naraporn?
1 (Did you do/Have you done)
Mr. Naraporn: Not exactly.

Interviewer: But you _____ jobs like this before?
2 (had/have had)
Mr. Naraporn: Yes, from 1990 until 1995 I _____ in a Nike shoe factory.
3 (worked/have worked)
Interviewer: Hmm. And what was that like?

Mr. Naraporn: It _____ very noisy. And I _____
4 (was/has been)   5 (did/have done)
the same thing over and over.

Interview with Ms. Adams:

Interviewer: Ms. Adams, I _____ at your resume. All of your
6 (looked/have looked)
previous jobs at health clubs were part-time positions.

Ms. Adams: Yes, that's right.

Interviewer: You _____ a full-time job?
7 (didn't want/haven't wanted)
Ms. Adams: Well, from 1993 until 1997 I _____ a student.
8 (was/has been)
Interviewer: I see. But you _____ with people of different ages?
9 (worked/have worked)
Ms. Adams: Oh, yes: children, adults, senior citizens. And last year I

_____ some seminars on sports medicine.
10 (took/have taken)

UNDERSTANDING THE GRAMMAR POINT

**1. Look at the verbs listed in the box. Find these verbs in the interviews.
Write the verb as it is written in the interviews.**

Verb	Simple Past	Present Perfect	Verb	Simple Past	Present Perfect
1. do		*Have you done*	6. look		
2. have			7. want		
3. work	*worked*		8. be		
4. be			9. work		
5. do			10. take		

2. Complete the following statements:

• We use the _____ tense to describe an action in the past that took place at a specific time.

• We use the _____ tense to describe an action that was completed during a specific period of time in the past.

• We use the _____ tense to describe an action that took place at some indefinite time in the past, when no specific time is mentioned.

CHECKING

Most of these sentences have errors. Correct the errors.

1. I ~~have applied~~ *applied* for a promotion last year.

2. I joined this company in 1978.

3. They spent more than a month looking for a new office manager.

4. She has changed jobs last week.

5. Have you looked at the classified advertisements yesterday?

6. Have you ever worked with teenagers and children?

7. I have learned word processing in 1992.

8. My sister has decided to go into banking as a career.

9. We have hired temporary office staff last month.

10. They have interviewed me in March.

TRYING IT

**Write a letter applying for a job you would like to have.
In your letter, describe your skills and work experience.**

LANGUAGE NOTE
Include the present perfect or past tense.

....

....

19

20 The Babysitter

Have you ever had to take care of someone's children?
What was it like?

LISTENING TO COMPREHEND 🎧

Jenny is babysitting for Mr. Blake's children.
Write True (T) or False (F) for each statement.

____ The babysitter is going to take care of one child.

____ Jenny Thompson will be babysitting for this family for the first time.

____ Mr. and Mrs. Blake will not be home until midnight.

____ Jenny drove her own car to the Blakes' house.

WORD BOX
*a babysitter
* supper
* a refrigerator
* frozen pizza

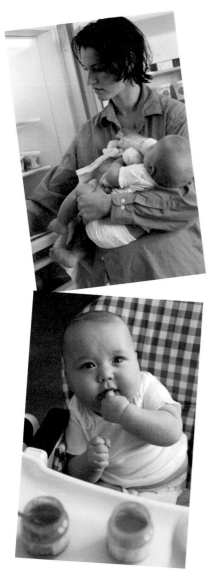

LISTENING TO NOTICE 🎧

Listen to the conversation again. Fill in the blanks with the word or words you hear.

Mr. Blake: Oh, hi, Jenny. Thanks for babysitting for us tonight.

Jenny: No problem. I love babysitting for you. Where ___*are you going*___ ? And when _____ home?

Mr. Blake: We're going out to eat and to a concert. The concert ends at 10:00, so we should be home by 10:30 or so.

Jenny: You'll have to remind me of a few things. How _____ to spend time after supper? When _____ to sleep? What _____ to get ready for bed? I seem to have forgotten.

Mr. Blake: Well, after supper, they like to watch television. About 8:30 they should get ready for bed. They should take a bath and put on their pajamas. Then if you could, please read them a story.

Jenny: OK, no problem. And, um, Mr. Blake, how much _____ me?

Mr. Blake: I think seven dollars an hour. Is that all right?

Jenny: That's fine.

Mr. Blake: And if you're hungry...

Jenny: Oh, good, I haven't eaten yet. What _____ for supper?

Mr. Blake: Help yourself to anything in the refrigerator. There's a frozen pizza, I think.

Jenny: Great. Oh, one more question. How _____ home?

Mr. Blake: Mrs. Blake or I will drive you home.

Jenny: Oh, just one more question. How _____ you?

Mr. Blake: The telephone numbers are right here. Jenny, you do remember the children's names, don't you?

Jenny: Of course, Mr. Blake.

UNDERSTANDING THE GRAMMAR POINT

1. Write each of the questions from the conversation in the box.
   Put one word in each column.

1	2	3	4	5
1. *Where*	*are*	*you*	*going?*	
2. *When*		*you*	*be*	*home?*
3.			*like*	
4.	*should*			*to sleep?*
5.		*they*		
6. *How much*				
7.	*can*			*for supper ?*
8.			*get*	
9.		*I*		

2. Now label columns 1 – 4 using these terms:
   auxiliary verb (are, can, do . . .)   *wh-word*   *main verb*   *subject*

CHECKING

Most of these sentences are incorrect. Correct the errors.

1. ~~Where are going we tonight?~~ *Where are we going tonight?*

2. What should say if the telephone rings?

3. How I can contact you?

4. What do you like to eat?

5. When are you coming back?

6. Where she lives?

7. She should call in an emergency who?

8. How much pay we the babysitter?

9. When the children go to bed?

10. What time do we pick her up?

TRYING IT

Some friends or relatives have asked you to take care of their house or apartment. Make a list of questions you want them to answer.
When does the newspaper arrive each day? Who should I call if there's a problem?

....

....

Complete the passage below. Choose from the words and phrases in the box. Use each item one time only. There are some extra items.

at	have had	you won't	say	angry
refused	enters	angrily	to	won't you
does he do	on	have	he does	has refused
says	entered	want	in	appreciate

Trouble at the First Community Bank

The police were called to the First Community Bank _____ Washington
(1)

Avenue yesterday afternoon when a man _____ to leave the bank.
(2)

Frank Mardell, age 60, _____ the bank _____ 4:59 p.m.,
(3) (4)

just one minute before closing time. Mardell told a bank employee, "I _____
(5)

to deposit five thousand dollars — all in pennies." He pointed to several heavy bags next to him.

The employee said it was too late to help him. Then Mr. Mardell shouted _____:
(6)

"Your television commercial _____ , ' We _____ every
(7) (8)

cent you bring us.' Why _____ take my money now?"
(9)

According to the branch manager, this is not the first time they _____ trouble
(10)

with Mr. Mardell. He explained, "One day _____ 1998, he came into the
(11)

bank fifteen times. Each time he took out one dollar from his account. Why _____
(12)

these things?"

Complete the passage below. Choose from the words and phrases in the box. Use each item one time only. There are some extra items.

enjoys	learns	simply	lives	lived
she	in	at	to	how
on	did	eats	learned	does
enjoy	does she	is eating	has given	

The Oldest Living Woman

The Guinness Book of World Records _____ the title of the oldest living
₁

woman to 117-year-old Sarah Knauss. Knauss _____ in a nursing home
₂

_____ Allentown, Pennsylvania. Yesterday, she _____ she was
₃ ₄

the oldest woman alive. _____ she get excited? No. Ms. Knauss said
₅

_____ , "So what?"
₆

Knauss was born _____ September 24, 1880. She has lived through several
₇

wars, the sinking of the Titanic, and the Apollo space mission _____ the
₈

moon. How _____ she usually spend her time now? Knauss says she
₉

_____ watching golf on television and looking after her 93-year-old daughter.
₁₀

She dislikes vegetables ("I won't eat them," she reported), but she _____
₁₁

chocolate, potato chips, and other junk food.

And what _____ advise people to do? "Keep busy. Work hard. And don't
₁₂

worry about your age," Knauss said.

21

Hobbies

Do you have a hobby?
Why is it special to you?

LISTENING TO COMPREHEND 🎧

Francesca, Linda and Yana are describing how they spend their free time. What are their hobbies?

Francesca _____

Linda _____

Yana _____

WORD BOX
* precise routine
* stretch
* muscles
* containers
* spray
* insects

LISTENING TO NOTICE 🎧

Listen again. Put a check (✔) in the places you hear an adverb.

regularly	*usually*	*immediately*	*perfectly*	*always*
frequently	*repeatedly*	*continuously*	*normally*	*slowly*

This is Francesca.

My name is Francesca. Do you want to know about my hobbies?

Well, I'm not a good athlete, but I enjoy running. I follow a precise routine.

After I stretch my muscles for a few minutes, I begin jogging. I start to run.

This is Linda.

My name is Linda. Here's how I spend my free time. I have no place for a

garden, so I grow flowers and vegetables in containers on our balcony. It's

enjoyable, but it's not easy. In the summer, I water the plants twice a day. I

find insects, and I spray them.

This is Yana.

I'm Yana. I'd like to tell you how I spend my leisure time. A few years

ago, I started piano lessons. I practice my lessons in the afternoon. I enjoy

practicing; I play the same tune. (My neighbors complain.) I keep hoping

that I'll play a piece. (My neighbors hope so, too.)

UNDERSTANDING THE GRAMMAR POINT

1. Look at these sentences from the text. Underline the adverbs.

1. I enjoy running regularly.
2. I usually follow a precise routine.
3. Slowly I start to run.
4. I always water the plants twice a day.
5. Frequently I find insects.

6. I spray them immediately.
7. Normally I practice my lessons in the afternoon.
8. I play the same tune repeatedly.
9. My neighbors complain continuously.
10. I keep hoping that I will play a piece perfectly.

2. In which sentences does the adverb come:

(a) at the beginning of the sentence? _____

(b) in front of the verb? _____

(c) at the end of the sentence? _____

3. Why is this sentence incorrect?

✗ She studied seriously ballet.

CHECKING

Which of these sentences contain an error? Correct the errors.

1. Mr. Tanaka takes ~~seriously~~ stamp collecting *seriously*ₐ

2. Occasionally I go scuba diving, but it's not one of my hobbies.

3. He is an experienced bird watcher; he patiently waits for the birds to come to the area he has chosen.

4. Ana is a dedicated runner; she enters races regularly.

5. My grandmother loves reading; she has usually a book with her.

6. My sister plays the piano all the time; she practices her lessons constantly.

7. Often I have thought of learning photography.

8. Over the years he has built up patiently an extensive stamp collection.

9. I quickly developed an interest in Japanese pottery when I lived in Japan.

10. My husband loves gardening; he spends always his weekends in his garden.

TRYING IT

What are some things you really like doing? Write sentences about 5 things.

LANGUAGE NOTE
Use adverbs: usually, carefully, a lot ...

....

....

21

22

Weather Forecast

*What is the weather like where you live?
What do you think the weather will be like tomorrow?*

ERROR BOX

✗ There will be a little clouds today.

✗ There will be a few rain today.

LISTENING TO COMPREHEND

Listen to the weather forecast. Check the correct boxes.

WORD BOX
* recently
* forecast
* 80% chance of...
* overcast
* degrees
* temperature

	today	tomorrow	Saturday	Sunday
sunny	☐	☐	☐	☐
cloudy	☐	☐	☐	☐
rainy	☐	☐	☐	☐
snowy	☐	☐	☐	☐

LISTENING TO NOTICE

Listen again. Fill in the blanks with one of these words or phrases.

little   a little   few   a few

We've had very nice sunny weather recently, with _____ clouds 1

and _____ rain. But that's going to start changing soon. This afternoon's 2

forecast calls for mostly cloudy skies. Tonight there's an 80% chance of rain,

although _____ areas will get more than a couple of millimeters. Lows 3

tonight will be about 5 degrees Celsius.

Tomorrow we'll have _____ periods of sunshine in the morning 4

and then overcast skies for the rest of the day. Tomorrow night there's a 50%

chance of rain. _____ thunderstorms are possible, especially in the areas 5

to the west. Highs around 10 degrees, lows around 3.

Saturday will be clear and cold, with _____ wind. The high tem- 6

peratures will be only around 5 degrees Celsius. Saturday night some areas in

the north could get _____ snow. 7

On Sunday morning it will be cloudy and cold, although by later in the

day we should get _____ sunshine. High temperatures will again be 8

about 5 degrees.

**For Grammar Explanation,
See The Yellow Pages p.130** ▶

UNDERSTANDING THE GRAMMAR POINT

1. Look back at the weather forecast. Complete the table below.

a few	few	little	a little
	few clouds		

2. What kinds of words follow *a few* and *few*?
   What kinds of words follow *a little* and *little*?

3. Can you explain the difference in meaning between *a few* and *few*?
   Between *a little* and *little*?

CHECKING

Which of these sentences contain an error? Try to correct all the errors.

1. Sydney will have ~~a few~~ *a little* sunshine in the morning, but the afternoon will be cloudy.

2. It was very windy in Vancouver today, with a few gusts of more than 60 kilometers per hour.

3. Tomorrow Paris will be mostly sunny, with only a little clouds.

4. This weekend, there is little rain in the forecast for New York; it will be clear and mild through Sunday.

5. It's not unusual for Washington, D.C. to receive a few snow in the winter.

6. The weather throughout Japan looks very good for the New Year's Day period; there should be a few travel problems.

7. In Berlin, it will be sunny and warm for the rest of the afternoon, but tonight few thunderstorms could pass through the area.

8. In the San Francisco Bay area, it will become increasingly cloudy this evening, and we may see a few rain.

9. Beijing will be cold and overcast, possibly with a few snow flurries.

10. Looking ahead to Thursday and Friday, Hong Kong will be warm and sunny, with few wind.

TRYING IT

LANGUAGE NOTE
Try to use few/a few and little/a little

How has the weather been in your town?
Write a weather forecast answering these questions.
What was it like yesterday? What will the weather be like tomorrow?

....

....

22

23

Quiz Show

Do you like quiz shows?
Would you like to go on a quiz show?
Why or why not?

ERROR BOX
✗ Of all the animals, the chee tah is fast.
✗ Mt. Everest is tall than Mt. Fuji.

LISTENING TO COMPREHEND

Do you think these statements are true or false?

	True	False
The heaviest animal in the world is the elephant.	☐	☐
Mt. Fuji is the highest volcano in the world.	☐	☐
The largest pyramid in the world is in Egypt.	☐	☐

Listen to the quiz show. Check your answers.

LISTENING TO NOTICE

WORD BOX
* contestant
* pyramid
* mistakes
* statement
* monument

Listen again. Complete the conversation.

Quiz-Show Host: Today's contestant, from Toronto, is Alison MacTavish. Welcome, Alison. Please say "True" or "False" after each statement I read to you. Remember, if you make three mistakes, the game is over, and you lose. Ready?

Alison: Yes.

Quiz-Show Host: All right. Number 1: The ___*heaviest*___ animal in the
                     1 (heavy/heavier/the heaviest)
world is the elephant.

Alison: True.

Quiz-Show Host: I'm sorry, that's not correct. Elephants are
_____ , but the blue whale is _____ than the elephant.
2 (heavy/heavier/the heaviest)   3 (heavy/heavier/the heaviest)
Let's try Number 2: Mt. Fuji is _____ volcano in the world.
                                4 (high/higher/the highest)

Alison: Yes, that's true.

Quiz-Show Host: Wrong again. Mt. Fuji is _____ , but several
                                            5 (high/higher/the highest)
volcanoes are _____ than Mt. Fuji. Here's Number 3:
              6 (high/higher/the highest)
_____ pyramid in the world is in Egypt.
7 (large/larger/the largest)

Alison: True?

Quiz-Show Host: Oh, I'm sorry: Wrong again. The Great Pyramids of
Egypt are _____ . But the pyramid of Quetzalcoatl in Mexico is
          8 (large/larger/the largest)
_____ . In fact, it's _____ monument in the world.
9 (large/larger/the largest)   10 (large/larger/the largest)
Better luck next time, Alison.

UNDERSTANDING THE GRAMMAR POINT

1. Look back at the quiz show. Write the adjectives from the blanks in the correct column.

adjective	adjective + -er	adjective + -est
heavy		*heaviest*

2. Which form of the adjective do we use to compare two things? Which form of the adjective do we use to compare three or more things?

CHECKING

Correct the errors in these sentences.

1. What is the ~~fast~~ *fastest* elevator in the world?

2. The fastest elevator in the world travels over 40 kilometers per hour.

3. What is the long snake ever found?

4. The longer snake ever found is over 10 meters long.

5. Mt. Fuji is not the high volcano in the world.

6. I thought the Egyptian pyramids were largest in the world.

7. Blue whales are much heavier than elephants.

8. Chicago is not bigger as New York.

9. New York bigger than Chicago.

10. New York is the big city in the United States.

TRYING IT

Do you know any special facts or world records? Make up some quiz questions about these things.

LANGUAGE NOTE
Use comparative and superlative forms of adjectives.

....

....

....

23

24

Animal Idioms

Do you think you are like a particular animal?
Which one? Why?

as stubborn
as a mule

like a fish
out of water

as slow as
a tortoise

LISTENING TO COMPREHEND

Listen to the radio show, "The Language Minute."
Match each animal with a word or phrase.

tortoise	busy
fish	happy
bull	head cut off
chicken	in a china shop
mule	in a hen house
beaver	out of water
clam	slow
ox	strong
fox	stubborn

WORD BOX
*clumsy   *clam
*bull   *ox
*china shop *fox
*henhouse
*disorganized

LISTENING TO NOTICE

Listen again. Fill in the blanks with the words you hear.

Welcome to "The Language Minute." I'm your host, Sara Glass. Our topic today is idioms. We will compare human characteristics with characteristics of animals.

Do you take a long time to get ready in the morning? We'll often say, "You're ___*as slow as*___ a tortoise." Do you feel unhappy and uncomfortable in
1
certain situations? We may say that you are " _____ out of water." We
2
may describe someone who is very clumsy by saying he's " _____ in a
3
china shop." And here's one of my favorites: saying that someone is so disorganized that she's running around " _____ with its head cut off"!
4
Does someone refuse to see your point of view? We may want to say,
"You're _____ a mule." How about someone who is always working?
5
" _____ a beaver." And how about these: " _____ a clam";
6 7
" _____ an ox"; " _____ in a henhouse." This last one describes
8 9
someone who can't be trusted.

Well, that's all for today. Next time we'll look at how other languages use animals in idioms. Until then: See you later, alligator!

UNDERSTANDING THE GRAMMAR POINT

1. Complete the table using the eight expressions in the lecture.

as _____ as . . .	like a _____
as slow as a tortoise	*like a fish out of water*

2. What kind of word do we use between *as...as*? **What kind of word or phrase do we use after** *like*?

CHECKING

Which of these sentences contain errors? Correct the errors.

1. Tom and his brother look the same and act the same; they're ~~as~~ *like* two peas in a pod.

2. My daughter is as gentle a lamb with her baby brother.

3. When my husband goes into a sporting goods store, he's like a child in a candy shop.

4. He always keeps his promises; his word is as good like gold.

5. What did you put in this bookbag? It feels like a ton of bricks.

6. I often don't even know if Yoshi is in his room; he is as quiet as a mouse.

7. I thought they would be finished two hours ago! They're as slow molasses.

8. She spends so much time washing her car; it's always as clean as a whistle.

9. They only met once; they were as two ships passing in the night.

10. Do you know that people used to compliment someone by saying he was as healthy a horse?

TRYING IT

Write down three idioms involving people and animals from your language.

1. ....
2. ....
3. ....

Can you translate these idioms into English?

1. ....
2. ....
3. ....

LANGUAGE NOTE

use the patterns
as + ADJECTIVE + as
and like + NOUN
PHRASE

24

25

European Cities

Have you ever visited a European city?
What was it like?

LISTENING TO COMPREHEND

What cities are being compared?   Find one way in which each pair of cities is different.

Cities	Difference
_____ and _____	_____
_____ and _____	_____

LISTENING TO NOTICE

Listen again. Fill in the blanks with the missing preposition in the box below.

to   from   as   with   than   0 (no preposition)

WORD BO
* compare
* contrast
* artistic spiri
* dignified
* variety

        Moscow and St. Petersburg: the two great cities of

Russia. We Russians love to compare them. The two cities are very different

___*from*___ each other. Compared _____ Moscow, St. Petersburg is a
       1   2

fairly new city. But today Moscow has in many ways become the more mod-

ern city. And the cities are unlike _____ each other in many other ways.
                                          3

For example, we say that in contrast _____ St. Petersburg, which is a
                                         4

European city in Russia, Moscow is a truly Russian city: in its size, in its

variety, in its complexity.

        Madrid is different _____ Barcelona in several ways. First, unlike
                                5

_____ Barcelona, which is a Mediterranean city, Madrid is deep in the
    6

interior of the country, far from the sea. Second, in contrast _____
                                                                    7

Barcelona, which is a city of great artistic spirit, Madrid is more dignified and

stately — our center of government. No, Madrid is not like _____
                                                              8

Barcelona; Madrid is our nation's brain, but Barcelona is its heart.

UNDERSTANDING THE GRAMMAR POINT

1. Look back at the descriptions of the cities. Find the preposition that follows each of these comparative terms. Write the comparative expression and the preposition.

Comparative term	Preposition
different	*from*

2. Study what preposition is used with each comparative expression.

CHECKING

Which of the following sentences are incorrect? Correct the errors.

1. Compared $\overset{with}{\wedge}$ the normal winter in Minneapolis, winters in Washington are quite mild.

2. Boston differs from San Francisco in a number of ways.

3. Vancouver is unlike as Seattle in some ways.

4. Like as Denver, Atlanta has grown fast during the last 25 years.

5. Although they are both cosmopolitan cities, Montreal's atmosphere is different from Toronto's.

6. Compared from New York, Boston has the feel of a small city.

7. In contrast to Miami, San Diego gets very little rain.

8. Unlike Los Angeles, which is located on the Pacific Coast, Phoenix is hundreds of miles from water.

TRYING IT

Compare any two cities in your country. Think about: location, climate, size, age, customs, etc.

LANGUAGE NOTE

Use similar to, different from and other comparative expressions.

....

....

....

26

Following Directions

Have you ever gotten lost? Did you look at a map? Did you ask for directions?

LISTENING TO COMPREHEND

Listen to a runner in Singapore getting directions. He wants to go to the Botanical Gardens. Mark the route he describes on the map.

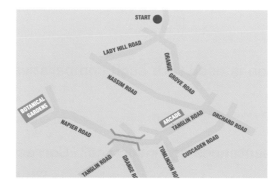

WORD BOX
*botanical gardens
*intersection
*arcade
*directions
*pedestrian

LISTENING TO NOTICE

Listen to the directions again. Fill in the blanks with *there's* or *it's*.

You want to go jogging in the Botanical Gardens? That's one of my favorite places to go, especially when __*it's*__ sunny. No, _____ not too far from here. Turn left on Orange Grove Road and go all the way to Tanglin Road. If you're walking, _____ about five minutes. Go right on Tanglin Road. The road curves a little, and _____ a short arcade along the way. _____ a pedestrian bridge at a big intersection. Use it, because _____ dangerous to cross at the intersection. Actually, I think _____ illegal, also. From the corner of Orange Grove Road and Tanglin Road, _____ less than a kilometer. OK, take a right when you come down from the bridge. Walk for a few more minutes. You won't miss it. _____ a big ornate gate at the entrance, just what you'd expect. At this time of day, _____ pretty quiet in the Gardens.

(blank numbers: 1, 2, 3, 4, 5, 6, 7, 8, 9, 10)

For Grammar Explanation, See The Yellow Pages p.132 ▶

UNDERSTANDING THE GRAMMAR POINT

1. **Find the words** *it's* **and** *there's* **in the directions to the Botanical Gardens. Find the words that follow them. Complete the table.**

it's	there's
sunny	*a short arcade*

2. **When do you use** *it's*? **When do you use** *there's*?

CHECKING

Complete the following text by filling in each blank with either *it's* **or** *there's*.

I'm going to give you directions to our house. Now, you have to take Highway 5 west out of the city.

___*It's*___ 12 miles to the junction of Highway 5 and Silver Lake Road. _____ about fifteen or twenty
  1   2

minutes, a little more if _____ a lot of traffic. _____ a small shopping area on the left just before
                              3   4

you get to Silver Lake Road. Turn right on Silver Lake Road and go about three miles. Silver Lake Road is

narrow, and _____ one very steep hill, so drive carefully, especially if _____ raining or foggy. Our
                 5   6

house is on the left. _____ a group of pine trees in the front just before our driveway. _____ very
                          7   8

quiet out here in the country; you'll know you're not in the city.

TRYING IT

Is your home close to the airport or railroad station? Describe how to get from the airport or railroad station to your house or apartment.

....

....

....

....

LANGUAGE NOTE
Be sure to use *it's* and *there's*.

26

Alzheimer's Disease

27

Do you know anyone with Alzheimer's disease? What is he or she like?

LISTENING TO COMPREHEND

Listen to the lecture about Alzheimer's disease. Complete the table.

All people...	People with Alzheimer's disease...
1. forget things but remember them later	*may forget something and never remember it*
2. sometimes forget the right word	
3. sometimes get lost	
4. sometimes lose something	
5. sometimes are moody	

LISTENING TO NOTICE

Listen to the lecture again. Fill in the missing verbs.

WORD BOX
* recognize
* a wallet
* a disease
* moody
* Alzheimer's disease
* calm

Today I want to tell you how you can recognize when someone has Alzheimer's disease.

Most people forget things but they usually remember them later. People with Alzheimer's disease ___*may*___ forget something and never remember it.

We all have trouble finding the right word sometimes. People with Alzheimer's disease _____ forget even very simple words.

We all get lost sometime or other. People with Alzheimer's disease _____ get lost on their own street!

We sometimes lose something like our wallet or our keys. People with Alzheimer's disease _____ lose things all the time. For example, they _____ put a wristwatch in the sugar bowl.

We are all moody sometimes. People with Alzheimer's disease _____ be calm one minute and angry the next — for no reason. For example, they _____ suddenly say you have stolen something from them.

Next, I'd like to talk about the treatment of Alzheimer's disease...

UNDERSTANDING THE GRAMMAR POINT

1. Look back at the lecture. Complete the table.

Modal Verbs	Main Verbs
may	*forget*

2. Now complete this sentence about the use of modal verbs like *may*:

A modal verb is followed by _____ .

a. to + verb   b. verb+ing   c. a simple verb   d. a past participle.

3. What is the difference in meaning between the verbs in these sentences?

• Maria often forgets things.

• She may forget her own name one day.

CHECKING

Complete the sentences. Use a modal verb or a simple present tense.

People with Alzheimer's disease ___*forget*___ things. They ___*may prepare*___ a meal and then forget they cooked it.
                                        1 (forget)   2 (prepare)

We all _____ strange things sometimes, but people with Alzheimer's disease _____ things that do
            3 (say)   4 (say)

not make any sense at all. Some people _____ in strange ways but people suffering from Alzheimer's dis-
                                                    5 (dress)

ease _____ several shirts or dresses at the same time. They also _____ some very odd things. For
        6 (put on)   7 (do)

example, someone with Alzheimer's _____ an iron in a freezer. Everybody _____ sometimes, but
                                            8 (put)   9 (cry)

people with Alzheimer's disease _____ into tears for no reason at all.
                                        10 (burst)

TRYING IT

How can you tell whether someone has a common cold? Write about the symptoms.

A person with a common cold ....

....

....

LANGUAGE NOTE

Remember to use modal verbs to say what may possibly happen.

27

28

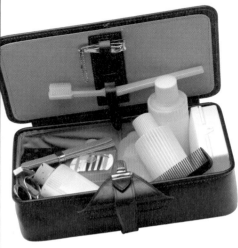

A Trip to Russia

*Imagine you're going to visit Russia.
What would you want to know before you leave?*

LISTENING TO COMPREHEND

Boris is giving Roberta information about Russia. Put a check next to each item they talk about.

getting a passport	buying film
✓ getting a visa	confirming hotel reservations
bringing traveler's checks	confirming the return flight
bringing gifts	sightseeing
buying souvenirs	learning Russian

LISTENING TO NOTICE

Listen again. Fill in the blanks with the word or words you hear.

WORD BOX
* currency
* trouble
* advice
* reconfirm
* fascinating

Roberta: I'm planning a trip to Russia. I know you've been there several times. What do I need to do to get ready for my trip?

Boris: Well, first you ___*have to*___ get a visa ahead of time. You can't enter the
          1
country without one, and you can't get one when you arrive. And when you arrive, you _____ fill out a currency declaration form. And don't lose it;
                    2
you _____ turn it in at passport control when you leave.
        3
    Oh, and you _____ reconfirm your return flight; if you don't,
                              4
you'll lose your reservation. These are things you must do.

Roberta: Those are the rules? OK, I'll be sure to follow them. Do you have any advice about what I should bring or what I should do while I'm there?

Boris: Yeah, a few things. You _____ use bottled water. And you
                                        5
_____ bring plenty of film and extra batteries for your camera; film is
      6
very expensive in Russia, and you may have trouble replacing your camera battery. And you _____ bring small gifts — souvenirs of the place you live
                            7
are nice; it isn't necessary, of course, but it's a nice thing to do. And you
_____ try to see as much as you can; it's a fascinating country.
      8
Roberta: Thanks for your help.

UNDERSTANDING THE GRAMMAR POINT

1. Here are the sentences from the conversation with *have to* **and** *should*. **Rewrite each sentence using** *"It is necessary to..."* **or** *"It is a good idea to...".*

"Well, first you have to get a visa ahead of time."
It is necessary to get a visa ahead of time.
"You have to fill out a currency declaration form."

"You have to turn it in at passport control when you leave."

"You have to reconfirm your return flight."

"You should use bottled water."

"And you should bring plenty of film and extra batteries for your camera."

"And you should bring small gifts."

"And you should try to see as much as you can."

2. What is the meaning of *have to*? **What is the meaning of** *should*?

CHECKING

What is the best way to complete each sentence? Use *should* **or** *have to*.

1. You _____ show a photo I.D. at the check-in counter. This is a federal law.

2. You_____ bring plenty of film. Film is very expensive there.

3. You _____ get a visa in advance. You cannot get one when you arrive.

4. You _____ turn in your currency declaration form. You are required to turn it in when you leave.

5. It's not necessary, but you _____bring flowers or a small gift if you are invited to someone's home.

6. At some airports, you _____ pay an airport service fee or departure tax.

7. Instead of a large sum of cash, you _____ bring traveler's checks.

8. At the airport, you _____ go through airport security.

IDEA BOX

dress code, work time, places to eat

TRYING IT

Imagine that a new student comes to your school or that a new employee comes to your place of work. List the rules that that person *has to* **follow. Then provide advice and suggestions about what the person** *should* **do.**

Letters of Reference

Look at the word box. Choose the three words you would most like someone to include in a job reference for you.

IGG
215 First Street
Los Angeles 90021 CA

To whom it may concern:

Marcia Lewis has worked in our sales department for the past five years. She began as a sales assistant, with responsibilities for small businesses in the Los Angeles area. Because of her extraordinary ability to find new clients, we quickly promoted her to sales manager for all of southern California. This is the position she currently holds.

In her job Ms. Lewis has demonstrated perseverance and drive. She consistently searches out potential clients who have relocated in the area and develops a plan to introduce our products and services. As a result of her careful research and planning, she has been personally responsible for landing us several major accounts over the past three years.

Although Ms. Lewis has often alienated some of her colleagues in the department with her excessive demands, I have found her to be a highly desirable employee. For some time, I have realized that her career goals would eventually lead her to look for employment with a larger national or international firm. I imagine that when she finds colleagues with equally ambitious goals, she will fit in very well and continue to exhibit her fine skills at selling.

I will be sorry to see Ms. Lewis leave our firm. I have found her influence on our company to be very beneficial.

I highly recommend her for a challenging position in sales and marketing.

If you have any questions, please feel free to contact me.

Sincerley,

Lydia S. Thone
Marketing Manager

LISTENING TO COMPREHEND

1. Listen to the references of three workers. Complete the table.

Name	Place of Work	Job(s)
Maria Garcia	_____	• sales assistant
		• _____
Julie England	_____	• receptionist
		• _____
_____	Berlitz School	• _____

WORD BOX

* dependable
* skillful
* personal charm
* professional
* popular

LISTENING TO NOTICE

Listen to the references again. Write in the correct form of the verb.

1. Maria Garcia ___*has been*___ at Bloomingdale's since 1990. To begin with, she
1 (be)
_____ in the cosmetics department as a sales assistant. For the last five years
2 (work)
she _____ as assistant manager in the women's apparel department. She
3 (act)
_____ herself dependable and highly professional. We will be sorry to see
4 (show)
her leave.

2. Julie England _____ as a hostess at the Essex Club since 1995. Initially,
5 (work)
she _____ as a receptionist, greeting customers as they arrived. However,
6 (act)
for the last 12 months she _____ charge of some of the club's most impor-
7 (take)
tant customers. Julie has a lot of personal charm and _____ extremely
8 (be)
popular. We strongly recommend her.

3. Mike Byson _____ at the Berlitz School since 1993. He _____
9 (work)   10 (come)
to us with no teaching experience but since _____ into a highly skillful
11 (develop)
teacher of English. He is now very popular with the students. For the last few
months, however, Mr. Byson _____ to follow his own method of teaching
12 (chose)
English rather than the methods used by the school. For this reason we have
asked him to find other employment.

UNDERSTANDING THE GRAMMAR POINT

1. **Look back at the references. Circle the verbs in the simple past tense (e.g.** *worked*). **Underline all the verbs in the present perfect tense (***has worked***).**

2. **Complete these sentences:**

   • Use the _____ tense to refer to actions that took place in the past and are *now completed.*

   • Use the _____ tense to refer to an action that started in the past and is *still continuing* at the time of speaking.

3. **Which tense is used with** *for* **and** *since*?

4. **Complete these explanations of how to use** *for* **and** *since*. **Fill in the example sentence.**

   • Use _____ with the present perfect to refer to a time when an ongoing action first started.
   She has been at Bloomingdale's _____ 1990.

   • Use _____ with the present perfect to refer to a period of time an action has been going on.
   _____ *the last five years she has worked as an assistant manager.*

CHECKING

Choose the present perfect tense or the simple past tense.

Rod Ellis was born in England. He _____ overseas for most of his life. In 1967 he _____ to
                                    1 (live)   2 (go)
Zambia where he _____ for 10 years. In 1978 he _____ work in London. He _____ there
                  3 (live)   4 (start)   5 (work)
from 1978 to 1989. In 1989 he _____ London to work for Temple University in Japan and then in
                                6 (leave)
Philadelphia. He _____ at Temple for nine years. In July 1998 he _____ to Auckland in New
                  7 (teach)   8 (move)
Zealand where he _____ since. He _____ working at the University of Auckland and expects to stay
                  9 (live)   10 (enjoy)
there many more years.

TRYING IT

Write a reference for a friend who is applying for a job. Or write a reference about yourself.

LANGUAGE NOTE

Make sure you use the present perfect tense with *for* and *since*.

....

....

....

....

....

29

30

The Sad Story of Miss Leeson

You are going to hear a story. Look at the words in the word box. Can you imagine what happened to Miss Leeson?

LISTENING TO COMPREHEND

Read the sentences below. Then listen to the story about Miss Leeson. Write True or False for each statement.

1. _____ Miss Leeson did not have much money.
2. _____ Miss Leeson left the guest house early every day.
3. _____ Miss Leeson was a typist.
4. _____ Miss Leeson did not eat enough food.
5. _____ Miss Leeson died in hospital.

WORD BOX
*a guest house
*an ambulance
*starvation
*recover

LISTENING TO NOTICE

Listen to the story again. Fill in the blanks with the correct form of the verb in parentheses ( ).

Miss Leeson ___*found*___ a small room at the top of Mrs. Parker's guest house.
1 (find)

It cost her only a few dollars.

Every day Miss Leeson _____ the guest house early. She came back late.
2 (leave)

Sometimes she _____ back papers and copied them on her typewriter.
3 (bring)

Often, though, she _____ no papers to copy. Then she just _____
4 (have)   5 (sit)

with the other guests. They talked and laughed together.

One winter day Miss Leeson did not come down from her room. Clara, the

maid, _____ on her door but she did not answer. Clara forced the door
6 (knock)

open. Miss Leeson _____ very still on her bed. She _____ her out-
7 (lie)   8 (still wear)

door clothes. She _____ . An ambulance _____ and took Miss
9 (hardly breathe)   10 (come)

Leeson to the city hospital. When the doctor _____ at her he said that
11 (look)

she _____ from starvation but that she would recover.
12 (suffer)

For Grammar Explanation, See The Yellow Pages p.134 ▶

UNDERSTANDING THE GRAMMAR POINT

1. Circle the verbs in the simple past tense (*found*). Underline the verbs in the past continuous tense (*was lying*).

2. When is the past continuous tense used?
    a. To refer to a past action that happened several times in the past.
    b. To refer to a past action that took place at a definite point in the past.
    c. To refer to a past action that took place over a period of time.

3. The simple past has two uses. Find examples of these two uses in the story.

Past action completed at a definite point in the past	Past action happening several times
found	*left*

4. Which of these sentences is correct? Can you explain why?
    a. Every day Miss Leeson left the guest house early.
    b. Every day Miss Leeson was leaving the guest house early.

CHECKING

Here is another story. Study the verbs. Are they in the correct tense? Change the ones that are wrong.

Jimmy Spencer was a burglar. Every month he ~~was robbing~~ *robbed* a different bank.

Sometimes he **was getting** a lot of money but he always **was spending** it quickly. Jimmy

Spencer liked the good life.

One day he **was visiting** a small town in Arkansas. He **booked** into the local hotel and then

walked over to the bank. A beautiful young woman **was going** into the bank.

"Who's she?" he asked a man.

"That's Polly Simpson. She's the bank manager's daughter," the man told him.

So Jimmy **decided** not to rob the bank after all. Instead he **was staying** on in the town and

opened a shoe shop. It was very successful. Jimmy **started** a savings account at the bank.

Within a year he **was marrying** Polly Simpson.

LANGUAGE NOTE
Try to use both the simple past tense and the past continuous tense.

TRYING IT

Do you know any stories or folk tales?
Tell a story that you know well.

Complete the passage below. Choose from the words and phrases in the box. Use each item one time only. There are some extra items.

Note: In this passage one gap needs to be left blank. For this blank, write 0.

best	will	should	were showing	are suffering
poorly	often	it	smart	as
smarter	like	to	there	were suffering
from	little	have shown	a little	few
may	poor			

Dealing with Pain

Do men and women deal with pain in the same way? Several studies _____
                                                                                    1
that women deal with pain better than men.

One study at Ohio University involved 99 women and 48 men. During this study, all of these
people _____ from arthritis, which is a common illness of the bones and
                         2
joints. The research had two important findings.

First, the study concluded that women may be _____ than men about dealing
                                                                    3
with pain. What do women do differently? Generally, in comparison _____
                                                                                          4
men, women stay busy. They don't think about the pain. On the other hand, men
_____ focus on the pain they are feeling. They seem to have
                5
_____ ideas about how to deal with pain.
                6

Second, unlike _____ women, men choose to suffer in silence. They are not
                                  7
as likely _____ women to ask their doctor for advice. In this way also, most
                    8
men cope with pain _____ .
                                 9

One thing is clear. These studies_____ definitely produce more debate about
                                                    10
differences between men and women. What can we learn from this research now?
_____ is one obvious piece of advice: Men _____ learn
               11   12
more about how to deal with pain.

Complete the passage below. Choose from the words and phrases in the box. Use each item one time only. There are some extra items.

has worked	might	unexpected	little	it
unexpectedly	there	it is	have enjoyed	as
from	warmer	must	have to	few
was working	like	enjoyed	a few	to
warm				

From Chicago to Florida

Last year at this time Jessica Anderson _____ in Chicago, one of the coldest

cities in the United States. Now she is working in a hotel in the Florida Keys, one of the warmest

spots in the country. _____ just a short walk from her office to palm trees and

white sand beaches.

"This is _____ a dream for me," Jessica said. "I have a challenging job, and I

live in a great place. And Florida is a lot _____ than Chicago. My company,

Hotels International, _____ transferred me to Orchid Beach Resort last

March. I had only _____ weeks to prepare for the move. And I had

_____ time to learn my new job. I'm Director of Guest Services. It's different

_____ my last job, but I _____ it. I like to stay busy, and

_____ is something to do every minute.

I tell my staff that we _____ remember: our guests come here for the best

vacation possible. Our motto is: 'You can't stay forever at Orchid Beach Resort, but you

_____ want to!'"

31

Famous Modern Buildings

What famous building have you seen?
What does it look like?

LISTENING TO COMPREHEND

Listen to the description of Kansai Airport.
Which of these places are mentioned?

☐ Osaka Bay　　　　☐ the domestic lobby
☐ Italy　　　　　　☐ McDonald's
☐ the ground floor　☐ shops
☐ the shuttle trains　☐ the train station
☐ the international departure lobby
☐ the international arrival lobby

WORD BOX

*terminal
*architect
*international
*a lobby
*a departure gate
*a shuttle train

LISTENING TO NOTICE

Listen again. Do you hear *the*? Write *the* or *O* (no *the*) in the blanks.

Welcome to ___*O*___ Kansai International Airport, KIA. The airport is located
　　　　　　　　1

on _____ Airport Island in _____ Osaka Bay. KIA has _____ world's largest
　　　　2　　　　　　　　　　3　　　　　　　　　4

passenger terminal. It was designed by _____ Renzo Piano, _____ famous
　　　　　　　　　　　　　　　　　　　　5　　　　　　　　6

Italian architect.

On arrival you will enter _____ main terminal. You will find _____ international
　　　　　　　　　　　7　　　　　　　　　　　　　　　　8

arrival lobby on the first floor of the main terminal. _____ international
　　　　　　　　　　　　　　　　　　　　　　　　9

departure lobby is on the fourth floor. _____ domestic lobby for both arrivals
　　　　　　　　　　　　　　　　　　　10

and departures is on the second floor.

There are 26 restaurants, including _____ McDonald's, and 44 shops situated
　　　　　　　　　　　　　　　　11

on the second and third floors.

Your departure gate will be in _____ north or south wing. Shuttle trains leave
　　　　　　　　　　　　　　12

the main terminal every two minutes.

UNDERSTANDING THE GRAMMAR POINT

1. Complete the table with the noun phrases from the passage.

O + Noun Phrase	THE + Noun Phrase
Kansai International Airport	*the world's largest passenger terminal*

2. When should you not use *the*? When should you use *the*?

CHECKING

Read the paragraph about Trump Tower. Find the errors and correct them.

Trump Tower

Trump Tower was designed by Philip Johnson, one of ^the^ leading architects in the U.S. It overlooks the Central

Park in the heart of Manhattan. At bottom of the tower is Trump International Hotel. Above this there are a

number of luxury apartments. Some of apartments cost as much $10 million. Residents can use all the ameni-

ties of hotel, including gourmet restaurant, Jean-Georges, and fitness center. In grand atrium of the tower you

can find world's most exclusive shops. For example, in lobby you will find the Cartier and Galeries Lafayette

while on second floor there is the Club Chagall. You can be sure that in the Trump Tower you will rub shoul-

ders with some very rich and famous people.

LANGUAGE NOTE
Think about whether
or not to use the
before nouns.

TRYING IT

Write a short description of a building you know well.
OR Write a description of your hometown, mentioning
some of the special places.

....

....

....

32

True Stories

*Sometimes people do very strange things.
Do you know a funny story about someone?*

LISTENING TO COMPREHEND

Listen to the stories and answer these questions.

Story 1
What happened to Jason and Mary Ellen Jones?

_____

Story 2
What did the man steal?

_____

WORD BOX

* stubbornness
* drowning
* topple
* a well
* available
* frustration
* unemployed

LISTENING TO NOTICE

Listen again. Write *a(n)* or *O* (no *a(n)*) in each space.

1. __*An*__ unfortunate accident occurred in rural Texas yesterday. The accident
   1
occurred when Jason B. Jones and his wife, Mary Ellen Jones, died from
_____ drowning. Apparently, _____ chicken had fallen into _____ well on
   2   3   4
their farm. Jason, known locally for _____ stubbornness rather than _____
                                     5   6
intelligence, climbed in to rescue it. When he got stuck he called his wife, who
lowered _____ rope into the well. Jason grasped the rope and started to pull
        7
himself out. Unfortunately, he was too heavy for his wife, who toppled into the
well. They both fell into the water at the bottom.
Only the chicken survived.

2. _____ unusual event took place in Ypsilanti, Michigan, yesterday. _____
   8   9
unemployed man tried to rob _____ diner. He walked into the diner at 11:05
                            10
in the morning and threatened the owner with _____ gun. However, the
                                             11
owner said he could not open the cash register unless the man ordered _____
                                                                      12
food. The man ordered _____ bacon and eggs, but the owner told him break-
                      13
fast finished at 11 o'clock. The man then asked for _____ soup, but the owner
                                                    14
told him it was not available. Full of _____ frustration, the man walked away.
                                       15

UNDERSTANDING THE GRAMMAR POINT

1. Look at the stories again. Circle the word in each blank and the noun or noun phrase that follows. Complete this table.

Nouns with a(n)	Nouns without a(n)
an unfortunate accident	*drowning*

2. Which kind of noun is *a(n)* used with? Which kind of noun should *a(n)* **not** be used with?

3. Study the nouns in the table. Which ones have *a*? Which ones have *an*? Make a rule to explain when to use *a* and when to use *an*.

CHECKING

Here is another unusual story. Can you find the errors and correct them?

A man in San Antonio, Texas, was arrested for stealing cell phone and a money from a car. The owner of the car, feeling an anger, decided to trick the thief. He pretended that he was from radio station. He called his cell phone number and the thief answered. He told the thief that he had won a $5,000 prize from the radio station and he had to come to the radio station to pick it up. When the thief arrived to pick up his prize, the police were waiting. They arrested him for a possession of stolen property.

LANGUAGE NOTE
Be careful about using a(n) and the.

TRYING IT

**Do you know a true story like the ones above? Write it out.
If you do not know one, you can make one up.**

A man/woman ....

....

....

....

....

Fantastic Toys

33

Have you ever had a pet?
What did you have to do to take care of it?

LISTENING TO COMPREHEND

Listen to the newspaper report about the tamagochi.
Answer these questions:

1. What is a tamagochi?
2. What does the owner of a tamagochi have to do?
3. What kind of tamagochi did the Chinese street seller make?
4. Why did Mariko Tada lose her job?

WORD BOX
* hatch   * insect
* cage   * discipli
* chick   * fired
* bamboo   * gadget
* chirping   * invent

LISTENING TO NOTICE

Listen again. Choose *a* or *the* to complete the newspaper report.

   __A__ tamagochi is a computerized toy invented in Japan. The name
means a cute little egg. _____ tamagochi has become very popular all around
the world. The gadget hatches _____ chick. _____ chick makes a chirping noise
every few minutes. _____ owner has to push buttons to feed, play with, clean
up and discipline the chick. If _____ owner stops caring for the chick, it dies.

   However, the electronic toy is expensive and many people cannot afford
to buy one. _____ street seller in China had a good idea. He decided to make
a live tamagochi. He made _____ small cage out of bamboo. Then he caught
_____ insect. He put _____ insect inside _____ cage. _____ street seller was
able to sell the tamagochi for three yuan (about 40 cents). Now he has become
rich selling live tamagochis.

   Some people think that the tamagochi is a bad thing. "I bought a tamagochi and spent a lot of time looking after it," explained Mariko Tada, a sales
assistant in _____ downtown Tokyo store. She spent so much time caring for
her tamagochi that _____ store fired her!

UNDERSTANDING THE GRAMMAR POINT

1. Read the story again. Fill in the table.

a(n) + noun	the + noun
a tamagochi	*the tamagochi*

2. When is *a* used? When is *the* used?

3. Look through the story again. Study the other noun phrases with *a* and *the*
(a computerized toy; the gadget). Can you see why *a* is used in some noun phrases and
the in others?

CHECKING

Read the following descriptions of other toys. Fill in the blanks with *a(n)* or *the*.

1. TUGGLES is __*a*__ cuddly pet with a leash. When you pull on _____ leash the pet walks by itself. Kids
   love taking Tuggles for _____ walk.
   1   2
                                      3

2. JOSEPHINA MONTOYA is _____ realistic doll that looks Hispanic. It is accompanied by _____ book.
   _____ book tells you all about how to care for _____ doll.
                                          4   5
   6   7

3. BULLDOG DOZER is _____ construction set together with _____ bulldozer. _____ bulldozer keeps
   knocking down _____ construction you are making. Kids will love it!
                          8   9   10
               11

TRYING IT

LANGUAGE NOTE
Be careful about
using a and the.

Think of a toy you would like to invent. Write a description of
the toy. OR Think of a toy that you loved as a child. Describe it.

....

....

....

....

....

34

Brothers and Sisters

Do you have a lot of brothers and sisters?
Do you have friends from large families?

LISTENING TO COMPREHEND 🎧

Listen to Amy, Bruce and Carla talk about their families. Answer each question by putting a check (✔) in the correct space.

	Amy	Bruce	Carla
Who has the largest family?	☐	✔	☐
Whose family has the most males?	☐	☐	☐
Whose family has the most females?	☐	☐	☐
Who has the smallest family?	☐	☐	☐

WORD BOX

* twin
* single
* worry
* career

LISTENING TO NOTICE 🎧

Listen again. Fill in the blanks with *other*, *the other* **or** *another*.

AMY

The person in my family I spend the most time with is my twin sister. I have two ___*other*___ sisters, but one reason I spend so much time with my twin sister is that we understand each other perfectly. _____ reason is that we both love to cook.

1

2

BRUCE

I come from a large family: There are four brothers. One of my brothers lives near Chicago, where we grew up; _____ brother lives in Boston; and _____ brother lives in Miami. I love visiting him, especially in the winter! And then there are two sisters. Both of my sisters are in Chicago. One still lives at home; _____ sister lives only a few miles away.

3

4

5

CARLA

I have two brothers. One lives in London; _____ brother lives in Sydney. Their lives are different in _____ ways, too. One difference is that my brother in London has a big family, but my brother in Sydney is single. _____ difference is that my brother in London worries about everything, especially his career. My brother in Sydney never worries at all. _____ difference is that my brother in London has plenty of money, but my brother is Sydney is always broke.

6

7

8

9

For Grammar Explanation, See The Yellow Pages p.136 ▶

UNDERSTANDING THE GRAMMAR POINT

1. Complete this chart with information from the texts.

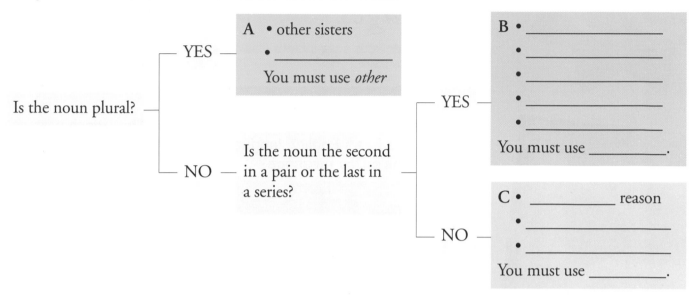

Is the noun plural?

— YES —
A • other sisters
• _____
You must use *other*

— NO — Is the noun the second in a pair or the last in a series?

— YES —
B • _____
• _____
• _____
• _____
• _____
You must use _____.

— NO —
C • _____ reason
• _____
• _____
You must use _____.

2. Now complete each of the following statements:

a. When we want to refer to the second (or last) of two or more persons or things, we use _____

b. When we want to identify the next item in a group, we use _____

c. With plural nouns, we use _____

CHECKING

Which of the following sentences are incorrect? Correct the errors.

1. My father's brother has two boys. One of them is much older than me; another is about my age.

2. I know some of the people in Hiroko's family, but there are another members of her family I've never even met.

3. His sisters look alike and act alike. Other similarity is that they both love sports.

4. Some people think it would be nice to have a twin brother or sister; other people wouldn't like to have a twin.

5. I know you've met one of my two brothers. Have you met another?

6. Two of her four grandchildren are lawyers, and another is a doctor.

7. There are three children in my family; two of us are girls, and other is a boy.

8. I have three sisters; two of them are older than me, but other is five years younger.

> **LANGUAGE NOTE**
> Use the other, another and other.

TRYING IT

Describe a large family you know. Identify and describe the people in the family. Talk about their ages, their jobs, their hobbies, etc.

35

Valentine's Day Messages

Have you ever sent a Valentine's Day message to somebody? What did you say?

LISTENING TO COMPREHEND

1. Listen to the Valentine's Day messages. They were written by students in an English language program. Who sent each Valentine's Day message?

To:	From :
1. Marcos	_____
2. Melisa	_____
3. Yong Jin	_____
4. Grace	_____

2. Which of the four lovers are unhappy? Why?

WORD BOX
* a heartthrob
* avoid
* broken-hearted
* can't stand somethin

LISTENING TO NOTICE

Listen to the Valentine's Day messages again. Choose the correct verb.

1.

To Marcos

My darling Marcos! I miss __*seeing*__ you
      1(to see/ seeing)
every day. You are the nicest and kindest
guy I have ever known. And you are so sexy.
Please keep _____ about me always!
    2 (to think/ thinking)
         Your heartthrob

2.

To Melisa

I will never forget you even though you have
forgotten me. You promised _____
           3 (to write/writing)
to me but I have heard nothing. But I shall
never stop _____ of you.
    4 (to think/ thinking)
         Broken hearted

3.

To Yong Jin

I want _____ you a big kiss for
    5 (to give/ giving)
Valentine's Day! I look forward to every
day because I know I shall enjoy
_____ you.
6 (to see/ seeing)
        True lover

4.

To Grace

I think only of your face, your hair, your lips.
But I know you avoid _____ to me and
        7 (to talk/ talking)
you can't stand _____ at me. Never
      8 (to look/ looking)
mind. I refuse _____ hope. You are the
     9 (to give up/ giving up)
only woman for me! I swear never
_____ you.
10 (to forget/forgetting)   Lost lover

UNDERSTANDING THE GRAMMAR POINT

1. **Look back at the letters. What verb comes before the blanks? Circle it.
Write these words in the correct column.**

Verbs followed by an infinitive (to + V)	Verbs followed by a gerund (V + ing)
promise	*miss*

2. **Here are some more verbs. Do they take an infinitive or a gerund?**

| try | deny | suggest | fail | agree |
| finish | consider | decide | prepare | delay |

CHECKING

Here are some more Valentine messages. Can you find the errors? Correct them.

1. I have enjoyed ~~to spend~~ *spending* time with you.

2. I cannot avoid to see you.

3. I promise never to forget you.

4. I miss to hold you in my arms.

5. I keep to look at the photo of you.

6. I refuse to forget you!

7. Do not be so cruel! Why do you avoid to meet with me?

8. Please, never stop to think of me!

9. I want to live my whole life with you!

10. I want to think of you every day of my life.

11. I fancy to hold you in my arms.

12. Soon I shall risk to ask you to be my lover.

TRYING IT

**Think of someone who is special to you.
Write a Valentine's Day message to that person.**

....

....

LANGUAGE NOTE
Use some of the verbs you have been studying in this unit.

35

LET vs. MAKE

36 Working Relationships

Have you ever had a difficult teacher or employer?
How was he or she difficult?

LISTENING TO COMPREHEND

What are the conversations about?

Conversation 1 is about:
(a) current events
(b) deciding what to read
(c) politics and environment

Conversation 2 is about:
(a) Mr. Arroyo
(b) finishing a project
(c) making plans for the weekend

WORD BOX
* current event
* deadline
* topic
* breathe
* proposal
* environment
* politics

LISTENING TO NOTICE

Listen to the conversations again. Fill in each blank with let or make.

Conversation 1:

Teacher: This month you're going to read about current events.

Student 1: What topic will we be reading about?

Teacher: I'm going to ___*let*___ you choose a topic. I'm not going to _____ you all read about the same topic.

1   2

Student 2: You won't _____ us read about politics?

3

Teacher: No, if you'd rather read about the environment, I'll _____ you choose that topic.

4

Student 1: When do we have to decide on our topic?

Teacher: I'll _____ you think about it until next week. Any other questions?

5

Conversation 2 :

Secretary: Sorry I'm late. I was afraid Mr. Arroyo wouldn't even _____ me leave for lunch.

6

Friend: What happened?

Secretary: There's a big proposal to finish, and Mr. Arroyo _____ everyone stop whatever they were doing to work on it.

7

Friend: Was he angry?

Secretary: No, but he's afraid we won't meet the deadline. He'll _____ us come in this weekend if we don't finish by the end of the week.

8

Friend: Well, enjoy your lunch. It sounds as if he's going to _____ you work hard for the next few days.

9

Secretary: He's not going to _____ us breathe until this proposal is done!

10

For Grammar Explanation,
See The Yellow Pages p.137 ▶

UNDERSTANDING THE GRAMMAR POINT

1. Study the use of *let* and *make* in the conversations. Which one means "require"? Which one means "allow"?

2. Look at these pairs of sentences. How are they different?

   • I'm going to let you choose a topic.

   • I'm going to allow you to choose a topic.

   • I'm not going to make you read it.

   • I'm not going to force you to read it.

3. Rewrite the sentences in the conversations with *make* and *let*.
   Use *allow...to* or *require...to /force...to.*

CHECKING

Which of these sentences contain an error? Can you correct the errors?

1. He found so many errors in the report that he ~~let~~ *made* his secretary retype it.

2. Our science teacher makes us use the laboratory after school if we want to do extra work.

3. Our office manager doesn't make us use our office telephones for personal calls.

4. Our company lets us to leave an hour early if we work through the lunch hour.

5. The plant manager lets everyone working in the factory wear safety glasses.

6. My English teacher makes us ask questions whenever we want.

7. Our supervisor lets us provide a receipt for even the smallest travel expense.

8. Because I had been sick, my teacher made me take the exam again.

> **LANGUAGE NOTE**
> Use expressions with make and let:
> I would make...
> I would not make...
> I would let...
> I would not let...

TRYING IT

Imagine that you are the manager of an office or the teacher of a class. Write some of the policies and rules you would have.

....

....

37 A Personal Problem

Do you read the personal problem letters in newspapers or magazines sometimes? What kinds of problems do these letters talk about?

LISTENING TO COMPREHEND

Listen to Angela read the letter she wrote to a newspaper. She is asking for advice. What do you think Angela should do? Why?

a. She should marry Rick because she loves him.
b. She should leave Rick because he is always fighting with her.
c. She should wait to see if Rick's behavior gets better.
d. She should . . .

WORD BOX
* a quandary
* caring
* alcohol
* spend money
* frightening

LISTENING TO NOTICE

Listen to Angela's letter again. Write in all the *-ing* words.

Dear Anne,

I am in a real quandary so I hope you can help me. I have been ___living___₁

with Rick, my boyfriend, for over a year now and I love him very much.

He is a very ___₂___ guy and sometimes he can be really ___₃___.

Most of the time he also is very ___₄___. However, he sometimes

goes out ___₅___ with his friends and when he comes home, he starts

___₆___ with me. He's always ___₇___ all his money on alcohol

and starts ___₈___ with me. Sometimes I find him really ___₉___.

Now he says we should get married. But I'm not so sure.

A very ___₁₀___ lover,

Angela

UNDERSTANDING THE GRAMMAR POINT

1. Read Angela's letter again. Write the words from the blanks in the correct column.

Verb *-ing*	Adjective *-ing*
living	*interesting*

2. Which of these words go with the verbs? Which of these words go with the adjectives?

	always	very	really	sometimes
go with the verbs	☐	☐	☐	☐
go with the adjectives	☐	☐	☐	☐

CHECKING

Which of these sentences are incorrect? Correct the errors.

1. Rick is ~~very~~ *always* quarreling with Angela.

2. He is a very interesting guy.

3. He is also really amusing sometimes.

4. Sometimes he is really caring.

5. But he is very drinking with his friends.

6. Angela is a very loving person.

7. He is very spending his money on alcohol.

8. He is very fighting with Angela.

9. He can be really frightening.

10. Now Angela is very doubting she loves him.

TRYING IT

Are you having a personal problem with someone? Do you know someone who is? Write a letter asking for advice about the problem.

LANGUAGE NOTE
Use some -ing words with very, really, sometimes and always.

....

....

....

....

38

Mission in Space

Imagine you are part of the crew of a space station.
What would it be like?

LISTENING TO COMPREHEND

1. **Listen to the news report about the Spiv space station. What do the cosmonauts plan to do? Complete their schedule.**

   August 12th: *Two new cosmonauts blast off*

   August 14th: _____

   September 15th: _____

2. **What will the new cosmonauts do on Spiv?**

   _____

WORD BOX

* a cosmonaut
* a crew member
* risky
* to relieve
* damaged
* a space module
* a solar panel

LISTENING TO NOTICE

Listen again. Write down the form of the verb you hear.

Two new cosmonauts _____ off August 12th. They _____ Russian
<u>1 (blast / will blast)</u>   <u>2 (relieve / will relieve)</u>

crew members on the Spiv space station.

Cosmonauts Markov Zhlinksi and Boris Petrogrov _____ at 1536 GMT
<u>3 (depart / will depart)</u>

Tuesday from the space center in Kazakhstan. They _____ two other
<u>4 (join / will join)</u>

Russians and Brad Leaky, a U.S. astronaut, on Spiv. The Russian cosmonauts

_____ to earth on August 14th. Leaky, however, _____ until
<u>5 (return / will return)</u>   <u>6 (stays / will stay)</u>

September 15th when another American astronaut _____ him.
<u>7 (replaces / will replace)</u>

The cosmonauts _____ out repairs to the damaged energy systems on
<u>8 (carry / will carry)</u>

Spiv. The two Russians _____ inside a darkened space module. They
<u>9 (work / will work)</u>

_____ electric cables to the solar panels in the module. Their work
<u>10 (attach / will attach)</u>

_____ risky. Leaky, the American, however, _____ in the Spivlet
<u>11 (is / will be)</u>   <u>12 (waits / will wait)</u>

space vehicle. Zhlinksi, a veteran cosmonaut, said, "I expect everything

_____ according to plan. We _____ the repairs in a few days."
<u>13 (goes / will go)</u>   <u>14 (finish / will finish)</u>

UNDERSTANDING THE GRAMMAR POINT

1. Read the news report again. Is it about something that:

a. will happen?   b. is happening now?   c. often happens?   d. has already happened?

2. List the verbs you wrote in the correct columns below. What time do the verbs in the two columns refer to?

Simple present tense	Future tense
blast	*will carry*

3. When can you use the simple present tense to refer to the future?

a. To predict when something is going to happen. (It rains tomorrow.)
b. To refer to future actions that are part of a journey (I leave for Australia next week.)
c. To refer to specific future actions. (I buy a house soon.)

CHECKING

Read the following news report. All the verbs are in the simple present tense but some should not be. Correct them by changing them to the future tense.

Shuttle Discovery and its crew of six **blast** off from the Kennedy Space Center in Florida at 10:41 a.m.

Thursday. The shuttle **releases** a German satellite which **studies** the earth's upper atmosphere. It **provides** scien-

tists with very useful information. The cosmonauts **carry** out a number of space walks. They **test** a Japanese

robot. The shuttle **returns** after 11 days.

> **LANGUAGE NOTE**
> Use the present tense and future tense appropriately.

TRYING IT

The president of the United States is coming to your town for a one-day visit.
Write a press release about the planned visit.
The president of the United States is scheduled to visit _____ next month. He arrives

....

....

....

39

Summer Plans

What plans do you have for your next summer holiday?

LISTENING TO COMPREHEND

Listen to Sara and Jim's conversation. They are brother and sister. Answer these questions.

1. What does Sara want to do?
2. Why does Sara need money?
3. What does Jim like to do most?
4. How would Jim spend any money he had?

WORD BOX
* diving school
* lend
* ambitious
* certified
* big-screen TV

LISTENING TO NOTICE

Listen again. Fill in the blanks with the correct word(s) in parentheses.

Sara: I'm going to get a part-time job.

Jim: Why? If you __*need*__ some money, Mom or Dad _____ lend you some.
1 (need/needed)   2 (will/would)

Sara: I know, but I want to earn my own money. If I _____ working at a part-
3 (start/started)
time job now, I _____ earn a lot of money by the beginning of summer.
4 (will/would)

Jim: If I _____ a part-time job, I _____ have time to spend with
5 (take/took)   6 (won't/wouldn't)
my friends.

Sara: That's true.

Jim: If I _____ to choose between working and spending time with my
7 (have/had)
friends, I _____ rather spend time with my friends.
8 (will/would)

Sara: Well, me too, but if I _____ two thousand dollars, I _____
9 (earn/earned)   10 (will/would)
be able to spend a month at Waikiki Diving Camp in Hawaii.

Jim: If I _____ two thousand dollars, I _____ buy a big-screen TV.
11 (have/had)   12 (will/would)

Sara: Yeah, I could buy something, but if I _____ to that diving school, I
13 (go/went)
_____ become a certified diving instructor by the end of the summer.
14 (will/would)

Jim: Wow, you're so ambitious!

UNDERSTANDING THE GRAMMAR POINT

1. Look back at the conversation. Find the sentences with *if*. Put them in the table below.

IF + simple present tense + *will* + VERB	IF + past simple tense + *would* + VERB

2. What is the difference in meaning between the conditional sentences in the two columns?

3. Which type of conditional does Sara use? Which type of conditional does Jim use? Why?

CHECKING

Which of these sentences contain an error? Correct all the errors you find.

1. If she doesn't get the promotion, she ~~would~~ *will* look for another job.

2. If we won the lottery, we will buy an apartment in Paris

3. I doubt that I'll be assigned to our office in Buenos Aires. If I had the opportunity to go there, I would accept it in a minute.

4. If my husband loses his job, he will start a new career.

5. If I had a daughter studying English, I would encourage her to go on a homestay program.

6. If we buy a new car, we'll probably get a sport utility vehicle.

7. He said he's going to call in a few minutes. If we have to cancel our vacation plans, I would be disappointed.

8. If we went to live in another country, I try to learn the language of that country right away.

TRYING IT

Complete each of the following sentences in as many ways as you can.

• *If I learn to speak English very well,*...

....

• *If I visited the United States,*..

....

40

Life Choices

What important choices have you made in your life?

LISTENING TO COMPREHEND

Cynthia, Lynn and Lance are talking about their lives. Complete the table.

	What he or she is:	What he or she would like to be:
Cynthia	_____	_____
Lynn	*forester*	_____
Lance	_____	*accountant*

WORD BOX
* courage
* garden designer
* accountant
* forester

If I changed careers now,...

LISTENING TO NOTICE

Listen again. Fill in the blanks with the correct word or words in parentheses.

Cynthia: I work for a large bank. About three years ago, I started to do gardening. If I ___*changed*___ careers now, I _____
1 (changed / had changed)   2(would become / would have become)
a garden designer. I took up gardening only because we moved from an
apartment into a house. If we _____ in that apartment,
                    3(stayed / had stayed)
I _____ interested in gardening.
4 (would never become/would never have become)

Lynn: I've worked for the Forest Service all my adult life. Twenty years ago, if
you _____ me about my future plans, I _____ ,
   5 (asked / had asked)   6 (would answer / would have answered)
"Working outside, taking care of the forests!" I'm very happy with my
work. If I _____ the last 20 years working in a city office, I
       7 (spent / had spent)
_____ very unhappy.
8 (would be / would have been)

If I had had more courage...

Lance: I have wanted to get out of sales work for many years. If I
_____ more courage, I _____ it a long time ago.
   9(had / had had)   10 (would do / would have done)
Of course, if I _____ harder, I _____ to a
         11 (studied / had studied)   12 (would go / would have gone)
university, to become an accountant. If I _____ to start a new
                          13(decided / had decided)
career now, I _____ an accountant.
      14 (would become / would have become)

If you had asked me...

For Grammar Explanation,
See The Yellow Pages p.139 ▶

UNDERSTANDING THE GRAMMAR POINT

1. Look at the monologues again. Find all of the sentences that contain *if*. Circle the verbs in the sentences. Write the sentences in the correct box.

If I + past tense, I would + verb	If I had + past participle, I would have + past participle
	If we had stayed in that apartment, I would never have become interested in gardening.

2. Which group of sentences describes situations that are *imaginary but* possible (hypothetical)? Which group of sentences describes situations that are *imaginary and* impossible (unreal)?

CHECKING

Look at the following sentences. Which ones describe *hypothetical* situations? Which ones describe *unreal* situations?

1. If I hadn't had a family to support, I would have quit my job to go back to school. *unreal*

2. If she had wanted to travel, she would have applied to one of the overseas posts in her company. _____

3. She has said that if she ever stopped teaching, she would become a counselor. _____

4. If I had known how interesting gardening is, I would have started doing it years ago. _____

5. If we had a child now, our lifestyle would change drastically. _____

6. If we lost our possessions in a fire or some other disaster, we would stay right here and rebuild our lives. _____

7. If I had the chance to spend a year working in Japan, I would do it. _____

8. If Mr. Lee had been in better health, he would not have retired. _____

TRYING IT

Imagine that you are writing to someone about these topics:
If I had been a male (or a female) ...
If I went to live in another country ...
What ideas would you want to express?

....

....

40

Complete the passage below. Choose from the words and phrases in the box. There are some extra items. You need to use *a* 2 times, You need to use *the* 2 times also.
Note: In this passage one gap needs to be left blank. For this blank, write O.

to solve	interesting	solve	interested	a
the other	solving	another	travel	one
were traveling	a	will	the	read
the	would	reading	traveled	

Detective Stories by Agatha Christie

Not everyone enjoys detective stories but almost everyone has read _____

book by Agatha Christie. She is _____ most popular writer of detective stories
                                     2
of all time.

Christie popularized the "puzzle novel." She made her readers _____ the
               3
crime themselves.

Her two best-known detectives were Hercule Poirot and Miss Marples. _____
                   4
was a very odd Belgian gentleman. _____ was a very proper English lady.
             5
Both characters are very _____ .
           6

Many of her novels were set in a very enclosed space. For example, *Death on the Nile* was about a

group of people who were traveling down _____ Nile River on a boat when a
            7
murder occurred. In yet _____ of her novels, *Murder on the Orient Express,*
         8
the setting is _____ train.
      9

Next week I _____ to _____ South America. I know that
         10   11
if I don't take two or three Agatha Christie thrillers with me, I _____ not
                                        12
enjoy the journey.

Complete the passage below. Choose from the words and phrases in the box. Use each item one time only.

Note: In this passage one gap needs to be left blank. For this blank, write O.

the other	to	would	surprised	to live
worrying	made	have started	eating	start
the	another	a	surprising	others
worried	let	to eat	would have	living

Drugs for Animals

Bart Zinkel is the director of Alcona Zoo in _____ Warshaw, Tennessee.
₁

Bart was very _____ about the mental health of some of the animals in the
₂

zoo, so he gave them a drug called Prozac. Although many people questioned the effectiveness of

the drug on animals, Bart was not _____ that it was successful. "I knew it
₃

would work," Bart said.

Two lionesses refused _____ when an old lion in the zoo died. One of the
₄

lionesses got Prozac and recovered quickly, but _____ became seriously ill.
₅

_____ baboon became very moody until Bart _____ him
₆   ₇

take Prozac. Now _____ baboon is enjoying life again.
₈

"If we had not given drugs to these animals they _____ died. With Prozac they
₉

enjoy _____ in the zoo," Bart said.
₁₀

"Next month we _____ a second experiment using another drug, Valium,"
₁₁

Bart said. "Then perhaps the animals will stop _____ and get a decent night's
₁₂

sleep!" he joked.

41

Personal Opinions

What topics do you have strong opinions about?

LISTENING TO COMPREHEND 🎧

Listen to people give their opinions about these topics. Do you agree or disagree with them?

	Agree	Disagree	Not sure
1. Tax	☐	☐	☐
2. Diet	☐	☐	☐
3. Government	☐	☐	☐
4. Old people's clothes	☐	☐	☐
5. Tests	☐	☐	☐
6. Punishing children	☐	☐	☐
7. Cars	☐	☐	☐
8. Angry people	☐	☐	☐
9. Politicians	☐	☐	☐
10. Salaries	☐	☐	☐

WORD BOX
* efficient
* wealthy
* creative
* democratic
* politicians
* damage
* tax
* honest

LISTENING TO NOTICE 🎧

Listen again. Choose the correct word to complete the sentence.

1. I think ___*wealthy*___ people shouldn't have to pay a lot of tax. They should

_{1 (wealthy /wealth)}
   be able to keep their money.

2. I don't think we should bother about having a _____ diet. It's more
   important to just enjoy your food. _{2 (healthy /health)}

3. I think an _____ government is more important than a _____
   _{3 (efficient / effciciency)}
   government. Who cares whether they can vote if the government works? _{4 (democratic / democracy)}

4. I think old people shouldn't wear _____ clothes. It makes them look
   really silly. _{5 (sexy / sex)}

5. I think teachers should never give _____ tests. It's not fair to students
   if they can't do well on a test. _{6 (difficult / difficulty)}

6. I think children should never be punished, even if they are _____ . It
   might damage their personalities. _{7 (naughty /naughtiness)}

7. I think it is more important to have cheap cars than _____ cars.
   What's the sense of a car being safe if nobody can afford it? _{8 (safe / safety)}

8. I think it is best to let _____ people have their own way. Arguing
   with them just makes things worse. _{9 (angry / anger)}

9. I think there are no _____ politicians. If I had my way I'd get rid of
   all of them. _{10 (honest / honesty)}

10. I think hard-working people should earn more money than _____
    _{11 (creative / creativity)}
    people. In my opinion, creative people just sit around all day doing nothing.

UNDERSTANDING THE GRAMMAR POINT

1. Compare these sentences:

- He is a very wealthy person. (**wealthy** is an adjective) • He has considerable wealth. (**wealth** is a noun)

Here is a test to find out whether a word is an adjective or a noun:

- A word is an adjective if it can complete this sentence:
She is a very _____ person.
- A word is a noun if it can complete this sentence:
I like/don't like _____ .

2. Look at the pairs of words in the opinions. Complete this table.

adjective	noun		adjective	noun
1. *wealthy*	*wealth*	6.		
2.		7.		
3.		8.		
4.		9.		
5.		10.		
		11.		

3. Which of these statements is correct?

a. If a word ends in a -y it must be an adjective.
b. If a word ends in a -y it must be a noun.
c. If a word ends in a -y it can be an adjective or a noun.

CHECKING

Which of these sentences are incorrect? Correct the errors.

1. Michael Jackson is a very creativity person.

2. Some countries do not have democratic governments.

3. Rap musicians sometimes seem to be very angry people.

4. Japanese cars are recognized as very safety cars.

5. Vegetarians have a very health diet.

6. Famous film actors and actresses are very wealthy people.

7. Pop singers generally wear sexy clothes.

8. My country faces a lot of difficulty problems.

9. Children are often not punished for their naughty behavior.

10. I have never met a completely honesty person.

LANGUAGE NOTE
Use the adjectives and nouns you have studied in this unit.

TRYING IT

Choose 5 topics from the list below. Write your opinion about each one: *sports, music, marriage, friends, air travel, food, film stars, clothes, money, old people.*

....

....

42

Admirable People

Who are some people you really admire?
Why do you admire them?

LISTENING TO COMPREHEND

Listen to the story about Dien Tranh. Complete the time line.

1959.................1971...............1979.................1984.................1994

Dien Tranh
is born

Dien has
six stores.

LISTENING TO NOTICE

Listen to the stories again. Fill in the blanks with one of the verbs in parentheses.

Dien Tranh: My neighbor Dien Tranh was born in 1959 in Vietnam, in the

city of Hue. By the time he was 12, he ——————— both his
1(lost / has lost / had lost)

parents. Somehow he cared for himself and his younger sister. By the time he

was 20 he ——————— in the United States as a refugee, and
2 (arrived / has arrived / had arrived)

he ——————— working two and sometimes three jobs at a
3 (began / has begun / had begun)

time. Within five years, he ——————— enough
4 (already saved / has already saved / had already saved)

money to help bring many of his relatives to the United States, and he

——————— a small florist shop. By 1994 — 10 years after
5 (bought / has bought / had bought)

he bought that small shop — Tran ——————— his business
6 (expanded / has expanded / had expanded)

to include six stores and more than 30 employees.

UNDERSTANDING THE GRAMMAR POINT

1. Study this diagram about how to use the past perfect tense.

Time 1 Past Perfect	Time 2 Simple Past

past   now   future

Example: By the time Dien was 12, he had lost his parents.

Now complete the table with sentences from the story.

	Time 1 (Past Perfect)
By the time Dien was 12	
By the time he was 20	
By the time he was 20	
Within five years	
Within five years	
By 1994	

2. Make up a rule to explain the use of the past perfect tense.

CHECKING

Can you find the sentences that contain an error? Correct all the errors you find.

1. Before she came to the United States, Cecilia Sanchez has never traveled more than 100 miles from Mexico City.

2. When she came to the United States with her family, she has very little education.

3. Within a few years, however, Cecilia had learned English.

4. When she entered junior high school, her physical education teacher notices Cecilia's natural ability as a runner.

5. She had joined her school's track team a few weeks later.

6. Even before she began her last year of high school, several universities offer her an athletic scholarship.

7. After graduating from college, Cecilia had become a track coach.

8. By her 40th birthday, Cecilia had received numerous awards for her work in the community.

TRYING IT

Make a timeline for your own life. Write sentences about what you had already done by a certain time.

LANGUAGE NOTE
Use expressions like,
*By the time I was
twelve, I had already ...*

....

....

Computer Care

What valuable things do you have that you need to take care of?

How do you take care of them?

ERROR BOX

✗ A damp cloth is use to clean it.

✗ Computers must care for properly.

LISTENING TO COMPREHEND

Listen to the lecture about how to take care of a computer. What does the speaker say we should do? Put a check (4) to show what is right and wrong.

What should you do?	Right	Wrong
1. Keep it in a cool place.	☐	☐
2. Keep it away from sunlight.	☐	☐
3. Keep drinks away from it.	☐	☐
4. Clean it with chemical cleaner.	☐	☐
5. Turn it off and on quickly.	☐	☐

WORD BOX
*humid
*spill
*consume
*dust
*spray
*switch

LISTENING TO NOTICE

Listen again. Write the correct form of the verb in parentheses ( ).

Today we are going to learn about computer care. Ready?

Now, a computer ___*should be kept*___ in a cool room — not too hot and not
1 (should keep)

too cold and not too humid and not too dry.

Also, a computer _____ in a place that is free of dust. Bright
2 (should put)

sunlight _____ . Liquids like coffee or Coke _____
3 (should avoid)   4 (must never consume)

near a computer. And if some liquid _____ onto your system,
5 (spill)

the power must _____ off immediately. It must be completely
6 (switch)

dry before it _____ on again. A computer _____
7 (turn)   8 (should clean)

regularly. A slightly damp cloth is best. No chemical cleaners. All right? But a

glass cleaner _____ onto the monitor screen to clean it. And one
9 (can spray)

last thing. When a computer _____ off it _____
10 (switch)   11 (should not turn)

on again right away. Now, can you remember all this?

**For Grammar Explanation,
See The Yellow Pages p.141** ▶

UNDERSTANDING THE GRAMMAR POINT

1. Compare these sentences:

a.

AGENT	+	VERB (ACTIVE)	+	PATIENT	
You		should keep		a computer	in a cool place.

b.

PATIENT	+	VERB (PASSIVE)	
A computer		should be kept	in a cool place.

Are the verbs in the lecture active or passive?

2. Now fill in the table. Read the lecture if you need help.

Active verb	Passive verb	Active verb	Passive verb
1. should keep	*should be kept*	7. turn	
2. should put		8. should clean	
3. should avoid		9. can spray	
4. must never consume		10. switch	
5. spill		11. should not turn	
6. must switch			

3. How is the passive of the present tense formed?

4. Why do you think the lecturer used the PASSIVE rather than the ACTIVE?

CHECKING

Can you correct the errors in these sentences?

1. The overall life of the car can be ~~increase~~ *increased* if it is ~~service~~ *serviced* regularly.

2. The oil in your car should check frequently.

3. The oil must changing after 10 thousand kilometers.

4. The tires must checked for wear.

5. The tires should rotate from time to time.

6. The spare wheel must inspect occasionally.

7. The brakes must replacing after 30 thousand kilometers.

8. The car should be wash every week.

9. It is best if the car is keeping in a garage.

10. Above all, a car should be driving carefully.

TRYING IT

LANGUAGE NOTE
Use passive verbs.

Choose something you use frequently (a bicycle, a car, a CD player, a Walkman, a guitar). Prepare a set of rules about how to care for it.

....

....

Dreams

Do you remember your dreams?
What do you dream about?

LISTENING TO COMPREHEND

Brad and Sook are talking about their dreams. Check (✔) the things they dream about.

Brad
- [ ] a swim suit
- [ ] father
- [ ] a cake
- [ ] mother
- [ ] a window
- [ ] an orchestra

Sook
- [ ] dentist
- [ ] mother
- [ ] a car
- [ ] a ball
- [ ] father
- [ ] a forest

WORD BOX
* disappear
* consist
* conduct (an orchestra)
* increase

LISTENING TO NOTICE

Listen to Brad and Sook talk about their dreams again. Choose the correct form of the verb.

Brad's dreams

I often dream about my mother. Sometimes I dream that she is dying. You see, my mother _____ when I was still a small child. Sometimes I dream I am
  1 (died / was died)
outside a house and the door _____ . I can see my mother standing there
  2 (opens / is opened)
but somehow I can't go in to join her. Then after a while she _____ .
  3 (disappears / is disappeared)
Sometimes, though, I have nice dreams about my mother. Once I dreamed it was my birthday and my mother had given me a big cake which _____
  4 (consisted / was cons[...])
entirely of ice cream. And once something really funny _____ in a
  5 (occurred / was occurred)
dream. My mother was dressed in a swim suit conducting an orchestra.

Sook's dreams

I often have nightmares about my father. Once I dreamed I was at the dentist and the dentist _____ into my father. Another time I dreamed my father
  6 (changed / was changed)
was driving a car that was trying to hit me. I ran and ran and just as the car was about to hit me it _____ . Then there was the time I dreamed I was in a
  7 (stopped / was stopped)
dark forest and a tree _____ on me. Except it wasn't a tree — it was my
  8 (fell / was fallen)
father! The other night something really strange _____ in my dream. My
  9 (happened / was happened)
father threw a ball to me. The ball _____ in size until it was bigger than me.
  10 (increased / was increased)

UNDERSTANDING THE GRAMMAR POINT

1. What is wrong with these sentences?

✗ My mother was died.
✗ My mother was disappeared.
✗ A strange thing was happened.

✗ A funny thing was occurred.
✗ A tree was fallen on me.
✗ The cake was consisted of ice cream.

Complete the statement about these verbs.

• Some verbs, such as *die* and *disappear*, describe events that have no known cause.

These verbs can be used only in the _____ voice. They cannot be used in the _____ voice.

2. Other verbs have an active and a passive. Can you explain the difference in meaning?

a. My mother died.
b. My mother was killed.

a. The car stopped.
b. The car was stopped.

a. The door opened.
b. The door was opened.

a. The size was increased.
b. The size increased.

3. Which of these verbs can be used only in the active?

become   continue   fall in love   decrease   hurt   break   sink
decline (grow less)   develop   close   rise   disappear   dry

CHECKING

Which of these sentences are incorrect? Can you correct them?

1. Last year my father ~~was died~~ *died* suddenly.

2. It happpened a strange thing to me.

3. The window opened by itself.

4. My head suddenly was increased in size a lot.

5. It occurred a strange thing the other day.

6. It grew very dark the evening.

7. A slate from the roof was fallen on me.

8. It consisted of chocolate and icing the cake.

9. The weather was suddenly changed for the better.

10. It stopped suddenly the rain.

TRYING IT

Do you remember your dreams? Write three or four sentences about some of your own dreams.

LANGUAGE NOTE
Try to use some of the verbs you have studied in this unit.

....

....

....

....

45

Where Should We Go?

Where do you want to go on your next vacation? Why?

LISTENING TO COMPREHEND

Listen to Paula and Alonzo's conversation. They are discussing where to go on vacation. Which places are they still considering? Which places have they decided not to visit? Complete the table.

Place	Still considering? Yes	No	If not, why not?
Hawaii	☐	☐	_____
_____	☐	☐	_____
_____	☐	☐	_____

LISTENING TO NOTICE

Listen again. Fill in the missing words.

Paula: OK, where should we go during the holidays? How about Hawaii? I've always had a good time there.

Alonzo: _____. And I love those beaches!
        ₁

Paula: _____. But I don't want to keep going back to the same place every year.
     ₂

Alonzo: _____. All right, let's go someplace else this year.
        ₃

Paula: We've never been to Venice. I'd love to see Venice.

Alonzo: _____. But the crowds are terrible in the summer. And I don't want to find myself surrounded by so many other tourists.
        ₄

Paula: Well, _____. But I don't think it's as nice there during the winter.
         ₅

Alonzo: _____.
        ₆

Paula: What about the Rockies? I wouldn't mind having a vacation closer to home.

Alonzo: _____. Since we have only a week, I don't want to deal with jet lag.
        ₇

Paula: _____. And I think it would be nice to do a lot of hiking and bicycling.
        ₈

Alonzo: _____. I'll ask people I know about nice hotels and places to visit.
        ₉

Paula: _____.
     ₁₀

For Grammar Explanation, See The Yellow Pages p.142 ▶

UNDERSTANDING THE GRAMMAR POINT

1. Study this chart. Complete the chart with examples from the conversation.

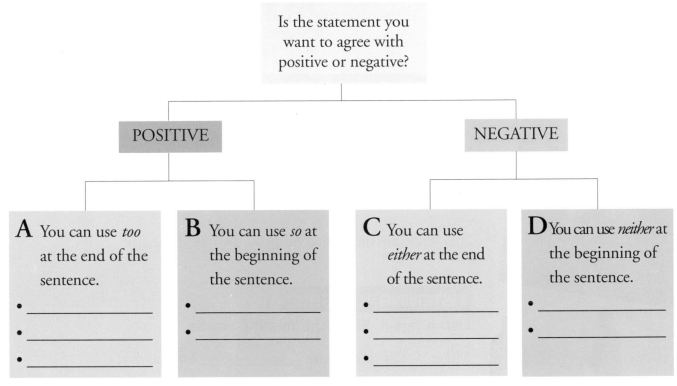

Is the statement you want to agree with positive or negative?

POSITIVE — NEGATIVE

A You can use *too* at the end of the sentence.

* _____
* _____
* _____

B You can use *so* at the beginning of the sentence.

* _____
* _____

C You can use *either* at the end of the sentence.

* _____
* _____
* _____

D You can use *neither* at the beginning of the sentence.

* _____
* _____

2. How is the word order in each pair of sentences different?

* *I do too. vs. So do I.*
* *I don't either. vs. Neither do I.*

Make up a rule to explain the word order differences.

CHECKING

Look at the following sentences. Can you find the errors? Correct each error you find.

1. A: Northwest Airlines flies from Tokyo to Beijing.
   B: Neither does Japan Airlines.
2. A: Hawaii is a very popular vacation spot.
   B: Florida is, too.
3. A: Trains to my town are not very frequent.
   B: Buses are neither.
4. A: Sydney is a fascinating city to visit.
   B: Melbourne does too.
5. A: I enjoyed our holiday in Thailand.
   B: So the rest of my family did.

LANGUAGE NOTE
Include words like: too, so, either, neither

TRYING IT

Write a short dialogue between yourself and a friend. Talk about where your friend should go for a holiday (or to study or work).

....

....

45

TOO vs. ENOUGH

46 *Moving In*

When did you last move to a new apartment?
What was the most difficult part about moving?

ERROR BOX

✗ The doorway is narrow to get the sofa through.

✗ He is enough strong to carry those boxes.

LISTENING TO COMPREHEND

Mike and Toni are moving. Answer these questions.

1. Where is this conversation taking place?

2. Why didn't they put the piano in the extra bedroom?

3. How are they going to spend the rest of the day?

LISTENING TO NOTICE

Listen again. Fill in the missing words.

Mike: Well, I think that's _____ for one day!
                                    1

Toni: Why didn't you put that big piano in the extra bedroom?

Mike: The doorway is _____. It's not _____ to get the
                                 2   3
piano through.

Toni: Did you try?

Mike: No, I know the opening isn't _____. Anyway, it's
                                              4
_____ to move, especially since neither of us is an Olympic
        5
weightlifter.

Toni: Never mind. Right now I'm _____ to care.
                                            6

Mike: I hope you're _____ to celebrate the big move. I made a
                               7
dinner reservation for 7:30. We have _____ to wash up and change
                                              8
clothes.

Toni: Well, I certainly have _____ to go out for a nice meal. But not
                                        9
at that Thai restaurant we went to last time, I hope. The food was

_____ to eat.
      10

UNDERSTANDING THE GRAMMAR POINT

1. Complete this table with phrases from the conversation.

too	enough	
	with nouns	with adjectives
	enough work	

2. • What kind of word always follows *too*?
   • Where does *enough* go when it is used with a noun?
   • Where does *enough* go when it is used with an adjective?
   • What form of the verb follows expressions with *too* and *enough*?

3. **Which sentence in each pair is closest in meaning to the target sentence?**

   The doorway is too narrow.
   • We can get the piano through the doorway.
   • We can't get the piano through the doorway.

   That's enough work for one day.
   • We should have done less work.
   • We don't need to do any more work.

4. **Complete these statements.**
   • We use the word _____ to express the idea of *excessive*; this has a negative meaning.
   • We use the word _____ to express the idea of *sufficient*; this has a positive meaning.

CHECKING
Which of these sentences have an error? Correct the errors.

1. The table was heavy enough for one person to lift.

2. It's too late to start moving our things; we'll begin tomorrow morning.

3. Are you tired to move anything else?

4. These boxes aren't heavy; they're light enough for me to carry.

5. The closet is enough big to store all our sports equipment.

6. The door was too wide to get the sofa through.

7. This apartment is expensive enough; we'll have to find a cheaper one.

8. I am too strong to lift this chair by myself.

TRYING IT

Write five sentences describing yourself with the words *too* and *enough*.

....

....

....

....

47

Travel Club

How do you find information about vacations and traveling?

LISTENING TO COMPREHEND

Listen to the advertisement about the All-Continent Travel Club. What are the advantages of joining this club? Check (✔) them.

- ☐ free hotel rooms
- ☐ the cheapest fares
- ☐ vacation planning
- ☐ free travel once a year
- ☐ homestay programs for teenagers
- ☐ discounts at restaurants and shops
- ☐ special services for senior citizens
- ☐ free membership for the first year

WORD BOX
* destination
* fares
* resort
* discount
* value
* full-service

LISTENING TO NOTICE

Listen again. Fill in the blanks.

How ___*can you get*___ more value for your travel dollar? If this is a
       1

question you've been asking, then you should find out what

_____ for you. All-Continent Travel Club is a full-service
       2

club. Where _____ to go? We'll help
       3

you find the cheapest fares. What _____ to do? We'll help
       4

you plan your ideal vacation. We'll tell you how _____
       5

discounts at hotels, restaurants and shops at your favorite destinations. How

much _____? Only 50 dollars a year. If you
       6

think about how much _____ the very first time you use
       7

our service, it's like having a free membership. Call us now at 1-888-543-6936.

You'll soon learn why _____ the traveler's best friend.
       8

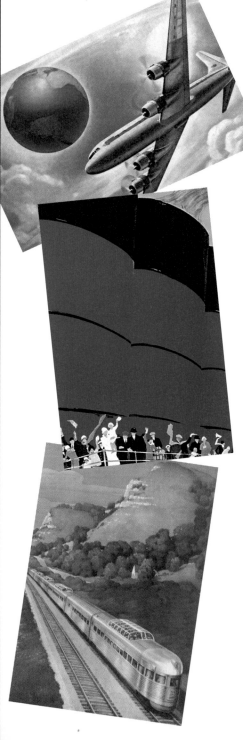

UNDERSTANDING THE GRAMMAR POINT

1. Complete the table with sentences from the conversation.

sentence starts with a WH question	WH question is embedded in a statement
• *How can you get more value for your travel dollar?*	• *...what the All-Continent Travel Club has for you.*
•	•
•	•
•	•

2. Study the word order in the questions and the statements. How is it different?

3. Can you say what is wrong with this sentence?

He wants to know what country am I visiting.

CHECKING

Most of these sentences have an error. Correct the errors you find.

1. Do you know when does the flight arrive?

2. Masako is not sure how long can she be away.

3. I wonder how long does the ship take to reach Shanghai.

4. Tell me where you want to go in Italy.

5. I don't know how much does a membership cost.

6. The travel agent asked me what kind of vacation I want to take.

7. I wonder how is the weather in Ireland at this time of year.

8. My friend Antonio asked when we would visit him in Costa Rica.

TRYING IT

What place would you like to visit? Write questions you want to ask a travel agent. Then write six sentences with WH statements. Use these expressions:

I'd like to know...   *I was wondering...*   *I need you to tell me...*

....

....

....

....

....

Special Dishes

What is your favorite food? Can you make it?

ERROR BOX

✗ Chirashi consists of raw fish which the chef arranges it over a bowl of rice.

✗ Maki-sushi consists of a long roll of rice is covered with seaweed.

LISTENING TO COMPREHEND

Here are the names of different kinds of sushi, a favorite Japanese food:
nigiri-sushi   chirashi   maki-sushi   sashimi
Listen to Michiko describe different types of sushi. Label the pictures.

LISTENING TO NOTICE

Listen again. Complete the sentences.

WORD BOX
* a chunk
* an assortment
* a roll
* shredded
* seaweed
* an appetizer
* strips

Hi, my name is Michiko. I want to tell you about my

favorite food — sushi! Mmmm!

Do you know what sushi is? Well, it consists of pieces

of raw fish _____ chunks of rice. There are
                                1

many different kinds of sushi. I hope you'll try them all.

Maki-sushi consists of a long roll of rice _____
                                                           2

seaweed. To make it the chef uses a bamboo mat

_____ seaweed, rice and strips of tuna.
            3

Nigiri-sushi consists of pieces of fish _____
                                                      4

on top of fingers of rice.

Sashimi is an assortment of raw fish _____ with
                                                     5

shredded radish, often as an appetizer. Chirashi consists of sashimi and

chopped vegetables _____ over a bowl of rice.
                                6

Sushi is usually eaten with soy sauce and wasabi (green horseradish)

_____ in a small bowl.
            7

Now, why don't you try some sushi? You'll love it!

UNDERSTANDING THE GRAMMAR POINT

1. All of Michiko's sentences contain relative clauses. Divide each sentence into two sentences. Write them in the table.

Sentence 1	Sentence 2
1. *Sushi consists of pieces of raw fish.*	*The chef serves the raw fish with chunks of rice.*
2.	
3.	
4.	
5.	
6.	
7.	

2. Look at Michiko's sentences again. Underline the relative pronoun in each sentence and draw an arrow to show the phrase it refers to.

Sushi consists of raw fish, <u>which</u> the chef serves with chunks of rice.

CHECKING

Here are some definitions of other national foods. Find the errors and correct them.

1. Tempura is a Japanese dish. It consists of seafood and vegetables and have been lightly fried in batter.

2. Chapati is an Indian food. It is a kind of bread that the cook makes it with wholemeal flour.

3. Paella is a Spanish dish. It is made with rice and the chef cooks with seafood.

4. Mtedza is a Malawian dish. It is a meat stew which the cook makes it with minced groundnuts.

5. Spaghetti bolognese is an Italian dish. It consists of a rich meat sauce who the chef serves over spaghetti.

6. A Cornish pasty is an English food. It is a small pie and the chef fills with potatoes and meat.

TRYING IT

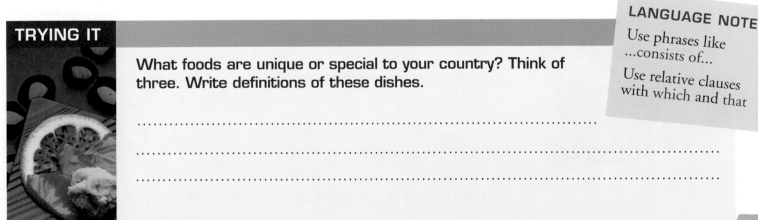

What foods are unique or special to your country? Think of three. Write definitions of these dishes.

LANGUAGE NOTE
Use phrases like ...consists of...
Use relative clauses with which and that

....

....

....

49

A Wedding in Paradise

If you could get married in any place in the world, where would you choose?

ERROR BOX

✗ Hawaii is a place where thousands of people get married there every year.

✗ Hawaii is a place where are many chapels.

LISTENING TO COMPREHEND

1. Listen to the advertisement about Hawaii. It mentions five places you can get married in Hawaii. What are they?

- _____
- _____
- _____
- _____
- _____

2. What are the three times you can get married?

- _____
- _____
- _____

WORD BOX

* a zoological garde...
* service
* a parachute
* a chapel
* a submarine
* a volcanic crater
* a minister

LISTENING TO NOTICE

Listen to the advertisement again. Fill in the blanks with *where*, or *when*.

Are you about to get married? Are you looking for a wedding with a difference
How about Hawaii? Hawaii is a place ___*where*___ thousands of couples say or
renew their vows every year. You can get married in a zoological garden,
_____ there is a chapel by the sea.

Or you can choose a volcanic crater, _____ the service is held in a helicopter
Or you can do it on a tennis court, _____ the minister calls out "Love-all."
Or you can choose underwater in a submarine, _____ you are surrounded
by tropical fish. Or you can get married in the sky, _____ the service is
held with everyone in parachutes.

And there are also different times _____ you can get married. You can get
married at dawn, _____ the sun rises over the mountains, or at midday,
_____ the sun beats down on the beaches, or in the evening, _____
the sun sets over the ocean.

Hawaii offers you a wedding that you will never forget. A wedding made in
paradise. Call the Hawaii Visitors Bureau at (808) 923-1811.

UNDERSTANDING THE GRAMMAR POINT

1. Read the advertisement again. Write the words that *where* and *when* refer to.

WHERE	*place*					
WHEN	*times*					

Can you explain how to use *where* and *when*?

2. Look at the sentences in the advertisement that have relative clauses.
Divide the sentences into two. Write them in the table.

	Sentence 1	Sentence 2
1.	*Hawaii is a place.*	*Thousands of couples say or renew their vows there every year.*
2.		
3.		
4.		
5.		
6.		
7.		
8.		
9.		
10.		

3. This sentence has an error. Can you find it? Can you say why it is an error?
   ✗ Hawaii is a place where thousands of couples say or renew their vows there every year.

CHECKING

All of these sentences have an error. Some have more than one error. Correct the errors.

1. Wolfgang and Maria got married last year ~~that~~ when they were on holiday ~~then~~ in Hawaii.

2. The service was held in an old church where the minister began the service there with a traditional Hawaiian song.

3. They were married early in the morning when was cool and the birds were singing then.

4. They stayed in a hotel and where newlyweds are especially welcome.

5. "That was a time when we were then perfectly happy," they said.

TRYING IT

What kind of wedding would you like? Describe the wedding of your dreams.

....

50

Book Notices

Do you like to read?
What is your favorite novel?

LISTENING TO COMPREHEND

Listen to the book notices. Match each book with its main character.

Book	Main Character
The Color Purple	a young Scottish woman
The Day of the Jackal	an African American traveler
The Invisible Man	an African American woman
The Remains of the Day	Henri, Napoleon's cook
The Ginger Tree	an English butler
The Passion	an assassin

WORD BOX
* sexist
* butler
* racism
* assassin
* loyalty

LISTENING TO NOTICE

Listen again. Fill in the missing words.
Here are some books you might like to read.

The Color Purple by Alice Walker

This novel is in the form of letters written by an African American woman
_____ is made miserable by her cruel husband.
₁

The Day of the Jackal by Frederick Forsyth

This thriller tells the story of an assassin _____ to shoot the French
president, Charles de Gaulle, nearly succeeds.[2]

The Invisible Man by Ralph Ellison

This novel tells the story of an African American man _____ through the
United States reveals the chronic racism of that country.[3]

The Remains of the Day by Kazuo Ishigur

This is the strange story of an English butler _____ is governed by his
complete loyalty to his master.[4]

The Ginger Tree by Oswald Wynd

This novel tells the story of a young Scottish woman _____ to a young
English officer in China is a failure.[5]

The Passion by Jeanette Winterson

This historical romance tells the story of Henri, Napoleon's cook, _____ is
happily accepted by Villanelle, the daughter of a Venetian boatman.[6]

UNDERSTANDING THE GRAMMAR POINT

1. **Read the book notices again. Divide each book notice into two sentences.**

The Color Purple	*This novel is in the form of letters written by an African American woman. Her life was made miserable by her cruel husband.*
The Day of the Jackal	
The Invisible Man	
The Remains of the Day	
The Ginger Tree	
The Passion	

2. **A relative pronoun always refers back to a previous noun phrase. Look back at the book notices. Underline the words in the table that correspond to *whose*. Draw an arrow to show the phrase it refers to.**

This novel is in the form of letters written by <u>an African American woman</u> <u>whose</u> life is made miserable by her husband.

CHECKING

Read these book notices. All of them have errors. Correct the errors.

The Murder by Grant Nelson
This is a story of a man who his murder leads to the resignation of the president of the United States.

Funeral Service by Colin Coffin
In this short novel we follow the story of a man whose his life is changed by the death of his father.

Sad Ending by Marilyn Hornchurch
This bittersweet comedy tells the story of two teenagers whom their parents try to destroy their marriage.

Broken Glass by Stephanie Bottle
This exciting thriller is about a woman whom the government imprisons her husband as a spy.

TRYING IT

**Choose two novels you know well.
Write short book notices about each one using whose.**
(Title and Author)

_____   This novel is about _____ whose _____ .

Complete the passage below. Choose from the words and phrases in the box. Use each item one time only.

increasing	which	she kept	will	so
whose	enough	dirty	am	where
do	allowed	increased	who	too
was	had	allow	dirt	did
she keep	are			

Animal Lovers

Ms. Blunsden is a 38-year-old woman who lives alone in Brooklyn, New York. She is not

_____ to keep any animals. A police officer told a Brooklyn court that he
  1

_____ found 15 dogs and 20 cats living in a small room _____
  2   3

measures just 10 feet by 12 feet. "There was not _____ space for one animal let
                                                    4

alone 35," he said. "The room was very _____ ."
                                          5

"The animals _____ taken care of properly," Ms. Blunsden told the court. "I
                6

take them all for walks in a shopping cart." When the judge asked Ms. Blunsden why

_____ so many animals she said, "Everybody loves animals and I
  7

_____ too. You may think that my room is _____ small
  8   9

for so many animals, but I think it is just right."

The judge ordered the animals to be taken to a place _____ they could be
                                                          10

properly taken care of. He also ordered Ms. Blunsden to get help from Dr. Eugene Wilson

_____ clinic is well-known for dealing with such cases.
  11

The court heard that keeping many animals is _____ and that Ms. Blunsden's
                                                12

situation is now quite common.

Complete the passage below. Choose from the words and phrases in the box. Use each item one time only.

fun	did she work	had	efficient	which
efficiency	is consisted	is	have	changes
she worked	enough	does	where	too
are	whose	had	funny	is changed
consists				

Brett's Ad Agency

Everyone dreams of the perfect job but Juliet Moskowitz may have found it. She works for Brett's

ad agency, _____ she is the marketing manager.

1

By the time she _____ finished her first year at Brett's, Juliet knew she would

             2

never leave. She loves her job and so _____ everyone else working at Brett's.

                 3

At Brett's nobody has a desk, just a locker and a mobile phone _____ they

                      4

carry around strapped to their waists. They can sit and work wherever they like.

Asked when _____ , Juliet explained that she had no fixed hours. She decided

           5

when she wanted to work.

Brett's is an ad agency _____ employees all feel valued and trusted. There are

             6

no secretaries doing boring work. The work force _____ of fifty percent men

               7

and fifty percent women. In Brett's everyone is _____ busy to gossip or complain.

                8

Everyone _____ encouraged to put ideas forward in a friendly manner.

        9

Juliet said, "Brett's new office culture is still developing. It _____ every week.

                    10

One thing is certain: It will be no less _____ than the traditional office culture

             11

and a lot more _____."

      12

LEVEL ONE ◇◆◆◆◆

1 Pronouns: *He, She, It*
2 *There is/There are*
3 *Be* vs. *Have*
4 Present Continuous and Simple Present Tenses
5 *Do/Does* in *Yes/No* Questions
6 Negatives: *No* vs. *Not*
7 Plural Nouns
8 Countable vs. Uncountable Nouns
9 Determiners with Nouns
10 *Be* in *Yes/No* Questions

LEVEL TWO ◇◇◆◆◆

11 Stative Verbs
12 Simple Past Tense
13 Prepositions in Expressions of Time
14 Prepositions of Location and Direction
15 Adjectives vs. Adverbs
16 *Yes/No* Questions in the Simple Past Tense
17 Transitive vs. Intransitive Verbs
18 Subject-Verb Agreement with Simple Present Tense
19 Present Perfect for Indefinite Past
20 *Wh-* Questions

LEVEL THREE ◇◇◇◆◆

21 Adverb Position
22 *Few/A Few, Little/A Little*
23 Comparative and Superlative Form of Adjectives
24 *Like* and *As*
25 Comparative Expressions with Prepositions
26 *There is* vs. *It is*
27 Modals of Possibility
28 Modals of Obligation and Necessity
29 Present Perfect with *For* and *Since*
30 Simple Past and Past Continuous

LEVEL FOUR ◇◇◇◇◆

31 Unique Reference with and without *The*
32 The Indefinite Article *A*
33 The Definite Article *The*
34 *Other, The Other, Another*
35 Verb Complements
36 *Let* vs. *Make*
37 Participial Adjectives
38 Simple Present Tense for Future Time
39 Possible vs. Hypothetical Conditionals
40 Hypothetical vs. Unreal Conditonals

LEVEL FIVE ◇◇◇◇◇

41 Adjectives and Nouns Ending in *-y*
42 Past Perfect with *By* and *Already*
43 Passive Voice in the Simple Present Tense
44 Process Verbs
45 Pro-forms: *Too, So, Either, Neither*
46 *Too* vs. *Enough*
47 Embedded Questions
48 Relative Clauses with *Which* and *That*
49 Relative Clauses with *Where* and *When*
50 Relative Clauses with *Whose*

1. Pronouns are words that we use to replace nouns or noun phrases. We use pronouns to avoid repeating the same noun or noun phrase:

    Anil Chaudari is our sales representative. He joined our company last year.

    In this example, *he* replaces the noun phrase *Anil Chaudari*.
2. Pronouns that replace singular nouns are: *he, she* and *it*. There is also one pronoun that replaces a plural noun: *they*.
3. Do not use a pronoun if it is not clear who or what the pronoun refers to.

HE	**SHE**	**IT**
Use *he* to refer to a male person:	Use *she* to refer to a female person:	Use *it* to refer to an object:
the man, Mr. Tanaka, the owner of the company.	the woman, my sister, Ms. Robertson.	the book, the company I work for, the environment.

COMMON ERRORS

1. Omitting a pronoun:
    ✗ My brother is a doctor. Works in a large hospital in Toronto.
2. Using *he* instead of *she*:
    ✗ My grandmother lives in another city. He loves to visit us.
3. Using *he* instead of *it*:
    ✗ I just bought a new computer. He is very powerful.

See Unit 26 for more information about the use of *there is*.

THERE IS	**THERE ARE**
1. Use *there is* with singular nouns and noun phrases: **There is a clock on the wall.**	1. Use *there are* with plural nouns and noun phrases: **There are dishes piled up in the sink.**
2. Use *there is* with the expressions *a group of* and *a set of*: **There's a set of dishes in the cabinet.**	2. Use *there are* with the expressions *a lot of, lots of, a couple of,* and *a number of*: **There are lots of pillows on the sofa.**
3. The written contraction for *there is* is *there's*. We usually say *there's* in speech.	
4. Use *There it is* and *There they are* to say that you have found something.	

COMMON ERRORS

1. Omission of *be*:
    ✗ There several books on the shelf.
2. Omission of *there*:
    ✗ Is a dresser on the wall on the left.
    ✗ Are three Chinese silk paintings of birds.
3. Use of *there's* for *there are* and vice versa:
    ✗ There's three chairs in the kitchen.
    ✗ There are a pair of gloves on the counter.

BE	HAVE
1. Use the verb *be* to equate someone (or something) with something: **He is my brother.** **She is a lawyer.** 2. Use the verb *be* to describe someone or something with an adjective: **Olga is tall.**	1. Use *have* to describe what someone (or something) possesses: **He has blond hair.** **She has freckles.**

COMMON ERRORS

1. Omitting *be* or *have*:
   - ✗ She 30 years old.
   - ✗ The man brown hair.
2. Using *be* for *have* and vice versa:
   - ✗ She is blue eyes.
   - ✗ My brother has 20 years old.

4 | PRESENT CONTINUOUS AND SIMPLE PRESENT TENSES

PRESENT CONTINUOUS TENSE	SIMPLE PRESENT TENSE
1. The present continuous tense uses the auxiliary *be* (*am*, *are* or *is*) and the present participle (*sitting*): **I am sitting in a restaurant.** 2. The present continuous tense is used to refer to an action that is taking place now: **The sun is setting.** 3. The following adverbials are often used with the present continuous tense: now - at the moment - for a few days - these days	1. The simple present tense uses the simple form of the verb: **I eat, you eat, we eat, they eat,** but adds an *-s* to the verb when the subject is *he*, *she* or *it*: **He eats.** 2. The simple present tense is used to refer to actions that take place habitually (often or always): **The sun sets at eight o'clock in summer.** 3. The following adverbials are often used with the simple present tense: always - often - usually - sometimes - every day - in the morning/afternoon/evening

COMMON ERRORS

1. Leaving out the auxiliary when using the present continuous tense:
   - ✗ We sitting in a restaurant.
2. Using the simple form of the verb rather than the present participle when using the present continuous tense:
   - ✗ We are sit in a restaurant.
3. Using the present continuous instead of the simple present tense to refer to actions that are habitual:
   - ✗ Every day we are going shopping.
4. Omitting the *-s* from the verb when using the simple present tense with *he*, *she* or *it*:
   - ✗ She live in San Francisco.

5

DO/DOES IN YES/NO QUESTIONS

See Unit 16 for more information about *do/does* in questions.

1. When you want to make a question using the simple present tense you should use the auxiliary verb *do*:
   Statement: I iron all the clothes.
   Question: **Do you iron all the clothes?**
2. A question begins with *do* or *does* and is followed by the subject and then the main verb
   Does   Jim   **help**   with the kids?
   Do/does + subject + main verb
3. The auxiliary *do* has two forms—*do* and *does*. *Do* is used when the subject is *I, you, we* or *they*.
   Does is used when the subject is *he, she* or *it*:
   Do you cook all the food?
   Does your husband sometimes cook?

COMMON ERRORS

1. Failure to use the word order for questions (*Do* + subject + main verb)
   ✗ He helps you with the kids?
   Note: You can use this word order in a question to verify whether something is true.
2. Using *do* instead of *does*.
   ✗ Do Jim help you with the kids?
3. Adding an *s* to the main verb in a question with *does*:
   ✗ Does Jim helps you with the kids?

NOT	**NO**
1. Use *not* with an adjective: **Anna is not very tall.**	1. Use *no* with a noun by itself: **Anna is no angel.** **Anna has got no money.**
2. Also use *not* with a verb: **Anna is not going on holiday this year.**	2. Use *no* with an adjective and a noun. **She has no free time this week.**
3. Use *not* if the noun has *a(n), the* or a possessive pronoun before it: **Anna is not an angel.** **Anna is not my idea of an angel.**	

COMMON ERRORS

1. Using *no* when you should use *not*:
   ✗ Anna is no very tall.
   ✗ Anna is no an angel.
2. Using *not* when you should use *no*:
   ✗ Anna has got not money.

7

PLURAL FORM OF COUNTABLE NOUNS

1. Countable nouns such as *forest* and *beach* can have a singular form (*a forest*) and a plural form (*forests*).
2. You can make most countable nouns plural by adding -*s* (**forest<u>s</u>**).
3. Nouns that end in -ch or -sh add -*es* (**beach<u>es</u>**).
4. Some nouns do not have a plural with -*s*. They are irregular: **men, women, people, children, feet, teeth.**
5. Some nouns are the same in the singular and the plural: **sheep, salmon**
6. There are a number of common expressions used with plural countable nouns:
    some - many - both - all - a lot of - several   We saw <u>several monkeys</u> in the forest.

COMMON ERRORS

1. Omission of plural -*s*. This error often occurs when the sentence contains one of the expressions in Number 6 above:
    ✗ We saw some monkey.
2. Adding an -*s* to an irregular plural noun:
    ✗ The childrens are playing.
3. Adding an -*s* to a noun that is the same in the plural:
    ✗ We saw a lot of sheeps.

8

1. Nouns in English are usually either *countable* nouns or *uncountable* (sometimes called *mass*) nouns. Countable nouns can have a plural form; uncountable nouns cannot.

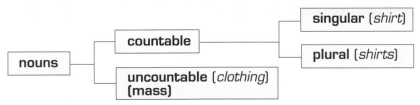

2. Countable nouns, such as *shoe* or *price*, can be preceded by *a* in the singular or in the plural by words such as *some*,
    several and *many*, or by a number: <u>**some** suitcases</u>   <u>**several** stores</u>   <u>**three** shirts</u>
3. Uncountable nouns cannot be preceded by *a(n)* and do not take the plural suffix:
    ✗ a furniture   ✗ two pieces of luggages   ✗ several sporting equipments
4. To express a specific number or quantity of an uncountable noun, we have to use certain phrases:
    <u>**three pieces of**</u> luggage   <u>**two** homework **assignments**</u>   <u>**four articles of**</u> clothing
    <u>**different kinds of**</u> trouble   <u>**lots of**</u> good advice
5. Some nouns in English can be both countable and uncountable:
    That was the first time I've gone into that shop to buy <u>coffee</u>; I didn't realize they have <u>coffees</u> from all over the world.

    My wife asked me to bring home some <u>cake</u>, but they had so many <u>cakes</u> that I had a hard time choosing.

    He stopped in the delicatessen to buy a little <u>cheese</u> to have for lunch, but when he saw all the <u>cheeses</u> they had, he ended up buying enough for a week.

COMMON ERRORS

1. Treating an uncountable noun as a countable noun:
    ✗ a furniture   ✗ some informations   ✗ four silverwares
2. Omitting the plural with countable nouns:
    ✗ four shirt   ✗ several week

1. Determiners are words like *some, much, many, a few, a little*. They go before nouns:
   a few people; <u>**several**</u> small children
2. Determiners answer the questions *How much?* or *How many?* They quantify a noun:
   <u>**Many**</u> **people** means a lot of people.
   <u>**Much**</u> **food** means a lot of food.
3. The table shows you which determiners go with mass nouns and plural nouns.

TYPE OF NOUN	EXAMPLES		DETERMINERS
mass noun	material money		the, some, much, any, a little, a lot of
plural noun	people cookies	pairs dishes	some, many, any, a few, several, a lot of, lots of

COMMON ERRORS

1. Using the wrong determiner to quantify a plural noun:
   ✗ There are not much things to buy.
2. Using the wrong determiner to quantify a mass noun:
   ✗ I bought a few bread.

See Unit 20 for more information about forming *Wh- questions*.

1. To form a *yes/no* question in English, reverse the order of the subject and verb.
   The question that corresponds to *The food is on the table* is:
   <u>**Is the food**</u> **on the table?**
2. If the verb has two parts, and the first part is a form of the verb *be*, invert the subject and the form of *be*.
   The question that corresponds to *He is reading the newspaper* is:
   <u>**Is he reading**</u> **the newpaper?**
3. In spoken English, people will sometimes ask *yes/no* questions by changing the intonation of a statement:
   You're a teacher? or **You're going to London tonight?**
   This is often done to verify that you have heard correctly what another speaker has said.

COMMON ERRORS

1. Adding *yes* or *no* to the end of a statement instead of inverting the subject and *be*:
   ✗ It's a bird, yes?
2. Omitting the subject:
   ✗ Are penguins?
3. Inverting the subject noun phrase and the entire verb phrase:
   ✗ Are poisonous those snakes?
4. Inverting the subject noun phrase and something other than *be*:
   ✗ Hungry the elephants are?
5. Including the verb *be* twice:
   ✗ Is that is an eagle?

11   STATIVE VERBS

1. Certain verbs, called *stative verbs*, do not usually occur in the present continuous form.
   These verbs can be classified into several categories of meaning:
   perception: see, taste, feel, hear, seem
   cognition: know, believe, understand, remember, realize
   description: include, contain, weigh, cost
   possession: have, own, want, desire, need

2. Some stative verbs *can* occur in the present continuous when they are used to describe *actions*:
   I think he will arrive tomorrow. vs.
   I <u>am thinking</u> of you all the time. (an action)

   The baby weighs 11 pounds. vs.
   The nurse <u>is weighing</u> the baby. (an action)

   I have a lot of friends whom we spend time with. vs.
   We <u>are having</u> some friends for dinner at our house. (an action)

COMMON ERRORS

1. Using a stative verb in the present continuous form:
   ✗ He is owning an exercise bicycle and a treadmill.
2. Using a stative verb in the imperative form:
   ✗ Weigh less!

12   SIMPLE PAST TENSE

See Unit 30 for more information about the *simple past*.

1. The simple past is the tense that is usually used to refer to actions that were completed in the past.
   It refers to actions that occurred at definite times in the past.

2. The past tense is used with adverbs like *yesterday*, *last week*, *in 1965*.
   However, it can also be used when the time is not mentioned:
   Johnny Cash <u>lived</u> in Arkansas.

3. Regular verbs like *play*, *fill* and *work* make the simple past tense by adding *-ed*:
   play<u>ed</u>, fill<u>ed</u>, work<u>ed</u>.

4. Irregular verbs like *come* and *give* make the simple past tense in a number of different ways.
   Here is a list of some of the most common irregular verbs:

beat (beat)	dig (dug)	give (gave)	leave (left)	run (ran)	shake (shook)	throw (threw)
begin (began)	drink (drank)	go (went)	let (let)	say (said)	sleep (slept)	wake (woke)
bite (bit)	eat (ate)	grow (grew)	lie (lay)	see (saw)	speak (spoke)	wear (wore)
bring (brought)	fall (fell)	have (had)	light (lit)	send (sent)	steal (stole)	write (wrote)
blow (blew)	feel (felt)	hear (heard)	lose (lost)	shine (shone)	stand (stood)	win (won)
buy (bought)	fight (fought)	hide (hid)	pay (paid)	shut (shut)	swim (swam)	
catch (caught)	find (found)	hold (held)	put (put)	sing (sang)	take (took)	
choose (chose)	forgive (fogave)	keep (kept)	read (read)	sit (sat)	teach (taught)	
come (came)	forget (forgot)	know (knew)	ride (rode)	spend (spent)	tell (told)	
cut (cut)	get (got)	lay (laid)	rise (rose)	shoot (shot)	think (thought)	

COMMON ERRORS

1. Using the simple form of the verb instead of the past form:
   ✗ Miles Davis' father give him a trumpet for his 13th birthday.
2. Using the regular form of the simple past for an irregular verb:
   ✗ Bob Dylan singed protest songs in the sixties.

13   PREPOSITIONS IN EXPRESSIONS OF TIME

Use **ON** with:	Use **IN** with:	Use **AT** with:

days of the week	year	month	specific time
on Monday	**in 1998**	**in February**	**at 3 o'clock**
dates	century	part of the day	**at the end of February**
on March 3rd	**in the 20th century**	**in the morning**	

There are also some common time expressions that do not have any preposition:
    next week, a week ago, tomorrow, yesterday

COMMON ERRORS

1. Using the wrong preposition in a time expression:
   ✗ on the night
   ✗ at 1998
   ✗ in 3 o'clock
2. Using a preposition with a time expression that does not take any preposition:
   ✗ He is visiting me in next week.

14   PREPOSITIONS OF LOCATION AND DIRECTION

1. Use *in* to describe location in cities, state, provinces, countries, and continents:
   Our regional office is in San Diego.
   We have sales representatives in Europe and Asia.
2. Use *at* with names of libraries, museums, universities:
   You can use the computers at the University of California.
3. *At* is also used to describe a general area:
   Let's meet at the stadium.   Note: We can also use : **by the stadium**   **in the stadium**
4. Use *at* to describe a location that includes an address number as well as a street or avenue:
   Their office is located at 3141 Crescent Road.
5. Use *on* when giving only the street or the avenue:
   Their office is on Crescent Road.
6. *On* is also used to describe locations for bodies of water:
   The town is on the Mississippi River.   **They have a cottage on Silver Lake.**
7. Use *to* to describe a destination:
   Since it was a nice day, we walked all the way to the park.
8. Use *toward* to describe motion in the direction of a destination:
   Walk toward the park. About 100 meters before the park, you'll see the pet store on the right side of the street.

COMMON ERRORS

1. Using *in* with an address:
   ✗ The office is located in 500 Kennedy Avenue.
2. Using *in* with *the corner*:
   ✗ The library is in the corner of Main Street and Fourth Avenue.
3. Using *at* instead of *to* to express direction:
   ✗ From here we can get at the park by walking along Lake Avenue.
4. Using *at* with a city:
   ✗ There are excellent museums at Boston.
5. Using *in* with a street:
   ✗ The medical center is in Main Street. (Note: This use of *in* is correct in British English.)

15 ADJECTIVES VS. ADVERBS

See Unit 21 for more information about the use of adverbs.

1. Adverbs of manner usually end in *-ly*: **carelessly**; **selfishly**.

2. An adverb of manner has a different form from an adjective: adverb - **carelessly**   adjective - **careless**

3. Adverbs of manner modify verbs (they say how an action was done):
The man <u>accidentally</u> broke the window.
Adjectives modify nouns:
It was an <u>accidental</u> action.

4. An adverb of manner can go in several places in a sentence:
   a. It can go at the beginning of a sentence:
   <u>Accidentally</u> the man broke the window.
   b. It can go between the subject and the verb:
   The man <u>accidentally</u> broke the window.
   c. It can go between an auxiliary and main verb:
   The man has <u>accidentally</u> broken the window.
   d. It can go at the end of the sentence:
   The man broke the window <u>accidentally</u>.
   However, the adverb cannot go between the verb and the direct object:
   ✗ The man broke accidentally the window.

COMMON ERRORS

1. Using an adjective where an adverb is required:
   ✗ He broke the window accidental.
2. Putting an adverb between a verb and a direct object:
   ✗ He broke accidentally the window.

---

16 *YES/NO* QUESTIONS IN THE SIMPLE PAST TENSE

See Unit 5 for information about how to make *yes/no* questions in the simple present tense.

1. When you want to make a *yes/no* question using the simple past tense you must use the past tense of the auxiliary verb *do*:
Statement: **Brad <u>did</u> not have a good holiday.**
Question: **<u>Did</u> Brad have a good holiday?**

2. A *yes/no* question in the simple past begins with the auxiliary *did* and is followed by the subject and then the main verb:
<u>Did</u>   +   Brad   +   have   +   a good holiday
Auxiliary   subject   main verb

3. The auxiliary *did* is used with all subjects:
<u>Did they</u> have a good holiday?

COMMON ERRORS

1. Failure to use the correct word order for questions:
   ✗ Brad did not have a good holiday?
2. Using the past tense of the main verb instead of the simple form:
   ✗ Did Brad had a good holiday?
3. Using the present tense auxiliary *do* or *does* instead of the past tense *did*:
   ✗ Does Brad have a good holiday when he was in London?

17 TRANSITIVE vs. INTRANSITIVE VERBS

See Unit 44 for more information on transitive and intransitive verbs.

1. Most verbs in English—including *enjoy*, *like* and *miss*—are always followed by a direct object:
   We missed the train. or **Yumiko enjoyed her year in Madison.** but not
   ✗ We missed. ✗ Yumiko enjoyed.   We call these verbs *transitive* verbs.

2. Some verbs in English—including *happen*, *die* and *disappear*—are never followed by a direct object:
   Her homesickness disappeared. but not
   ✗ She disappeared her homesickness.
   We call these verbs *intransitive* verbs. Other common intransitive verbs are: *live*, *arrive*, *walk*, *sleep*, *come* and *go*.

3. Some verbs in English—including *improve*, *change*, *grow* and *start*—are sometimes followed by a direct object; sometimes they are not followed by a direct object:
   Little by little, my English improved.
   My experiences with my host family have improved my attitude toward English-speaking people.
   These verbs can be transitive or intransitive.

COMMON ERRORS

1. Using a transitive verb without a direct object:
   ✗ How did I like the film? I enjoyed.
2. Using an intransitive verb with a direct object:
   ✗ She arrived the party late.
   ✗ He appeared a red spot on his face.

18 SUBJECT-VERB AGREEMENT WITH SIMPLE PRESENT TENSE

1. The simple present tense has a singular and a plural form of the third person:
   He/she/it runs.   They run.

2. Note that it is the singular form of the verb that has *-s*: **The cat runs.**
   This contrasts with nouns, where it is the plural form that has *-s*: **The cats run.**

COMMON ERRORS

1. It is easy to make a mistake after a relative pronoun:
   ✗ Geena Davis plays a school teacher who suffer from amnesia.
   Here *who* stands for *Geena Davis*, which is singular, so the verb must be in the singular form: **suffers**.
2. It is also easy to make a mistake after *and*:
   ✗ She suffers from loss of memory and want to find her past.
   Here *she* is the subject of *want*, so the verb must be in the singular form: **wants**.
3. Mistakes can occur after phrases such as *a pair of thieves*:
   ✗ A pair of thieves plan a robbery.
   Such phrases are singular, not plural (the main noun, *a pair* is singular),
   so the verb must be in the singular form, too:
   A pair of thieves plans a robbery.

PRESENT PERFECT FOR INDEFINITE PAST

See Unit 12 and Unit 29 for more information.

1. The simple past is used to describe an action completed at some specific time or during a specific period of time:
   I <u>had</u> a job interview <u>yesterday</u>.
   I <u>spent</u> <u>the first 20 years of my life</u> in Thailand.

2. If it is not important when the action took place, we usually use the present perfect:
   <u>Have</u> you <u>had</u> a tour of our plant?
   <u>Have</u> you <u>seen</u> that movie?

   Note: However, it is also OK to use the simple past for an indefinite time:
   <u>Did</u> you have a tour of our plant?
   <u>Did</u> you see that movie?

3. The present perfect often occurs with words like *ever*, *never*, and *always* to express an indefinite action in the past.

COMMON ERRORS

1. Using the present perfect to describe an action completed at a specific time in the past:
   ✗ I have spent a week in our Bangkok office last summer.
2. Using the present perfect to describe an action completed at a specific time or during a specific period of time in the past:
   ✗ I have worked at that company from 1988 to 1992.

20

WH- QUESTIONS

See Unit 10 for more information about forming *yes/no* questions.

1. Reverse the order of the subject and verb to form a *wh-* question—that is, a question beginning with words such as *who*, *what*, *where*, *when*, *why* and *how*.
   <u>Where</u> is the telephone?

2. If the verb has two parts, invert the subject noun phrase and the first part of the verb:
   When <u>are you</u> coming home?
   How <u>can I</u> reach you?

3. If the verb has only one part, you must use some form of *do*:
   Where <u>does</u> she live?
   How much <u>do</u> we pay her?

COMMON ERRORS

1. Failing to invert the subject noun phrase and the first part of the verb:
   ✗ What she should do in an emergency?
2. Failing to use a form of *do* when the verb consists of a single part:
   ✗ Where she lives?
3. Omitting the subject:
   ✗ When is coming?
4. Inverting the subject noun phrase and the entire verb phrase:
   ✗ When should go to sleep the children?

1. When you want to describe *where, when, how* or *how often* someone does something or something happens, you often use an *adverb*.

2. Many adverbs are formed by adding *-ly* to an adjective (sometimes with slight spelling changes):
   quick/quickly, careful/carefully, frequent/frequently, gentle/gently

3. Some adverbs are *not* derived from adjectives: **early, yesterday, there**
   Some adverbs differ a lot from the adjective closest in meaning: **good/well** or not at all: **fast/fast, hard/hard**

4. Adverbs can occur at different places in a sentence:
   (a) at the beginning of the sentence:
   Occasionally she would play the piano for her friends.
   (b) before a verb:
   He regularly met with other stamp collectors.
   (c) after the first part of the multi-part verb:
   He has slowly developed a reputation as a first-class gardener.
   (d) at the end of the sentence:
   My daughter doesn't take her music lessons seriously.

COMMON ERRORS

1. Putting the adverb between a verb and its object:
   ✗ She waters daily her flower garden.
2. Putting the adverb in front of a multi-part verb:
   ✗ He patiently is practicing his piano lesson.

---

22 *FEW/A FEW, LITTLE/A LITTLE*

See Unit 8 for information about determiners used with nouns.

1. Use *few* and *a few* with the plural of countable nouns:
   a few houses, few farmers, a few boys

2. Use *little* and *a little* with uncountable (mass) nouns:
   little hope, a little sugar, a little difficulty

3. Use *few* when you want to emphasize the idea of *not many*; use *little* when you want to emphasize *not much*.
   Few and *little* contrast with *many* and *a lot*:
   The forecast predicted a lot of thunderstorms for this week, but in fact we got little rain.

4. Use *a few* when you want to emphasize the idea of **a small number**; use *a little* to express the idea of **a small amount**. *A few* and *a little* contrast with *none* or *nothing*:
   They said it was going to be cold all week, but we did end up with a few sunny days.

5. The comparative form of *few* is fewer:
   There are usually fewer typhoons in August than in September.
   The comparative form of *little* is *less*:
   Last winter we had little snow, and this winter we've had less.

COMMON ERRORS

1. Using *a few* and *few* with uncountable nouns:
   ✗ Tomorrow there could be a few rain.
2. Using *a little* and *little* with countable nouns:
   ✗ The last few days have been sunny, with only a little clouds from time to time.
3. Confusing *few* and *a few* (or *little* and *a little*):
   ✗ The morning will be overcast, but by later this afternoon we may get little clearing.
   (The word *but* suggests that the weather will change, so *a little*, meaning more than *nothing*, is the correct choice.)

1. Use the comparative form of adjectives to compare two persons, things or situations:
   She is <u>taller</u> than her mother.

2. Use the superlative form of adjectives to tell which of three or more objects or persons or ideas has the most of some quality: **She is <u>the tallest</u> person in her family.**

3. The comparative form of one-syllable adjectives and of two-syllable adjectives that end in *y* is formed by adding -*er*:
   small, small<u>er</u>; high, high<u>er</u>; pretty, prett<u>ier</u>; busy, busi<u>er</u>
   The comparative form of adjectives of two or more syllables is usually expressed with the word *more*:
   convenient, <u>more</u> convenient; suitable, <u>more</u> suitable

4. The superlative form ends with -*est*: **<u>the</u> tall<u>est</u>**
   or, for words of two or more syllables, by adding the words *the most*: **<u>the most</u> convenient**

5. Be aware of certain spelling rules for comparative and superlative forms:
   a. For one-syllable adjectives ending in a vowel + consonant double the final consonant before adding -*er* or -*est*:
      big, big<u>ger</u>, big<u>gest</u>; hot, hot<u>ter</u>, hot<u>test</u>.
   b. For adjectives ending in a consonant + *y*, the *y* is changed to *i* before adding -*er* or -*est*: **pretty, prett<u>ier</u>, prett<u>iest</u>**
   c. For adjectives ending with *e* drop the *e* before adding -*er* or -*est*: **brave, brav<u>er</u>, brav<u>est</u>**

COMMON ERRORS

1. Not using the comparative form of an adjective to compare two persons or things:
   ✗ The blue whale is heavy than the elephant.
2. Not using the superlative form of an adjective when comparing three or more persons or things:
   ✗ The cheetah is the fast land animal in the world.
3. Omitting *the* when using the superlative form of an adjective:
   ✗ Mt. Everest is tallest mountain in the world.
4. Using both *more* and -*er* in comparing two persons or things:
   ✗ The pyramid of Quetzalcoatl is more larger than the Pyramids of Giza in Egypt.

24 LIKE AND AS

1. Use *as...as* with an adjective to describe what something is similar to.
   She is <u>as cold as</u> ice. She's not very friendly.

2. Use *like* with a noun or noun phrase to describe what something is similar to.
   (Use *unlike* to describe what something is *not* similar to.)
   He runs <u>like a snail</u>. He's so slow.

3. You can also use *as...as* with adverbs and expressions of quantity (*as much as, as many as*).
   The child spoke <u>as quietly as</u> a mouse.

4. Many speakers of American English will use *like* in place of *as if*:
   She said she feels <u>as if</u> she just ran a marathon!   She said she feels <u>like</u> she just ran a marathon!
   This use of *like* is not accepted by all speakers, especially for written English.

COMMON ERRORS

1. Using *as* instead of *like* with a noun or noun phrase:
   ✗ When my little brother goes into a toy store, he is as a bull in a china shop.
2. Using *like* instead of *as* with an adjective:
   ✗ My sister really likes her new job. She is happy like a clam.
3. Omitting the second *as* in the expression *as .... as*:
   ✗ My friend has been lifting weights. He is as strong an ox.

1. Use the following to show that two or more things are similar:
similar to, equal to, identical to, like

   <u>Like</u> its sister city of Kobe, Seattle enjoys a magnificent natural setting.
   Frankfurt is <u>similar to</u> Milan in several ways: Neither is a capital city, but both have great economic importance.

2. Use the following to show that two or more things are different:
different from, unlike, in contrast to, compared to or **compared with**

   Kyoto is <u>different from</u> Tokyo in many ways.
   <u>Unlike</u> Barcelona, Madrid is located in the interior of the country.
   <u>In contrast to</u> Vancouver's mild winter weather, Montreal's winters can be very cold and snowy.
   <u>Compared to</u> (<u>with</u>) Shanghai, many other large cities in China seem small.

COMMON ERRORS

1. Using the wrong word:
   ✗ Comparing with other capitals, Ottawa, the capital of Canada, is a small city.
2. Using the wrong preposition:
   ✗ Moscow is very different with St. Petersburg.
3. Using a preposition with *like* and *unlike*:
   ✗ In my opinion, Buenos Aires is in many ways like to a European city.

---

26 *THERE IS* VS. *IT IS*

See Unit 2 for more information about the use of *there is* and *there are*.

THERE IS

1. *There is* and *there are* are used to mention something for the first time:

   There is a big sign about 200 meters before the turn.

   There are several new buildings on the left side of the highway.

   In sentences like these, you can replace *there is* and *there are* with *You can see*.

2. Sometimes the word *there* refers to a place that has already been mentioned:

   You want to go to the Botanical Gardens? I go there almost once a week.

IT IS

1. The word *it* refers to something already mentioned:

   Do you see that tree by the entrance to the temple? It is a very old gingko tree.

2. Sometimes *it* does not refer to a noun. *It* is often used in expression of time, distance, situation and weather:

   It is a short ride to the museum.
   It is late.
   It is quiet in this room.

COMMON ERRORS

1. Omitting *there* or *it*:
   ✗ Is raining.
   ✗ Are four doors at the entrance; use the one on the far right.
2. Using *there is* for *it is*:
   ✗ There is not far to my office; we don't need to take a taxi.
3. Using *it is* for *there is*:
   ✗ It is a bookstore next to the north entrance to the train station.

27

MODALS OF POSSIBILITY

1. The modal verbs that express future possibility are: **may, might, can, could**
2. All these verbs are used with a main verb: **People with Alzheimer's disease <u>may forget</u> very simple words.**
3. The modal verbs *may, might, can* and *could* differ in meaning from *will*. They say what may *possibly* happen. *Will* says what will *definitely* happen:
   People with Alzheimer's disease <u>may get</u> lost.   People with a high fever <u>will feel</u> sick.
4. These four modals are close in meaning. For most speakers, *may* and *can* refer to something that is possible and likely:
   A person with Alzheimer's disease <u>may forget</u> things.
   A person with Alzheimer's disease <u>can forget</u> things
   For most speakers, *might* and *could* refer to something that is possible but not so likely:
   A person with Alzheimer's disease <u>might wear</u> two shirts or dresses.
   A person with Alzheimer's disease <u>could wear</u> two shirts or dresses.
5. Use the simple present tense to say what generally happens:
   Everybody <u>forgets</u> things.
   Use a modal verb to express what we think will possibly happen.
   A person with Alzheimer's disease <u>may forget</u> where she lives.
6. The modal verbs *might* and *could* should be used when the sentence is referring to the past:
   We <u>thought</u> that she <u>might</u> be suffering from Alzheimer's disease.

COMMON ERRORS

1. Using verb+ing, the infinitive with *to* or a past participle after a modal verb:
   ✗ People with Alzheimer's disease may forgetting things.
   ✗ People with Alzheimer's disease may to forget things.
   ✗ People with Alzheimer's disease may forgotten things.
2. Using *be able* and *can* in the same sentence:
   ✗ People with Alzheimer's disease can be able to forget things.
3. Using *will* instead of a modal verb of possibility:
   ✗ People with Alzheimer's disease will forget things.
4. Using *may* when referring to past possibility:
   ✗ We thought she may be suffering from Alzheimer's disease.

28

MODALS OF OBLIGATION AND NECESSITY

1. Use *should* to offer advice or to make a suggestion about something that you think is important:
   You <u>should</u> bring a warm jacket if you going to be in Moscow in October.
2. Use *might* to make a weaker offer of advice or to suggest something that you do not consider important:
   You <u>might</u> consider bringing an ATM card. They are quite convenient to use in Moscow and St. Petersburg.
3. Use *have to* to describe something that is necessary, or required:
   You <u>have to</u> have your visa before you board the flight for Russia.
   Have to and *must* express roughly the same degree of obligation.

COMMON ERRORS

1. Omitting *to* with *have*:
   ✗ I have get a visa.
2. Using *to* with *should* or *must*:
   ✗ You should to bring plenty of film and extra batteries.
   ✗ You must to reconfirm your return flight.
3. Using *should* to express necessity:
   ✗ You should reconfirm your return flight. You will lose your reservation if you don't.
4. Using *have to* or *must* to express advice:
   ✗ It isn't necessary, but you have to bring flowers or some small gift if you are invited to someone's house.

29 **PRESENT PERFECT WITH *FOR* AND *SINCE***

See Unit 19 for more information about *present perfect* tense.

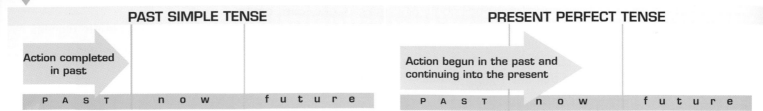

PAST SIMPLE TENSE	PRESENT PERFECT TENSE
Action completed in past	Action begun in the past and continuing into the present
P A S T　　n o w　　f u t u r e	P A S T　　n o w　　f u t u r e

FOR and SINCE

The present perfect tense is often used with *for* and *since*.

1. a. *For* is used with an expression referring to a period of time: <u>for</u> **five years**
   b. *Since* is used with an expression referring to a specific time in the past: <u>since</u> **1985** or <u>since</u> **the end of last month**

2. a. *For* can also be used with the simple past tense.
   In this case it refers to an action that took place over a period of time but is now completed:
   I lived in Zambia <u>for</u> 10 years between 1967 and 1977.
   b. *Since* can never be used with the past simple tense.

COMMON ERRORS

1. Using the simple past tense instead of the present perfect tense:
   ✗ He worked here since 1989.
   ✗ He worked here for three years and does not want to leave.
2. Using the present continuous tense instead of the present perfect tense:
   ✗ He is working here for three years.
3. Using *since* in place of *for*:
   ✗ He has worked here since two years.

1. Both the simple past tense and the past continuous tense refer to events that happened in the past and are now completed.

2. The past continuous tense is used to refer to past events that the speaker sees as lasting a period of time (the speaker wants to emphasize the *duration* of the past event): **Ms. Leeson <u>was starving</u> slowly.**

3. The simple past tense is used to refer to events that took place in the past more than once (they were *habitual*):
   Ms. Leeson sometimes <u>typed</u> papers in her room.
   Another way of referring to habitual actions in the past is to use *used to*:
   Ms. Leeson sometimes <u>used to</u> type papers in her room.

4. The simple past tense is also used to refer to past events that took place at a definite point in the past:
   An ambulance <u>took</u> Ms. Leeson to the hospital.

5. The same verb can be used in the simple past tense or the past continuous tense, depending on whether the speaker wants to emphasize the *completeness* of the past event or the *duration*:
   Ms. Leeson <u>stayed</u> in the top room of a guest house.
   Ms. Leeson <u>was staying</u> in the top room of a guest house.

COMMON ERRORS

A common error is to use the past continuous tense instead of the simple past tense to refer to habitual actions in the past:
   ✗ Ms. Leeson was sometimes typing papers in her room.

31 UNIQUE REFERENCE WITH AND WITHOUT *THE*

See Unit 8 and Unit 33 for more information.

1. Proper nouns, such as the names of places (Osaka Bay) or people (Renzo Piano), have unique reference — there is only one of them. They are used without any article:
Kansai International Airport is situated in Osaka Bay.

2. Other nouns are not proper nouns but can still have unique reference in context.
For example, there is only one *arrivals lobby* in an airport terminal and there can be only one *first floor*.
We use *the* to show unique reference with these nouns:
<u>The</u> arrivals lobby is on <u>the</u> first floor.

3. Usually we use *a* when we refer to something for the first time:
Kansai International Airport has <u>a</u> very modern airport terminal.
However, if a noun is unique in its context we must use *the* even if we are mentioning it for the first time:
<u>The</u> main terminal is very modern.

COMMON ERRORS

1. Using *the* with proper nouns:
✗ You can find the Japan Railways in the basement.
2. Omitting *the* when a noun has unique reference:
✗ Arrivals lobby is on first floor.
3. Using *a* instead of *the* in nouns with unique reference used for the first time:
✗ An arrivals lobby is on the first floor.

32 THE INDEFINITE ARTICLE *A*

See Unit 33 for use information about articles.

1. Use *a* before a noun that begins with a consonant: **<u>a</u> man**
Use *an* before a noun that begins with a vowel: **<u>an</u> English book**
Note: some words beginning with *h* use *an* because the *h* is silent when we say the word: **<u>an</u> hour.**
But some words beginning with *h* use *a* because the *h* is said: **a hotel.**

2. Do not use *a* with uncountable nouns:
He bought <u>food</u> for the journey.

3. Do not use *a* with abstract nouns.
He suffered from <u>depression</u>.

4. Do not use *a* with plural nouns.
He was attacked by dog<u>s</u>.

5. *A* is used when a noun is first mentioned and is therefore indefinite:
<u>A</u> man shot himself in a hotel in New York.

COMMON ERRORS

1. Omitting *a* with a countable noun:
✗ He shot himself in hotel in New York.
2. Omitting *a* before *half* and *hundred:*
✗ He gave the beggar half loaf of bread.
✗ She lost hundred dollars.
3. Using *a* with a countable noun:
✗ He gave me a good advice.
4. Using *a* with an abstract noun:
✗ A stubbornness can be very annoying.

See Unit 32 for more information about *articles*.

1. When we refer to a specific object or person for the first time we use *a*:
   A tamagochi is an electronic toy.

2. When we refer to the same object again we always use *the*:
   A tamagochi is an electronic toy. The tamagochi has become very popular.

3. *The* is also used with a different noun providing this noun refers to the same thing:
   A tamagochi is an electronic toy. The gadget has become very popular.

4. *The* is also used before a noun when the noun is followed by a phrase or a clause that makes it definite:
   The live tamagochi made by a Chinese street seller proved very popular.

COMMON ERRORS

1. Omitting *the* before a noun that has already been mentioned:
   ✗ A tamagochi is an electronic toy. Tamagochi has become very popular.

2. Using *a* instead of *the* before a noun made definite by a following phrase or clause:
   ✗ A streetseller who made live tamagochis has become rich.

OTHER

1. Use *other* with plural nouns:
   I have other siblings, but the person in my family I spend the most time with is my youngest sister.

THE OTHER

1. Use *the other* to identify the second of two (or the last of more than two) persons or things:
   One of my brothers is a businessman; the other is an accountant.

ANOTHER

1. Use *another* (*an + other*) to express the idea of additional:
   I've given you two reasons why it's nice to have a twin brother or sister. Here's another.
   In sentences like the one above, *another* refers to the next one in a list of two or more.

2. Use *another* when you want to express the idea of a *different* one:
   This photograph of my family isn't very good. Let me show you another one.

3. To emphasize that you are adding one more item to a list, use the phrase *still another*.
   My three sisters enjoy cooking, talking and shopping together.
   Still another thing they enjoy is going away together on holidays.

Note: *One another* and *each other* have the same basic meaning:
   They all like one another.   They all like each other.

COMMON ERRORS

1. Using *other* with a singular noun:
   ✗ I have other cousin who lives in the same city I do.

2. Using *another* with a plural noun:
   ✗ There are another things my sister and I enjoy doing together.

3. Using *other* instead of *the other*:
   ✗ Only one of my two sisters lives in Tokyo; other lives in Vancouver.

1. Some verbs such as *want* are followed by an infinitive:
   I want <u>to see</u> you.
   Other verbs such as *enjoy* are followed by a gerund:
   I enjoy <u>seeing</u> you.

2. Unfortunately, there is no easy rule to tell you which verbs take an infinitive and which ones a gerund.
   So you have to keep your ears and eyes open to spot whether a verb takes an infinitive or a gerund.

3. Common verbs that are followed only by the infinitive are:
   ask - demand - learn - forget - promise - refuse - swear - hope - decide - seem - want

4. Common verbs that are followed only by the gerund are:
   avoid - consider - deny - dislike - dread - enjoy - forgive - keep - miss - risk - suggest

5. A few verbs can take either the infinitive or the gerund:
   try - remember - stop
   There can be a difference in meaning between the infinitive and the gerund in sentences with these verbs:
   I remembered to see her. (I did not forget that I had to see her.)
   I remembered seeing her. (I recalled that I had seen her before.)

COMMON ERRORS

Using the wrong complement with a verb:
   ✗ I have enjoyed to spend time with you.
   ✗ He suggested to send her a Valentine card.

MAKE	LET
Use *make* to express the idea that someone is requiring someone to do something: **The teacher <u>made</u> the students rewrite the composition.**	Use *let* to show that someone has been *allowed*, or *given permission*, to do something, or that something has been made *possible*: **The teacher <u>let</u> the students choose the topic they would read about.**

Note: The verb *have* can also be used to express the idea of causing something to happen or causing someone to do something:
   Please <u>have</u> the next patient come in.
   The doctor <u>is having</u> me keep track of what I eat each day.

COMMON ERRORS

1. Using *let* to express the idea of requiring someone to do something:
   ✗ She let the staff stay until the report was finished.
2. Using *make* to express the idea of allowing someone to do something:
   ✗ If you finish your homework, I will make you watch television.
3. Using the word *to* before the verb complement:
   ✗ He made us to stop everything we were doing.
   ✗ I'll let you to choose the topic you want to read about.

1. Words that end in *-ing* can function as verbs (refer to actions) or as adjectives (describe nouns):
   Rick likes to go out <u>drinking</u>. (verb)
   Rick can be a <u>caring</u> person. (adjective)

2. Some common *-ing* verbs that function as adjectives are: *amusing - annoying - boring - caring - doubting - exciting - frightening - interesting - loving - threatening - worrying*
   These adjectives all come from transitive verbs (verbs that can take a direct object):
   He amuses me.   **He is an amusing person.**
   Intransitive verbs (verbs that do not take an object) cannot be made into adjectives:
   He <u>quarrels</u> all the time   ✗ He is a very quarrelling person.

3. Adverbs like *always* and *sometimes* modify *-ing* words that act as verbs and adjectives:
   Rick is <u>always</u> drinking.   **Rick is <u>sometimes</u> caring.**

   However, intensifiers such as *very* and *really* can modify only *-ing* words that act as adjectives:
   ✗ Rick is very drinking.   **Rick can be <u>very</u> loving.**

COMMON ERRORS

1. Using an intransitive verb as an adjective:
   ✗ He is a sweating person.
2. Using words like *very* with *-ing* words that function as verbs.
   ✗ She is very arguing.

SIMPLE PRESENT TENSE

1. The simple present tense CAN be used to refer to future actions that are part of a carefully planned schedule, such as a journey or a visit. Usually an adverb of time (*next week*) is included in the sentence:
   Two Russian cosmonauts <u>blast</u> off next week.   **They <u>stay</u> two months on Spiv.**
   Note: This is used more often in journalism than in everyday spoken language.

2. The simple present tense can be safely used to refer to future time with these verbs:
   open, close, begin, end, start, finish, arrive, return.
   Other verbs (*blast off, join*) can also be used when these refer to actions that are part of a definite schedule.
   The space mission <u>begins</u> next week.

FUTURE TENSE

1. You can also use the future tense to refer to a journey:
   Two Russian cosmonauts <u>will blast</u> off next week.   **They <u>will stay</u> two months on Spiv.**
   However, the simple present tense is sometimes preferred.

2. The future tense should be used to refer to actions that the speaker views as specific and not linked to a particular time:
   They <u>will repair</u> the damaged electrical systems.   **They <u>will work</u> inside the darkened space module.**

COMMON ERRORS

Using the simple present tense to refer to a specific action in the future,
especially when no particular time is mentioned:
✗ The astronauts work inside the darkened space module.

1. To describe a situation that is not yet taking place but that is possible or likely in the future, we usually put the verb in the *if*-clause in the simple present and the verb of the *result* clause in the simple future:
   If he <u>gets</u> the promotion he's been expecting, <u>we'll go</u> out and celebrate.

2. To describe what would happen in some imaginary, or hypothetical, situation, use the simple past in the *if*-clause and the conditional (*would* + main verb) in the *result* clause:
   If I <u>had</u> enough money [this suggests that you don't], **I <u>would buy</u> a new car** [this expresses what would happen].
   If I <u>won</u> the lottery, I <u>would retire</u> and move to the Caribbean.

3. Conditional sentences of this type can occasionally describe certain kinds of *imaginary situations*:
   If I <u>had</u> four legs, I <u>could run</u> like a horse.

COMMON ERRORS

1. Using the wrong verb tense in one or both parts of a conditional statement:
   ✗ If I earn enough money, I would move to a larger apartment.
   ✗ If I had enough money to buy a vacation home, I will look for a place in Hawaii.
2. Using the wrong kind of conditional statement:
   ✗ It's not going to happen, of course, but if I become the head of state of my country, I will make many changes.
3. Using a hypothetical conditional statement to describe a situation that is no longer possible:
   ✗ I didn't get the promotion. If I got the promotion, I would be very happy.

---

40 **HYPOTHETICAL** vs. **UNREAL CONDITIONALS**

See Unit 39 for more information about conditionals.

HYPOTHETICAL CONDITIONAL

1. Use a hypothetical conditional sentence to describe a situation that does not exist but that might possibly exist:
   If I <u>won</u> (past) **the lottery, I <u>would travel</u>** (would + verb) **first class all the time.**

2. In hypothetical conditionals, it is common to hear the phrase *I were* (or *he/she/it were*) in the *if*-clause:
   If <u>I were</u> in your situation, I would consider changing careers.

UNREAL CONDITIONAL

1. Use an unreal conditional sentence to describe an imaginary situation in the past that is contrary to the actual situation.
   If I <u>had known</u> (had + participle) **about the job opening earlier, I <u>would have applied</u>** (would have + participle) **for it.**
   The phrase *If I had known* tells us that the speaker in fact did not know about the job in time to apply. The speaker is therefore describing an unreal, or contrary-to-fact, situation.

2. Some speakers of American English use *would have* + participle in the *if* clause as well as the result clause:
   ✗ if I would have studied harder, I would have been admitted to a university.
   Although this kind of sentence is commonly heard, it is still not considered acceptable by most educated speakers of English.

COMMON ERRORS

1. Using the wrong verb forms:
   ✗ If I changed jobs, I had to move.
2. Expressing the wrong meaning with a conditional sentence:
   ✗ If he was unhappy in his job, he would leave.
   (**Intended meaning:** If he had been unhappy in his job (but he wasn't), he would have left (and he didn't).

1. You cannot always tell whether a word is a noun or an adjective from its ending. *Difficulty* is a noun but *healthy* is an adjective. So you will have to learn whether a word is a noun or a verb. Here is a list of some common noun/adjective pairs:

Noun	Adjective	Noun	Adjective	Noun	Adjective
anger	angry	efficiency	efficient	mud	muddy
creativity	creative	fun	funny	safety	safe
difficulty	difficult	health	healthy	sex	sexy
dirt	dirty	honesty	honest	wealth	wealthy

2. An adjective modifies a noun:
   a **difficult** question (a question that is difficult)
   a **wealthy** person (a person who is wealthy)
   a **naughty** child (a child who is naughty)

3. Nouns cannot be used to modify the nouns in these phrases:
   ✗ a difficulty question   ✗ a wealth person   ✗ a naughtiness child

4. A noun can modify another noun in phrases like these:
   a **health** plan (a plan for health)   a **wealth** tax (a tax of wealth)   a **sex** change (a change in sex)

COMMON ERRORS

1. Using a noun instead of an adjective to modify another noun:
   ✗ She is a difficulty person.
2. Using an adjective where a noun is needed:
   ✗ I don't like to talk about sexy.

1. Use the past perfect to indicate the relationship between the completion of some event or action and some other action or some point in time:
   Before she came to the United States, Cecilia <u>had never</u> <u>traveled</u> farther than 100 miles from her hometown.

2. Use the past perfect, like the present perfect, with *for* and *since* to express duration:
   They each <u>had</u> <u>lived</u> in Vancouver for 10 years before they met.

3. Words and phrases that typically occur in sentences calling for the past perfect include *when*, *by (the time)* and *already*.

4. Keep in mind that the words *before* and *after* often make the past perfect unnecessary:
   <u>After</u> he <u>(had) left</u> in anger, I realized that I should have chosen my words more carefully.

COMMON ERRORS

1. Using the past perfect to express only past time:
   ✗ Last year she had started a new career.
2. Using the past perfect to describe an action that was taking place at the same time as another action:
   ✗ While Mr. and Mrs. Sato were traveling in Southeast Asia, Mrs. Sato's sister had stayed in their apartment.

43

PASSIVE VOICE IN THE PRESENT TENSE

1. In making an active sentence passive, the *patient* becomes the grammatical subject, a passive verb is used, and the *agent* can be dropped:

You <u>should keep</u> a computer in a cool place.	A computer <u>should be kept</u> in a cool place.
AGENT + VERB (ACTIVE) + PATIENT	PATIENT + VERB (PASSIVE)

To include an *agent* in a passive sentence use *by*: **Drinks should not be consumed <u>by students</u> near a computer.**

2. A passive verb is formed with *be* and a past participle.
   a. A passive verb in the present tense consists of *am*, *is* or *are* and a past participle:

   The batteries <u>are located</u> at the back.
   _{*are* + past participle}

   b. A modal passive verb consists of: modal verb + **be** + past participle:

   A computer <u>should be cleaned</u> regularly.
   _{modal verb + be + past participle}

   c. Passive verbs can also be formed in other tenses:

   My computer <u>was stolen</u> yesterday.   **My computer <u>has</u> just <u>broken down</u>.**

3. The passive voice is used when the speaker wants to talk about what happens to the *patient* rather than what an *agent* does. Passive sentences often do not include the *agent*.

COMMON ERRORS

1. Using the simple form of the verb instead of the past participle:
   ✗ A damp cloth is use to clean it.
2. Omission of *be*:
   ✗ A computer should kept in a cool place.
3. Using an active verb in place of a passive verb:
   ✗ Computers must care for properly.

44

PROCESS VERBS

See Unit 17 for more information on intransitive verbs.

1. In a sentence like: **The door <u>opened</u>.**
   the action expressed by the verb (*opened*) takes place without any apparent cause (we do not know or do not want to concern ourselves with the agent of the action). The verb is *intransitive* and so the active voice must be used.

2. Verbs such as *open* can be both intransitive (as in the example above) and transitive, as in this sentence:
   Mary <u>opened</u> the door.
   When *open* is used as a transitive verb, we know who the agent of the action is. In this case, the passive voice can be used: **The door <u>was opened</u> (by Mary).**

3. Some verbs, like *happen*, are always intransitive and so can be used only in the active voice:
   A terrible murder <u>happened</u>.

4. a. Some common intransitive verbs that refer to actions that happen without a cause (or agent) are:
   become - consist - continue - die - fall - decline - develop - disappear - happen - occur - rise
   b. Some common transitive verbs that can refer to actions that happen without a cause are:
   break - change - close - decrease - dry - grow - hurt - increase - open - sink - stop

COMMON ERRORS

1. Using an intransitive verb in the passive:
   ✗ A very strange thing was happened.
2. Using *it* + intransitive verb:
   ✗ It happened a very strange thing.
3. Using the passive form of a transitive verb when the active form is needed:
   ✗ The wet clothes were dried quickly in the sun.

1. Use *so* and *too* to agree with a positive statement or to express a similar idea:
   A: I would like to visit Paris.
   B: **I would, <u>too</u>.** or **<u>So</u> would I.**

   C: My passport expires next year.
   D: **Mine does, <u>too</u>.** or **<u>So</u> does mine.**

2. Use *not...either* and *neither* to agree with a negative statement or to express a similar idea:
   A: I can't enjoy a place if it's crowded with tourists.
   B: **I <u>can't, either</u>.** or **<u>Neither</u> can I.**

   C: Our itinerary didn't give us enough time for shopping.
   D: **Ours <u>didn't, either</u>.** or **<u>Neither</u> did ours.**

3. The verb used in the statement of agreement is either some form of the verb *be* or some auxiliary verb (including *do*):
   Spain is a very interesting country to visit, and Morocco <u>is, too.</u>
   I can't be away for more than a week, and <u>neither can</u> my wife.
   The Komatsu family enjoy holidays by the sea, and <u>so do</u> our next-door neighbors.

COMMON ERRORS

1. Using *so* or *too* to agree with a negative statement or to express an idea similar to that of a negative statement:
   A: **I don't suffer too much from jet lag.**
   ✗ B: I do, too **or** So do I.
2. Using *either* to agree with a positive statement or to express an idea similar to that of a positive statement:
   A: **I like spending the days on the beach.**
   ✗ B: Either do I **or** I do, either.
3. Failing to invert the subject and verb with *so* or *neither*:
   ✗ So he does.   ✗ Neither they can.

46   **TOO vs. ENOUGH**

1. Use *too* to express the idea of *excess*. *Too* indicates *more* of a quality than *very*. Compare the following sentences:
   The table is <u>very</u> heavy.   **The table is <u>too</u> heavy (for us to lift).**
   The first sentence only describes the table. The second sentence describes the table and a result.

2. Use *enough* to express the idea of sufficient. Compare the following sentences:
   She is very strong.   **She is strong <u>enough</u> to lift the table by herself.**
   The first sentence only describes the person's strength. The second sentence states that the person's strength is sufficient for her to do something.

3. *Enough* always follows an adjective (or adverb); *enough* almost always comes before a noun:
   The table is <u>small enough</u> to fit nicely in that space.   **There is <u>enough room</u> to put the table there.**

COMMON ERRORS

1. Omitting *too* in a statement of result:
   ✗ The doorway is narrow to get the sofa through.
2. Using *enough* instead of *too*:
   ✗ The doorway is narrow enough to get the sofa through.
3. Placing *enough* before, instead of after, an adjective:
   ✗ She is enough strong to lift the table by herself.
4. Placing *enough* after, instead of before, a noun:
   ✗ We already have furniture enough in that room.

47 | **EMBEDDED QUESTIONS** | See Units 10, 16 and 20 for more information about forming questions.

1. Do not invert the subject and verb in a question if the question is part of (embedded in) another sentence:
   <u>I'd like</u> to know <u>how much</u> a round-the-world ticket costs.

2. When a *yes/no* question is part of another sentence, the question begins with the words *if* or *whether*:
   I'd like to find out <u>if</u> (<u>whether</u>) you have two-day cruises to the Bahamas.

COMMON ERRORS

1. Inverting the subject and first part of the verb in an embedded *wh*-question:
   ✗ The travel agent wants to know when are you going to pick up the ticket.
   ✗ I don't know how can I make reservations for that sightseeing tour.
2. Inverting the subject and verb in an embedded *yes/no* question:
   ✗ My wife wants to know will she have time to shop each day.
   ✗ I will ask them does this tour include all meals.
3. Omitting *if* (or *whether*) from an embedded *yes/no* question:
   ✗ She was wondering she could stay an extra day or two in Capetown.

48 | **RELATIVE CLAUSES WITH *WHICH* AND *THAT*** | See Units 49 and 50 for more information about *relative clauses*.

1. *Which* and *that* are relative pronouns that refer to things, such as types of food:
   Sushi consists of raw fish <u>which/that</u> is served with rice.
   Who and *whom* refer to people:
   A pastry chef is someone <u>who</u> makes pies, cakes and tarts.

2. When the relative clause is used to define the object (as in the sentence above) you can use either *which* or *that*. Both are correct. However, when the relative clause simply adds extra information about the object, only *which* is correct:
   Sushi, <u>which</u> is very popular in Japan, consists of raw fish and rice.
   ✗ Sushi, that is very popular in Japan, consists of raw fish and rice.

3. *Which* and *that* can be used to join two sentences:
   Sushi consists of raw fish.
   Sushi is served with rice.
   Sushi consists of raw fish <u>that</u> (<u>which</u>) is served with rice.

4. *Which* and *that* can function as the subject of the relative clause:
   Sushi consists of raw fish <u>which</u> (<u>that</u>) comes with rice.
   subject   verb
   Which and *that* can also function as the direct object of the relative clause:
   Sushi consists of raw fish <u>which</u> (<u>that</u>) you eat with rice.
   direct object subject   verb

COMMON ERRORS

1. Including an ordinary pronoun as well as the relative pronoun in the relative clause:
   ✗ Sushi consists of raw fish that it is served with rice.
   ✗ Sushi consists of raw fish which you eat it with rice.
2. Using *and* instead of a relative pronoun:
   ✗ Paella is made with rice and the chef cooks with seafood.
3. Leaving out the relative pronoun, when it functions as the subject:
   ✗ Sushi consists of raw fish is eaten with rice.
   Note: When the relative pronoun functions as direct object it can be omitted.
4. Using the relative pronoun *who* to refer to things:
   ✗ Sushi consists of raw fish who is eaten with rice.

1. *Where* and *when* can function as relative pronouns.
   Where refers to a place: **They got married in a zoological garden <u>where</u> there is a chapel by the sea.**
   When refers to a time: **They got married in the evening <u>when</u> it was cool.**

2. Relative clauses with *where* and *when* must have a subject for the verb (these relative pronouns cannot function as subjects themselves):
   They got married in a zoological garden <u>where there</u> is a chapel by the sea.
   They got married in the evening <u>when it</u> was cool.

3. Relative clauses with *where* do not also include *there* referring to place:
   Hawaii is a place <u>where</u> many people get married.

4. Similarly, relative clauses with *when* do not also include *then* referring to time:
   They got married in the evening, <u>when</u> it is cool.

COMMON ERRORS

1. Using *there* and *then* as relative pronouns instead of *where* and *when*:
   ✗ They got married in a zoological garden there is a chapel by the sea.
   ✗ They got married in the evening then it was cool.
2. Using *where* and *when* as subjects of the relative clauses:
   ✗ They got married in a zoological garden where is a chapel by the sea.
   ✗ They got married in the evening when was cool.
3. Using *there* and *then* in relative clauses with the same function as *where* and *when*:
   ✗ Hawaii is a place where many people get married there.
   ✗ They got married in the evening when it is cool then.
4. Using *where* and *when* instead of *which* or *that*:
   ✗ They stayed in a hotel where caters especially to newlyweds.
   ✗ "That was an experience when we will never forget," they said.

1. *Whose* is a relative pronoun that indicates possession. *Whose purse* refers to *the woman's purse* in the sentence:
   We helped the woman <u>whose purse</u> was stolen.
   Whose can refer both to people, as in the example above, and to objects and places:
   We visited Barbados, <u>whose beaches</u> are magnificent.

2. *Whose* is always followed by a noun (**whose <u>purse</u>**). The noun tells you what is possessed.
   Thus in the sentence above it is the *purse* that is possessed by the woman.

3. Like other relative pronouns (*who* and *which*) *whose* can be used to join two sentences:
   We helped the woman.   The woman's purse was stolen.
   We helped the woman <u>whose</u> purse was stolen.

4. *Whose +noun* can function as the subject of the relative clause: **We helped the woman <u>whose purse</u> was stolen.**
   subject   verb

   Whose +noun can also function as direct object of the relative clause: **We helped the woman <u>whose purse</u> the man stole.**
   direct object   subject   verb

COMMON ERRORS

1. Using *who* instead of *whose*:
   ✗ We helped the woman who her purse was stolen.
2. Including a possessive pronoun (*his* or *her*) or *the* after *whose*:
   ✗ We helped the woman whose her purse was stolen.
   ✗ We helped the boy whose the father is ill.

UNIT 1

ERROR BOX
That's Mary Smith. **She** is my boss.
Mary has a new office. **It** is located on the eighth floor.

LISTENING TO COMPREHEND

Employee	Position
Ms. Leslie Williams	**technical manager**
Ms. Sydney Mills	**senior programmer**
Mr. Anil Chaudari	**sales representative**
Mr. Jun Kim	**office secretary**

LISTENING TO NOTICE

Hello. I'm the president of Soft World. (1) **It**'s the world's best computer software company. Let me introduce you to the great team of people who work for Soft World.

Leslie Williams is our technical manager. When there's a problem with new software, (2) **she** finds a solution. I think (3) **she**'s a genius.

Sydney Mills is our senior programmer. (4) **She**'s a software wiz. (5) **She**'s from New Zealand. That's where she started designing and writing software programs. Sydney began working here last year; (6) **she** thinks (7) **it**'s the best place she has ever worked.

Anil Chaudari is our sales representative. (8) **He** joined the company two years ago. We call him "Language Man"; (9) **he** speaks five languages fluently. Then there's Jun Kim. (10) **He**'s the office secretary. (11) **It**'s a really important job. (12) **He** knows everything; his brain is just like a computer.

We're a great team.

UNDERSTANDING THE GRAMMAR POINT

he replaces:	she replaces:	it replaces:
Anil Chaudari	**Leslie Williams**	**Soft World**
Jun Kim	**Sydney Mills**	**office secretary**

2. We use **he** to refer to males.
We use **she** to refer to females.
We use **it** to refer to things or ideas.
3. *He* refers to males; *my sister* is a female.
My sister bought a new car two weeks ago, and **she** has already had an accident.
We use *it* to refer to things such as *books*.
I took a book out from the library last week, but I have not started reading **it**.

CHECKING

1. My brother is five years younger than me. **He** is an engineer.
2. My sister lives in Hong Kong. She is a computer programmer.
3. My father is a journalist. He has done many assignments for foreign newspapers.
4. My friend Carlos is a real estate agent. He owns his own agency. **It** is located in downtown Los Angeles.
5. His wife is a well-known psychologist. **She** works mostly with children and teenagers.
6. My neighbor started a catering business in 1994. **It** has grown a lot in the last several years.
7. My grandfather came to the United States when he was eight years old: By the time he was 20, **he** was a successful businessman.
8. My daughter is a buyer for a large department store. **She** spends a lot of time in other countries.

COMMON ERRORS (from the Grammar Explanation section)

1. My brother is a doctor. **He** works in a large hospital in Toronto.
2. My grandmother lives in another city. **She** loves to visit us.

3. I just bought a new computer. **It** is very powerful.

UNIT 2

ERROR BOX
There **are** several books on the table.
There **is** a painting on the wall.

LISTENING TO COMPREHEND

Mr. Stone (a magician)	Ms. Strain (a music professor)	Mr. Wolf (a private investigator)
✔ some chairs	___ a table	✔ a table
✔ a sink	✔ a computer	✔ some chairs
✔ a table	✔ a violin	✔ a pair of gloves
___ some books	✔ some dishes	___ a cup
✔ a pair of sunglasses	✔ some water	✔ a camera

LISTENING TO NOTICE

Mr. Stone:

(1) **There are** three chairs around a table. (2) **There's** a black cat on the table. (3) **There are** some things on the counter to the right of the sink: a false beard and a moustache, a bottle of hair coloring, and a pair of sunglasses. (4) **There are** a couple of magazines on the table, and (5) **there's** a stuffed rabbit next to them.

Ms. Strain:

(6) **There are** two chairs but no table. On one of the chairs (7) **there is** a laptop computer; on the other (8) **there's** a violin. (9) **There's** a clock over the sink, and (10) **there are** dishes piled up in the sink. Oh, and (11) **there are** several books on the counter next to the refrigerator. And (12) **there is** some water on the floor.

Mr. Wolf:

In the kitchen (13) **there is** a large, heavy wooden table. (14) **There are** six chairs neatly arranged around the table. (15) **There is** nothing at all on the table, but (16) **there are** a lot of things on the counter on either side of the sink: a pair of women's long evening gloves, a small cassette recorder, a camera, and opera glasses. (17) **There is** a toy fire engine on the floor.

UNDERSTANDING THE GRAMMAR POINT

THERE'S ...	THERE ARE ...
a black cat	**three chairs**
a stuffed rabbit	**some things**
a laptop computer	**a couple of magazines**
a violin	**two chairs**
a clock	**dishes**
some water	**several books**
a large, heavy wooden table	**six chairs**
nothing at all	**a lot of things**
a toy fire engine	

2. **Singular nouns** follow *there is*. **Plural nouns** follow *there are*.

CHECKING

We live in a large old house. (1) **There are** several rooms I like to spend time in, but my favorite room is my bedroom. Let me describe it for you.

When you walk in the room, (2) **there's** a dresser along the wall on the left. Above the dresser (3) **there are** three Chinese silk paintings of birds. Straight ahead is my bed. (4) **There are** lots of pillows on it, and (5) **there's** a nightstand on either side of the bed. Nearby (6) **there's** an antique coat tree that belonged to my grandfather. (7) **There are** always several shirts and other things on it. (8) **There's** a fireplace on the wall on the right. Even though it doesn't work, (9) **there are** logs in it, just for decoration. (10) **There are** also a couple of upholstered chairs in the room.

COMMON ERRORS (from the Grammar Explanation section)
1. There **are** several books on the shelf.
2. **There** is a dresser on the wall on the left.
   There are three Chinese silk paintings of birds.
3. **There are** three chairs in the kitchen.
   There is a pair of gloves on the counter.

UNIT 3

ERROR BOX
She **has** black hair.
My brother **is** 20 years old.

LISTENING TO COMPREHEND

Max (top picture)
✔ bald
✔ a beard
✔ a mustache
✔ glasses
___ a T-shirt
✔ 30 years old

Derrick (middle picture)
✔ 20 years old
___ glasses
✔ an earring
✔ a tattoo
___ a mustache
✔ blue eyes

Phillip (bottom picture)
___ an earring
✔ 50 years old
✔ tall
✔ a beige jacket
___ brown eyes
✔ a beard

LISTENING TO NOTICE
I just moved into a new apartment. These are my neighbors.

Max lives in Apartment 101. He (1) **is** bald. He (2) **has** a moustache and a beard. He also (3) **has** gold-rimmed glasses. I think he (4) **is** 30 years old, maybe older. Perhaps he (5) **is** a businessman or a lawyer.

Derrick lives with his parents in Apartment 103. He (6) **is** 20 years old, or even younger. He (7) **has** a ring in his left ear. He also (8) **has** a very small tattoo on the left side of his neck. He (9) **has** blue eyes; but he usually wears sunglasses. He (10) **is** a student, I'm sure.

Philip is in Apartment 104. This man (11) **is** about 50 years old. He (12) **is** tall. He (13) **has** short dark hair, and he (14) **has** a long gray beard. He always (15) **has** a beige jacket on. I think he's a writer or an artist.

UNDERSTANDING THE GRAMMAR POINT

HAVE	BE
has a moustache and a beard	is bald
has gold-rimmed glasses	is 30 years old
has an earing	is a businessman or a
has a very small tattoo	lawyer
has blue eyes	is 20 years old
has short cut hair	is a student
	is about 50 years old
	is tall

2. - We use *have* before a noun or noun phrase telling us about something that someone possesses.
   - We use *be* before a noun or noun phrase which tells us who someone is. We also use *be* when the next word is an adjective without an accompanying noun or noun phrase.

CHECKING
1. Mrs. Hayashi **is** 55 years old.
2. Roberto Garcia is tall and thin.
3. She **has** light brown hair.
4. Juliana **is** very smart.
5. He has a scar under his right ear.
6. My sister **is** 10 years old.
7. My father **has** a beard.
8. He's a businessman.
9. My sister **has** blue eyes.
10. One of my father's employees **has** a tattoo.

COMMON ERRORS (from the Grammar Explanation section)
1. She **is** 30 years old.
   The man **has** brown hair.
2. She **has** blue eyes.
   My brother **is** 20 years old.

UNIT 4

ERROR BOX
Every day I **sit** by the pool.
At the moment I **am drinking** a glass of wine.

LISTENING TO COMPREHEND
1. **b. On an island**
2. **a. In Paris**

LISTENING TO NOTICE
BRAD
This is the life! Every morning I (1) **have** breakfast by the pool. Then I (2) **go** for a walk along the beach or into town. In the afternoon I usually (3) **take** a trip somewhere on the island. In the evening I (4) **enjoy** the nightlife. At the moment I (5) **am listening** to some great jazz. Jealous? You should be! Brad.

GLORIA
Remember George Rush from London? Well, surprise surprise, he (6) **'s staying** at the same hotel for a few days. Well, (7) **are having** a great time. He (8) **is showing** me all the best places in Paris. Well, I must rush now. We (9) **are going** out to this new seafood restaurant right now. I (10) **love** you always. Gloria.

UNDERSTANDING THE GRAMMAR POINT
1. a. **have, go, take, enjoy, love**
   b. **am listening, is staying, are having, is showing, are going**
2. The adverbials are:
   Brad's postcard: **every morning, in the afternoon, in the evening, at the moment.**
   Gloria's postcard: **a few days, now, right now, always**
3.

SIMPLE PRESENT	PRESENT CONTINUOUS
every morning	**at the moment**
usually	**now**
in the evening	**for a few days**
always	
in the afternoon	

CHECKING
At the moment I am sitting in a little restaurant in Cocacabana. It is late and the sun **is** just **beginning** to set. I **am watching** some teenagers. They **are playing** volleyball on the beach. A middle-aged man is jogging past my table. Every day I **come** to the same restaurant. I **eat** a light meal - just a salad or some fish - and **drink** a glass of wine. Sometimes I chat with the waiter. He **tells** me about his young boy and I tell him about you. Life is almost perfect, except, of course, you are not here!

COMMON ERRORS (from the Grammar Explanation section)
1. We **are** sitting in a restaurant.
2. We are **sitting** in a restaurant.
3. Every day we **go** shopping.
4. She **lives** in San Francisco.

UNIT 5

ERROR BOX
Does Jim help you with the kids?
Does Jim **help** you around the house?

LISTENING TO COMPREHEND

	JIM	STEVE
...helps with the kids.	Yes	No
...washes the dishes.	Yes	No
...does the ironing.	No	No
...goes out with his wife for dinner.	No	Yes
...talks about things with his wife.	No	Yes

LISTENING TO NOTICE
Beth: What's Jim like? (1) **Does** he **help** with the kids?
Jill: All the time. What about Steve? (2)**Does** he **help** with the kids?
Beth: Never. He's out with his friends all the time.
Jill: What about around the house? (3) **Does** Steve sometimes **wash** the dishes?
Beth: Nope. What about Jim?
Jill: Yes, on the weekends. (4) **Does** Steve **do** any ironing?
Beth: You must be joking! (5) **Does** Jim?
Jill: Well, no. But I don't mind. I find ironing relaxing.
Beth: (6) **Do** you sometimes **go** out for dinner together?
Jill: No, never! Jim says he likes my cooking too much.
Beth: We often go out together.
Jill: Lucky you! (7) **Do** you **talk** about things with Steve a lot? (8) **Do** you **talk** about problems and all that?
Beth: Yeah, Steve's a great talker.
Jill: I can hardly get a word out of Jim.

UNDERSTANDING THE GRAMMAR POINT
1. **Q** 1. Does Jim help with the kids**?**
   S 2. Jim helps with the kids**.**
   Q 3. Does Steve wash the dirty plates**?**
   S 4. Steve washes the dirty plates**.**
   Q 5. Does Steve do the ironing**?**
   S 6. Steve does not do the ironing.
   Q 7. Do you sometimes go out to dinner with Jim**?**
   S 8. Jim never goes out to dinner with me**.**
   Q 9. Do you sometimes talk about things with Steve**?**
   S 10. Steve and I often talk about things**.**
2. A question in the simple present tense consists of:
   ***Do/does* + subject + main verb.**
   A statement in the simple present tense consists of:
   subject + main verb
3. *Does* is followed by someone's name (Jim) and also by *he* or *she* .
   Do is followed by *you* (also *we* and *they*).

CHECKING
1. **Do** you like watching television with your husband?
2. **Does** your wife have a job outside the home?
3. **Do you go** on vacation with your husband?
4. Does your wife **do** the gardening?
5. Do you and your wife **cook** together?
6. Does your husband **clean** the house?
7. **Does** your husband wash and iron clothes?
8. **Do** you and your wife have dinner parties?
9. **Do** you sometimes cook a special meal?
10. **Do** you and your husband **do** the shopping together?

COMMON ERRORS (from the Grammar Explanation section)
1. **Does he help** you with the kids?
2. **Does** Jim help you with the kids?
3. Does Jim **help** you with the kids?

UNIT 6

ERROR BOX
He's **not** exciting.
He's **not** working.
He's got **no** money.

LISTENING TO COMPREHEND
Across: 1. **boring**, 2. **dead**, 4. **lazy**, 5. **busy**, 9. **calm**
Down: 1. **broke**, 3. **happy**, 6. **amusing**, 7. **naughty**, 8. **awake**

LISTENING TO NOTICE
Across:
1. He is **not** interesting. He's . . .
2. She's showing **no** signs of life. She's . . .
4. He's **not** working. He's . . .
5. She has **no** free time this week. She's . . .
9. She is **not** nervous at all. She's . . .
Down:
1. He's got **no** money. He's . . .
3. She's got **no** worries at all. She's . . .
6. He's **not** a dull person. He's . . .
7. She's **not** a well-behaved child. She's . . .
8. He's **not** sleeping. He's . . .

UNDERSTANDING THE GRAMMAR POINT
1. **NOT** + adjective

NOT + a + adjective + noun	**NO** + noun
is + **NOT** + verb	**NO** + adjective + noun
not interesting	no signs of life
not working	no free time
not nervous	no money
not a dull person	no worries
not a well-behaved child	
not sleeping	

2. Use *not* before the adjective *very rich*.
   Use *no* before the noun *coward*.
   Use *no* before the noun *friend of mine*. (or *not a* friend of mine)
   Use *not* between *is* and verb.

CHECKING
1. She's got **no** free time this week.
2. He's **not** studying very hard.
3. She's got **no** idea of how to sew a dress.
4. He's **not** anxious to get a job.
5. She's **not** very patient with her friends.
6. He's **not** feeling very well.
7. She's **not** a very thoughtful person.
8. He's **not** very brainy.
9. She's **not** an angel.
10. He's got **no** clean shirts to wear.

COMMON ERRORS (from the Grammar Explanation section)
1. Anna is **not** very tall.
   Anna is **not** an angel.
2. Anna has got **no** money.

UNIT 7

ERROR BOX
The island is full of palm **trees**.

LISTENING TO COMPREHEND
✔ palm trees
✔ monkeys

- ✔ rain forests
- ✔ a volcano
- a golf course
- ✔ plantations
- discos
- a gambling casino
- ✔ a shipwreck
- museums

LISTENING TO NOTICE

Looking for somewhere special for a holiday? I have the answer – the sister (1) **islands** of St. Kitts and Nevis. They have everything – (2) **mountains**, sun, (3) palm **trees**. This is the place for you! You can keep the (4) **monkeys** company. You will enjoy the peace and quiet of the beautiful (5) **beaches**.

On St. Kitts you can walk through rain (6) **forests** and visit a (7) **volcano**. On Nevis you will find some old sugar (8) **plantations**.

In the beautiful Caribbean Sea you will see coral (9) **reefs** and perhaps a (10) **shipwreck** or two. Interested? Call 1-800-GET-AWAY.

UNDERSTANDING THE GRAMMAR POINT

1. | SINGULAR | PLURAL |
   |----------|--------|
   | volcano | islands |
   | shipwreck | mountains |
   | | trees |
   | | monkeys |
   | | beaches |
   | | forests |
   | | plantations |
   | | reefs |

2. **Plural nouns generally end in -s or sometimes -es. Singular nouns do not usually end in -s. If a noun has *a* in front of it, it is singular.**

CHECKING

1. In Dominica there are beautiful lake**s**.
2. Barbados offers miles of beaches lined with hotel**s**.
3. Enjoy the shop**s** and nightlife of the Bahamas.
4. Antigua welcomes all its visitor**s** with open arms.
5. In Jamaica you will find tropical garden**s** overlooking the sea.
6. Puerto Rico has some good museum**s**.
7. Grenada is a paradise of white beach**es** and tropical rain forests.
8. Dance the night away to the music of steel band**s** in Trinidad and Tobago.

COMMON ERRORS (from the Grammar Explanation section)

1. We saw some **monkeys**.
2. The **children** are playing.
3. We saw a lot of **sheep**.

UNIT 8

ERROR BOX

We are planning to buy some new **furniture**.

LISTENING TO COMPREHEND

Name of Department

___ Appliances	___ Sporting Goods
___ Men's Clothing	✔ Patio and Garden
✔ Children's Clothing	___ Jewelry
✔ Luggage	___ Small Electronics

LISTENING TO NOTICE

Dillard's, your favorite store, announces its summer sale. You'll find the lowest (1) **prices** of the year in all our (2) **departments**.

Looking for (3) **clothing** for the new school year? This weekend, you can save up to 25% on shoes, (4) **shirts**, jackets, and dresses in our children's department.

Are you planning an end-of-the-summer vacation? Then this is the time to replace your old (5) **luggage**. We have (6) **suitcases**, duffel bags, and backpacks — all on sale.

And remember: There are several more weeks of summer. Our patio and garden department has everything you need to enjoy the rest of the summer in style, including a large selection of outdoor (7) **furniture**.

Our staff is ready to provide expert (8) **advice**. We're open seven days a week.

UNDERSTANDING THE GRAMMAR POINT

1. | SINGULAR | PLURAL |
   |----------|--------|
   | clothing | prices |
   | luggage | departments |
   | advice | shirts |
   | furniture | suitcases |

2. The **plural nouns** are countable. The **singular nouns** are uncountable.
3. **Countable nouns** can have a plural form (usually *-s*). **Uncountable nouns** do not have a plural form.
4. **many, a, several, one, two, three...**

CHECKING

1. She buys almost all her sports **equipment** in that store.
2. In this jewelry store they always give good **advice** about gifts.
3. I couldn't find the small electronics department, so I went to the **Information** Desk and asked for directions.
4. Every time he takes a trip he has a different set of luggage!
5. This weekend I am going to buy some new **clothing**.
6. I think it's time to buy some new **silverware**.
7. The secretary ordered more photocopy **paper**.
8. I'm going to buy some new shoes and socks this weekend.
9. The furniture **is** on sale for this week only.
10. All the **employees** are helpful and courteous.

COMMON ERRORS (from the Grammar Explanation section)

1. a piece of **furniture**; some **information**; four pieces of **silverware**
2. four **shirts**; several **weeks**

UNIT 9

ERROR BOX

There are not **many** things to buy.
I bought **some** bread.

LISTENING TO COMPREHEND

1. **a new pair of shoes; material to make a dress; cookies**
2. **a loaf of French bread**

LISTENING TO NOTICE

Maria: Hi! Is that you, Bert?
Bert: Yeah, hi.
Maria: Sorry I didn't call before but just got back from shopping. There were so (1) **many** people in the store! I wanted to get a new pair of shoes. I saw (2) **several** pairs I liked but they were all too expensive!
Bert: Oh.
Maria: Then I looked for (3) **some** material to make a dress. I found just the color I wanted but there was only (4) **a little** material left on the roll, not enough for a dress. So I didn't buy (5) **any** material after all.
Bert: Yeah . . .

Maria: Next I headed for the food department. I wanted to buy (6) **a few** cookies but they looked stale so I didn't buy (7) **any**. I just bought a loaf of French bread. What a waste of time! Still, at least I didn't spend (8) **much** money.

Bert: Maria . . .

Maria: So where are we going this evening? I know a new Italian restaurant that has (9) **some** great dishes. Why don't you pick me up at eight o'clock?

Bert: Well, . . .

UNDERSTANDING THE GRAMMAR POINT

1.

many people	**a little** material	**any** cookies
several pairs	**any** material	**much** money
some material	**a few** cookies	**some** great dishes

2.

Type of noun	Examples	Determiners
Uncountable noun	material	**any, some, a little**
	money	**much**
Plural noun	people	**many**
	pairs	**several**
	cookies	**a few, any**
	dishes	**some**

3. **a little; much**
   many; several; a few
   some; any

CHECKING

1. There were only **a few** people in the store.
2. I bought some lovely shoes.
3. I bought **some** wine.
4. I wanted to buy **some/ a little** material to make a dress.
5. That new Italian restaurant has many great **dishes**.
6. You've brought too **many** cookies.
7. I ate a few cookies.
8. I also got a little blue cheese.
9. I had **some/ a little** beer in the restaurant.
10. I didn't have **much** time left so I had to rush.

COMMON ERRORS (from the Grammar Explanation section)

1. There are not **many** things to buy.
2. I bought **some** bread.

UNIT 10

ERROR BOX

Is it a zebra?
Are **the monkeys** dangerous?

LISTENING TO COMPREHEND

Circle the **penguin** and the **tiger.**

LISTENING TO NOTICE

Nina: Guess what animal I just saw!
Father: (1) **Is it** a lion?
Nina: No, it isn't a lion. You have to ask me questions.
Father: (2) **Is it** a mammal?
Nina: No, it's not a mammal.
Father: (3) **Is it** a bird?
Nina: Yeah, it's a bird.
Father: (4) **Is it** a tropical bird?
Nina: No, it lives in a cold region.
Father: (5) **Is it** able to fly?
Nina: No, it can't.
Father: I think I know.

Nina: You have to come this way. I didn't know they had these at this zoo!
Father: Are the kangaroos over there?
Nina: No, (6) **they're** not kangaroos. Try to guess.
Father: Are they from Africa?
Nina: Yes, (7) **some of them are**.
Father: Are they dangerous?
Nina: Yes, I think (8) **they're** dangerous.
Father: Are they striped?
Nina: Yes, they have stripes.
Father: I think I know. They're zebras. (9) **Am I** right?

UNDERSTANDING THE GRAMMAR POINT

QUESTION	ANSWER
Is it a lion?	No, it isn't a lion.
Is it a mammal?	No, it's not an animal.
Is it a bird?	Yeah, it's a bird.
Is it a tropical bird?	No, it lives in a cold region.
Is it able to fly?	No, it can't.
Are the kangaroos over there?	No they're not kangaroos.
Are they from Africa?	Yes, some of them are.
Are they dangerous?	Yes, I think they're dangerous.

2. - The verb **be** comes first in the questions.
   - The **subject (pronoun)** comes first in the answer (after *no* or *yes*).

CHECKING

1. **Is the zoo open today?**
2. Is that an otter? Yes, it is.
3. Are **those** panthers? No, those are leopards.
4. Are dolphins mammals?
5. Is the zoo ~~is~~ near the Museum of Natural History?
   Yes, it's only about a five-minute walk.
6. Are **those snakes poisonous**? Yes, they're very dangerous.
7. **Is the lion asleep**? Yes, lions sleep a lot during the day.
8. Is **that a rhinoceros**? No, that's a hippopotamus.

COMMON ERRORS (from the Grammar Explanation section)

1. **Is it** a bird?
2. Are **they** penguins?
3. Are **those snakes poisonous**?
4. **Are the elephants hungry**?
5. Is that ~~is~~ an eagle?

LEVEL 1 REVIEW TESTS

TEST A

1. is (Unit 3) 2. has (Unit 3) 3. sons (Unit 7) 4. do (Unit 5) 5. are (Unit 2) 6. many (Unit 9) 7. a lot of (Unit 9) 8. am (Unit 10) 9. she (Unit 1) 10. there's (Unit 2) 11. no (Unit 6) 12. am playing (Unit 4)

TEST B

1. has (Unit 3) 2. are (Unit 3) 3. runs (Unit 4) 4. thousands (Unit 9) 5. do (Unit 5) 6. no (Unit 6) 7. a lot of (Unit 9) 8. not (Unit 6) 9. is (Unit 2) 10. she (Unit 1) 11. it (Unit 10) 12. some (Unit 9)

UNIT 11

ERROR BOX

I **have** a headache.

LISTENING TO COMPREHEND

✔ headache	✔ medicine
✔ no appetite	___ sleeping problems
✔ losing weight	___ healthy diet
✔ exercise	✔ physical examination

Doctor: Well, Mr. O'Leary, here you are again. I (1) **notice** that this is your fourth visit this month. You (2) **are taking** the medicine I prescribed last time, aren't you?

Mr. O'Leary: Yes, I (3) **take** it every morning, but I (4) **need** something else. First of all, I (5) **have** a headache. I've had one for almost a week. And I (6) **am losing** weight. And my food (7) **tastes** funny; as soon as I start to eat, I (8) **lose** my appetite.

Doctor: Mr. O'Leary, I (9) **want** you to tell me whether you (10) **are trying** to get exercise.

Mr. O'Leary: Yes, I (11) **remember** your exact words: "It's important to exercise, and that (12) **includes** walking." And I (13) **try**. Some days I (14) **forget**, but when I exercise, I (15) **like** it.

Doctor: Well, Mr. O'Leary, it (15) **seems** that it's time for you to have a complete physical examination.

UNDERSTANDING THE GRAMMAR POINT

1.

Verb	Present Simple	Present Continuous
notice	notice	
take	take	are taking
need	need	
have	have	
lose	lose	am losing
taste	tastes	
want	want	
try	try	are trying
remember	remember	
include	includes	
forget	forget	
like	like	
seem	seems	

2. Their meanings deal with **perceiving, thinking, describing,** and **possessing**.
3. **Cost, understand, see, weigh,** and **recognize** do not usually occur in the present continuous.

CHECKING

1. I **realize** now I should get more exercise.
2. A healthy diet **includes** fruits and vegetables.
3. I **am trying** to remember when the pain started: maybe three days ago.
4. **Do you remember** when you first started to feel this pain?
5. She **owns** a lot of exercise equipment, but she never uses it.
6. He **weighs** 83 kilos; that's two kilos more than at the last checkup.
7. The doctor **is talking** to another patient right now; please take a seat and wait.
8. You **need** to make sure that your cast doesn't get wet.
9. That cut **seems** to be healing nicely.
10. I **want** you to continue taking your medicine.

COMMON ERRORS (from the Grammar Explanation section)

1. He **owns** an exercise bicycle and a treadmill.
2. ~~Weigh less~~! I wish he **weighed less**.

UNIT 12

ERROR BOX

Johnny Cash **wrote** his first song when he was 12.
Ella Fitzgerald **made** some popular albums.

LISTENING TO COMPREHEND

Name	Type of Music
Johnny Cash	**country and western**
Frederik Chopin	**classical**
Ella Fitzgerald	**jazz**

LISTENING TO NOTICE

1. Johnny Cash (1) **wrote** his first song when he was 12. In his twenties he (2) **recorded** a number of country and western albums for Sun Records. Later he (3) **worked** with Bob Dylan for Columbia Records. Now, he (4) **lives** in the United States with his second wife.
2. Frederic Chopin (5) **became** one of the most famous classical composers of the early 19th century. He **gave** piano concerts all over Europe. Unfortunately, he **died** while still young. His *Nocturnes* (8) **continues** to be a very popular piano piece.
3. Ella Fitzgerald (9) **began** her career in a singing contest in Harlem. She (10) **joined** Chick Webb's band and recorded several hits. Later, her *Songbird* albums (11) **made** her one of the most famous jazz singers of the 20th century. Ella was also very kind and religious. People (12) **remember** Ella as a person as well as a singer.

UNDERSTANDING THE GRAMMAR POINT

1. PAST: wrote, recorded, worked, became, gave, died, began, joined, made
   PRESENT: lives, continues, remember

2.

REGULAR PAST TENSE	IRREGULAR PAST TENSE
recorded	wrote
died	became
worked	made
joined	gave
	began

3. To make the regular past tense you add **-ed** (work**ed**) or, if the verb ends in a vowel, you add **-d** (die**d**).

CHECKING

Bob Dylan was born in 1941. He **taught** himself to play the guitar. In the1960s he **became** famous as a folk singer who **sang** protest songs. He **recorded** three famous albums — *The Freewheelin Bob Dylan, Times They Are a-Changin* and *Another Side of Bob Dylan*. These albums together with *Bringing it Back Home* **changed** rock music forever. They **influenced** bands such as the Beatles and the Rolling Stones. Dylan is the most original pop musician since the '60s. He still **tries** out new ideas.

COMMON ERRORS (from the Grammar Explanation section)

1. Miles Davis' father **gave** him a trumpet for his 13th birthday.
2. Bob Dylan **sang** protest songs in the sixties.

UNIT 13

ERROR BOX

The secretary called me **in** the morning.
Mr. Bean asked me to contact him **in** 2010.
I saw Mr. Bean **at** 3:00.

LISTENING TO COMPREHEND

1. **b.** Greg saw Mr. Bean but he did not get a job.

LISTENING TO NOTICE

Gloria: Well, have you got a job yet?

Greg: No way, but I've been trying. I made an appointment to see this Mr. Bean guy (1) **at** 3 o'clock (2) **on** a Monday in February. He's the manager of a big company.

Gloria: And did you see him?

Greg: No, his secretary called me (3) **in** the morning to cancel the appointment. Apparently he'd had a car accident.

Gloria: What a pity.

Greg: Anyway, I made another appointment to see him (4) **at** the end of February.

Gloria: Great!

Greg: No, not so great. When I got to his office he wasn't there. His secretary told me his wife had died (5) **at** 2 o'clock (6) **in** the morning and he wasn't coming in to work that day.

Gloria: So what did you do?

Greg: Well, his secretary suggested I reschedule for sometime (7) **in** March.

Gloria: And did you?

Greg: Yeah, I made an appointment to see him (8) **on** Monday March 5th.

Gloria: That was yesterday!

Greg: Yeah, and I actually saw the guy this time.

Gloria: And did he give you a job?

Greg: No, he told me all the positions had been filled (9) **in** February and suggested I contact him again (10) **in** 2010.

Gloria: Oh, no!

UNDERSTANDING THE GRAMMAR POINT

AT	IN	ON
at 3 o'clock	**in the morning** (x2)	**on a Monday**
at the end of February	**in March**	**on Monday**
at 2 o'clock	**in February**	
	in 2010	

2. Use **at** with times; use **in** with months, parts of the day (**morning**), years and centuries; use **on** with days.

CHECKING

1. Greg made an appointment to see Mr Bean **on** Monday.
2. The appointment was **at** 3 o'clock **in** the afternoon.
3. Unfortunately, Mr Bean had an accident **in** the morning.
4. Greg made another appointment **at** the end of February.
5. Mr. Bean's wife died **at** 2:00 in the morning.
6. Greg eventually saw Mr Bean **on** Monday, March 5th.
7. However, all the positions had been filled **in** February.
8. Mr Bean suggested Greg contact him again **in** 2010.

COMMON ERRORS (from the Grammar Explanation section)

1. **in** the night; **in** 1998; **at** 3 o'clock
2. He is visiting me ~~in~~ next week.

UNIT 14

ERROR BOX

The building where I work is **on** Madison Street.
You can meet us **at** the entrance to the park.

LISTENING TO COMPREHEND

EVENT:	LOCATION:
science fair	**Lake Avenue Elementary School**
concert	**Lincoln Park**
canoe trip	**56 Third St.**
dance registration	**Lake Avenue and Fourth Street**

LISTENING TO NOTICE

Welcome to the Riverton Youth Community Calendar. Here are some events taking place this weekend:

For future scientists: There will be a science fair (1) **at** Lake Avenue Elementary School. The fair will be held this Friday evening (2) **in** the school gymnasium. For rides (3) **to** the school, call 433-7894.

Music lovers: There will be a free concert from 2 to 4 on Saturday afternoon (4) **in** Lincoln Park. The main entrance to the park is (5) **on** Valley Avenue. Come (6) **to** Lincoln Park and enjoy some of the area's best musicians.

This next one is for you outdoor types: On Saturday, the Sierra Club is sponsoring a canoe trip (7) **on** Eagle River. Meet (8) **at** the Sierra Club office (9) **at** 56 Third Street at noon. Transportation (10) **to** the river will be provided.

For dance lovers: Saturday afternoon the Riverton Dance Studio is conducting registration for its next session. The studio is (11) **on** the corner of Lake Avenue and Fourth Street.

UNDERSTANDING THE GRAMMAR POINT

IN	AT	ON
the school gymnasium	Lake Avenue Elementary School	Valley Avenue
Lincoln Park	the Sierra Club Office	Eagle River
	56 Third Street	the corner of Lake Avenue and . . .

TO		
the school		
Lincoln Park		
the river		

2. We use *in* to tell the location of rooms or buildings.
We use *at* to tell the location of a specific street address.
We use *on* to tell the location of a street, corner, floor, body of water.

3. *To* tells the direction, not the location.

CHECKING

1. The American Red Cross building is located **on** the corner of Main Street and Sixth Avenue.
2. The Farmers' Market is held every Saturday morning **in** the parking lot of the Valley National Bank.
3. The Paramount Theater is located at 320 State Street.
4. Sunrise Day Care is **on** Washington Avenue.
5. Bus Routes 14 and 16 both stop **at** the entrance to the park.
6. The Silver Valley Community Center is on Maple Street, near the corner of Walden Avenue.
7. To get to post office, walk **to** the next traffic light, then turn right.
8. Our downtown office is on the third floor of the Skyline Building.

COMMON ERRORS (from the Grammar Explanation section)

1. The office is located **at** 500 Kennedy Avenue.
2. The library is **on** the corner of Main Street and Fourth Avenue.
3. From here we can get **to** the park by walking along Lake Avenue.
4. There are excellent museums **in** Boston.
5. The medical center is **on** Main Street.

UNIT 15

ERROR BOX

He broke the window **accidentally**.
He broke the window accidental**ly**.

LISTENING TO COMPREHEND

Story 1 Mother Abandons Child for Hawaiian Holiday
Story 2: Pachinko Addict Loses Family Fortune
Story 3: Husband Kills Himself
Story 4: Man Tricked with Promise of Marriage

LISTENING TO NOTICE

1. Tracy Smith (1) **selfishly** left her two children, ages five and eight, in her Philadelphia apartment while she went on a five-day holiday to Hawaii with her boyfriend. "She is a very (2) **selfish** woman," a neighbor said.
2. Yoko Kitazawa, a (3) **reckless** Japanese housewife, gambled away her family's savings in the local Pachinko parlor. "I did not know she could behave so (4) **recklessly**," her husband said.
3. When Garcia Mundo's wife threatened to leave him, he (5) **tragically** shot himself. "It's a (6) **tragic** mistake," she said. "I just told him that to make him pay more attention to me."
4. Hans Schmidt met a woman in a bar and (7) **foolishly** agreed to marry her. When the woman asked for $500 to buy a ring he gave her the money. The woman took the money and disappeared. "I guess I was a really (8) **foolish** man," Hans told the police.

UNDERSTANDING THE GRAMMAR POINT

1.

____ + verb or verb + _____	_____ + noun
selfishly left	**selfish woman**
behave so recklessly	**a reckless Japanese housewife**
tragically shot himself	**a tragic mistake**
foolishly agreed	**a really foolish man**

Words such as *selfishly* and *recklessly* that end in **-ly** are called **adverbs**. They modify **verbs** such as *left* and *agreed*.
-Words such as *selfish* and *reckless* are called **adjectives**. They modify **nouns** such as *woman* and *mistake*.

3. ✔ Yoko Kitazawa ✔ wasted ✗ the family savings ✔ .

CHECKING

YOUNG BOY DRIVES CAR 100 MILES

Samantha Lawson **thoughtlessly** left her five-year-old son in her car when she ran **quickly** into a shop to buy something. When she came out the car **mysteriously** had gone and so had her son. The boy drove the car **safely** for 100 miles before the gasoline ran out. "He is a very safe driver but it was very **thoughtless** of me," Lawson said. "I'll never do it again."

COMMON ERRORS (from the Grammar Explanation section)

1. He broke the window **accidentally**.
2. He **accidentally** broke the window.

UNIT 16

ERROR BOX

Did you have a great time?
Did you **see** Buckingham Palace?

LISTENING TO COMPREHEND

___ Buckingham Palace ___ Trafalgar Square ___ Tate Art Gallery
___ the British Museum ___ Covent Garden
___ the Tower of London ___ Hyde Park ___ the National Theater
✔ Guy's Hospital ___ The Houses of Parliament

LISTENING TO NOTICE

Georgia: So you're back from your holiday in London?
Brad: Yeah, I'm back.
Georgia: (1) **Did you have** a great time?
Brad: Well, ...
Georgia: No, don't tell me, let me guess what you did. (2) **Did you see** Buckingham Palace?
Brad: No.
Georgia: (3) **Did you visit** the Tower? The Tower's great.
Brad: No.
Georgia: Oh. (4) **Did you go** into the Houses of Parliament? They're a laugh.
Brad: The Houses of Parliament? No.
Georgia: (5) **Did you walk** around Covent Garden? That's fun.
Brad: No.
Georgia: What about Trafalgar Square? (6) **Did you go** there and see the pigeons?
Brad: No. I don't like pigeons.
Georgia: I know. (7) **Did you pay** a visit to the Tate Art Gallery? You like art, don't you?
Brad: Yes, I like art, but I didn't visit the Tate.
Georgia: The National Theater. (8) **Did you watch** a play?
Brad: No.
Georgia: Well, I give up. What did you do?
Brad: I fell down some stairs in my hotel and broke my leg on the first day. I spent the week in Guy's Hospital.
Georgia: Oh, you poor thing!

UNDERSTANDING THE GRAMMAR POINT

1. **Q** Did Brad have a great time**?**
   S Brad did not have a great time.
   Q Did Brad see Buckingham Palace**?**
   S Brad did not see Buckingham Palace.
   Q Did Brad visit the Tower**?**
   S Brad did not visit the Tower.
   Q Did Brad go into the Houses of Parliament**?**
   S Brad did not go into the Houses of Parliament.
   Q Did Brad walk around Covent Garden**?**
   S Brad did not walk around Covent Garden.
   Q Did Brad go to Trafalgar Square**?**
   S Brad did not go to Trafalgar Square.
   Q Did Brad pay a visit to the Tate Art Gallery**?**
   S Brad did not visit the Tate Art Gallery.
   Q Did Brad watch a play**?**
   S Brad did not watch a play.
   S Brad broke his leg.

2. Questions consist of: **Did + subject + verb**
   Statements consist of: **Subject + verb**

CHECKING

1. Did you **climb** the Eiffel Tower?
2. **Did** you **visit** Disneyland in Paris?
3. Did you go shopping in the Champs Elysees?
4. Did you **see** Notre Dame?
5. **Did** you **eat** in a restaurant on the Left Bank?
6. Did you **walk** in the Bois de Boulogne?
7. Did you **take** a trip to Versailles?
8. Did you go on a boat trip on the Seine?
9. **Did** you **spend** a day at the Pompidou Center?
10. Did you have a good time?

COMMON ERRORS (from the Grammar Explanation section)

1. **Did Brad** have a good holiday?
2. Did Brad **have** a good holiday?
3. **Did** Brad have a good holiday when he was in London?

UNIT 17

ERROR BOX

I enjoy **this class**.
Some interesting things happened **to** them.

LISTENING TO COMPREHEND

F Yumiko's family went with her to the United States.
F Yumiko grew up on a farm in Japan.
F Yumiko was homesick all the time she lived in Madison.
F Yumiko lived on a farm in Wisconsin.
T Yumiko kept a journal of her experiences.

LISTENING TO NOTICE

Yoko: Welcome back to Japan, Yumiko. Did you (1) **enjoy** your year in Wisconsin?
Yumiko: I (2) **loved** it! But not at first. When I (3) **arrived** in the United States, it was terrible. I (4) **cried** every day because I (5) **missed** my family, and I (6) **hated** so many things. After a few weeks, though, my homesickness (7) **disappeared**.
Yoko: What (8) **happened**?
Yumiko: Well, I made some friends, and my English (9) **improved**. Those two things really (10) **improved** my outlook.
Yoko: Did you (11) **like** Madison?
Yumiko: Oh, it's a great place. And it has (12) **grown** and (13) **changed** a lot since you lived there. But I also spent some time on a farm near

Madison.

Yoko: A farm?

Yumiko: Yeah, I became friends with a girl whose family had a dairy farm, and they also (14) **grew** corn. That was my first time on a farm — in my whole life! After my first visit, I (15) **started** a journal. When I read it, I know how much this past year has (16) **changed** me.

UNDERSTANDING THE GRAMMAR POINT

1.

Verbs followed by a direct object	Verbs not followed by a direct object	Verbs occurring with or without a direct object
enjoy your year	arrived	
loved it	cried	improved
missed my family	disappeared	grew/grown
hated so many things	happened	changed
improved my outlook	improved	
like Madison	grown	
grew corn	changed	
started a journal		
changed me		

2. a. Some verbs in English—including *enjoy*, *like*, and *miss*—are always followed by a **direct object**. We call these verbs transitive verbs.

   b. Intransitive verbs — including *arrive*, *happen* and *cry* — are never followed by a **direct object**.

   c. Some verbs in English—including *improve*, *change*, *grow*, and *start*—are sometimes followed by a direct object; sometimes they are not followed by a direct object. These verbs can be **transitive** or intransitive.

CHECKING

1. Did you enjoy **Madison? (or the movie, dinner, etc.)**
2. How soon did your homesickness disappear ~~you~~?
3. You've grown!
4. Do you think you've changed?
5. Did you miss your family?
6. When did you arrive **in** Australia?
7. Did your English improve?
8. Do you like **big cities? (or jazz, animals, etc.)**
9. What happened ~~it~~?
10. I'm happy to hear that you liked Madison.

COMMON ERRORS (from the Grammar Explanation section)

1. She arrived **at** the party late.
2. **A red spot appeared** on his face.

UNIT 18

ERROR BOX

Gwyneth Paltrow **plays** Emma.
Three former college friends **plan** revenge.

LISTENING TO COMPREHEND

Film	Type	Subject
1. **Grace of My Heart**	drama	**singing career of Edna Buxton**
2. **Big Night**	**bittersweet comedy**	**two Italian immigrants opening a restaurant**
3. **Hoop Dreams**	documentary	**14-year-old basketball players**
4. **The Long Kiss Goodnight**	action thriller	**a woman's search for her identity**

LISTENING TO NOTICE

1. Grace of My Heart

This drama (1) **follows** the singing career of Edna Buxton as she (2) **moves** through the pop music world of the late '50s and '60s.

2. Big Night

This bittersweet comedy tells the story of two Italian immigrants who (3) **open** a restaurant in New Jersey. But their American Dream (4) **turns** sour and things end up badly.

3. Hoop Dreams

This documentary follows four years in the lives of 14-year-olds Arthur Agee and William Gates, two exceptionally talented basketball players. They (5) **grow** up poor in downtown Chicago and (6) **dream** of careers as highly paid professionals.

4. The Long Kiss Goodnight

This action thriller stars Geena Davis playing a schoolteacher who (7) **suffers** from amnesia. She hires a detective, played by Samuel L. Jackson, and together they (8) **search** for her past and true identity.

UNDERSTANDING THE GRAMMAR POINT

	SUBJECT	VERB
1.	drama	follows
2.	she	moves
3.	who (two Italian immigrants)	open
4.	American Dream	turns
5.	they	grow
6.	they	dream
7.	who (a schoolteacher)	suffers
8.	they	search

2. With singular subjects use verb + *s* (*follows*).
   With plural subjects use the simple verb form (*open*).

CHECKING

1. The Relic

Penelope Ann Miller and Tom Sizemore (1) **star** in this thriller. They (2) **become** partners when a number of murders (3) **takes*** place in the museum where biologist Margo Green (4) **works**.

* The verb is singular because the subject is the singular noun *number*. However, many English speakers would use the plural verb (*take*) with number, because they consider "a number of"="several".

2. Romeo and Juliet

Leonardo DiCaprio and Clare Danes (5) **star** in this remake of Shakespeare's classic story of two doomed lovers. The action takes place in a gang-filled Los Angeles neighborhood. A rocking soundtrack (6) **keeps** the action moving.

COMMON ERRORS (from the Grammar Explanation section)

1. Geena Davis plays a school teacher who **suffers** from amnesia.
2. She suffers from loss of memory and **wants** to find her past.
3. A pair of thieves **plans** a robbery.

UNIT 19

ERROR BOX

She **started** a new job last week.

LISTENING TO COMPREHEND

| Mr. Naraporn | **airport baggage handler** |
| Ms. Adams | **aerobics instructor** |

LISTENING TO NOTICE

Interview with Mr. Naraporn:

Interviewer: (1) **Have you done** this kind of job before, Mr. Naraporn?

Mr. Naraporn: Not exactly.

Interviewer: But you (2) **have had** jobs like this before?

Mr. Naraporn: Yes, from 1990 until 1995 I (3) **worked** in a Nike shoe factory.

Interviewer: Hmm. And what was that like?

Mr. Naraporn: It (4) **was** very noisy. And I (5) **did** the same thing over and over.

Interview with Ms. Adams

Interviewer: Ms. Adams, I (6) **have looked** at your resume. All of your previous jobs at health clubs were part-time positions.

Ms. Adams: Yes, that's right.

Interviewer: You (7) **didn't want** a full-time job?

Ms. Adams: Well, from 1993 until 1997 I (8) **was** a student.

Interviewer: I see. But you (9) **have worked** with people of different ages?

Ms. Adams: Oh, yes: children, adults, senior citizens. And last year I (10) **took** some seminars on sports medicine.

UNDERSTANDING THE GRAMMAR POINT

1.

Verb	Simple Past	Present Perfect
1. do		**Have you done**
2. have		**have had**
3. work	**worked**	
4. be	**was**	
5. do	**did**	
6. look		**have looked**
7. want	**didn't want**	
8. be	**was**	
9. work		**have worked**
10. take	**took**	

2. - We use the **simple past tense** to describe an action in the past that took place at a specific time.
 - We use the **simple past tense** to describe an action that was completed during a specific period of time in the past.
 - We use the **present perfect tense** to describe an action that took place at some indefinite time in the past, when no specific time is mentioned.

CHECKING

1. ~~have~~ **applied** for a promotion last year.
2. I joined this company in 1978.
3. They spent more than a month looking for a new office manager.
4. She **changed** jobs last week.
5. **Did** you **look** at the classified advertisements yesterday?
6. Have you ever worked with teenagers and children?
7. I **learned** word processing in 1992.
8. My sister has decided to go into banking as a career.
9. We ~~have~~ hired temporary office staff last month.
10. They ~~have~~ interviewed me in March.

COMMON ERRORS (from the Grammar Explanation section)

1. I **spent** a week in our Bangkok office last summer.
2. I **worked** at that company from 1988 to 1992.

UNIT 20

ERROR BOX

What **should we** eat?

LISTENING TO COMPREHEND

_F_ The babysitter is going to take care of one child.

_F_ Jenny Thompson will be babysitting for this family for the first time.

_F_ Mr. and Mrs. Blake will not be home until midnight.

_F_ Jenny drove her own car to the Blakes' house.

LISTENING TO NOTICE

Mr. Blake: Oh, hi, Jenny. Thanks for babysitting for us tonight.

Jenny: No problem. I love babysitting for you. Where (1) **are you going**? And when (2) **will you be** home?

Mr. Blake: We're going out to eat and to a concert. The concert ends at 10:00, so we should be home by 10:30 or so.

Jenny: You'll have to remind me of a few things. How (3) **do the children like** to spend time after supper? When (4) **should they go** to sleep? What (5) **do they do** to get ready for bed? I seem to have forgotten.

Mr. Blake: Well, after supper, they like to watch television. About 8:30 they should get ready for bed. They should take a bath and put on their pajamas. Then if you could, please read them a story.

Jenny: OK, no problem. And, um, Mr. Blake, how much (6) **are you paying** me?

Mr. Blake: I think seven dollars an hour. Is that all right?

Jenny: That's fine.

Mr. Blake: And if you're hungry...

Jenny: Oh, good, I haven't eaten yet. What (7) **can I eat** for supper?

Mr. Blake: Help yourself to anything in the refrigerator. There's a frozen pizza, I think.

Jenny: Great. Oh, one more question. How (8) **will I get** home?

Mr. Blake: Mrs. Blake or I will drive you home.

Jenny: Oh, just one more question. How (9) **can I reach** you?

Mr. Blake: The telephone numbers are right here. Jenny, you *do* remember the children's names, don't you?

Jenny: Of course, Mr. Blake.

UNDERSTANDING THE GRAMMAR POINT

1.

1	2	3	4	5
1. **Where**	**are**	**you**	**going?**	
2. **When**	**will**	**you**	**be**	**home?**
3. **How**	**do**	**the children like**		**to spend time?**
4. **When**	**should**	**they**	**go**	**to sleep?**
5. **What**	**do**	**they**	**do**	**to get ready for bed?**
6. **How much are**		**you**	**paying**	**me?**
7. **What**	**can**	**I**	**eat**	**for supper?**
8. **How**	**will**	**I**	**get**	**home?**
9. **How**	**can**	**I**	**reach**	**you?**

2. Column 1: *wh*- word; 2. auxiliary verb; 3. subject; 4. main verb

CHECKING

1. **Where are we going tonight**?
2. What should **I** say if the telephone rings?
3. How **can I** contact you?
4. What do you like to eat?
5. When are you coming back?
6. Where **does** she **live**?
7. **Who should she call in an emergency**?
8. How much **do we pay** the babysitter?
9. When **do** the children go to bed?
10. What time do we pick her up?

COMMON ERRORS (from the Grammar Explanation section)

1. What **should she** do in an emergency?
2. Where **does** she live?
3. When is **she** coming?
4. When should **the children** go to sleep?

LEVEL 2   REVIEW TESTS

TEST A

1. on (Unit 14) 2. refused (Unit 12) 3. entered (Unit 12) 4. at (Unit 13) 5. want (Unit 11) 6. angrily (Unit 15) 7. says (Unit 18) 8. appreciate (Units 17) 9. won't you (Unit 20) 10. have had (Unit 19) 11. in (Unit 13) 12. does he do (Unit 20)

TEST B

1. has given (Unit 19) 2. lives (Unit 18) 3. in (Unit 14) 4. learned

(Unit 12) 5. did (Unit 16) 6. simply (Unit 15) 7. on (Unit 13) 8. to (Unit 14) 9. does (Unit 20) 10. enjoys (Units 17) 11. eats (Unit 18) 12. does she (Unit 20)

UNIT 21

ERROR BOX
She plays the piano **poorly**.

LISTENING TO COMPREHEND
1. Francesca: **running**
   Linda: **gardening**
   Yana: **playing the piano**

LISTENING TO NOTICE
Francesca

My name is Francesca. Do you want to know about my hobbies? Well, I'm not a good athlete, but I enjoy running **regularly.** I **usually** follow a precise routine. After I stretch my muscles for a few minutes, I begin jogging. **Slowly** I start to run.

Linda

My name is Linda. Here's how I spend my free time. I have no place for a garden, so I grow flowers and vegetables in containers on our balcony. It's enjoyable, but it's not easy. In the summer, I **always** water the plants twice a day. **Frequently** I find insects, and I spray them **immediately**.

Yana

I'm Yana. I'd like to tell you how I spend my leisure time. A few years ago, I started piano lessons. **Normally** I practice my lessons in the afternoon. I enjoy practicing; I play the same tune **repeatedly**. (My neighbors complain **continuously**.) I keep hoping that I'll play a piece **perfectly**. (My neighbors hope so, too.)

UNDERSTANDING THE GRAMMAR POINT
1. 1. I enjoy running <u>regularly</u>.
   2. I <u>usually</u> follow a precise routine.
   3. <u>Slowly</u> I start to run.
   4. I <u>always</u> water the plants twice a day
   5. <u>Frequently</u> I find insects.
   6. I spray them <u>immediately</u>.
   7. <u>Normally</u> I practice my lessons in the afternoon.
   8. I play the same tune <u>repeatedly</u>.
   9. My neighbors complain <u>continuously</u>.
   10. I keep hoping that I will play a piece <u>perfectly</u>.
2. a. **3, 5, 7**; b. **2, 4** c. **1, 6, 8, 9, 10**.
3. An adverb cannot come between a verb and its object

CHECKING
1. Mr. Tanaka takes **stamp collecting seriously**.
2. Occasionally I go scuba diving, but it's not one of my hobbies.
3. He is an experienced bird watcher; he patiently waits for the birds to come to the area he has chosen.
4. Ana is a dedicated runner; she enters races regularly.
5. My grandmother loves reading; **she usually has a book with her.**
6. My sister plays the piano all the time; she practices her lessons constantly.
7. Often I have thought of learning photography.
8. Over the years he has **patiently** built up a collection of stamps.
9. I quickly developed an interest in Japanese pottery.
10. My husband **always spends** his weekends gardening.

COMMON ERRORS (from the Grammar Explanation section)
1. She waters her flower garden **daily**.
2. He is **patiently** practicing the piano.

UNIT 22

ERROR BOX
There will be **a few** clouds today.
There will be **a little** rain today.

LISTENING TO COMPREHEND

	today	tomorrow	Saturday	Sunday
sunny	✔	✔	✔	✔
cloudy	✔	✔		
rainy	✔	✔		
snowy			✔	

LISTENING TO NOTICE
We've had very nice sunny weather recently, with (1) **few** clouds and (2) **little** rain. But that's going to start changing soon. This afternoon's forecast calls for mostly cloudy skies. Tonight there's an 80% chance of rain, although (3) **few** areas will get more than a couple of millimeters. Lows tonight will be about 5 degrees Celsius.

Tomorrow we'll have (4) **a few** periods of sunshine in the morning and then overcast skies for the rest of the day. Tomorrow night there's a 50% chance of rain. (5) **A few** thunderstorms are possible, especially in the areas to the west. Highs around 10 degrees, lows around 3. Saturday will be clear and cold, with (6) **little** wind. The high temperatures will be only around 5 degrees Celsius. Saturday night some areas in the north could get (7) **a little** snow. On Sunday morning it will be cloudy and cold, although by later in the day we should get (8) **a little** sunshine. High temperatures will again be about 5 degrees.

UNDERSTANDING THE GRAMMAR POINT
1. <u>a few</u>   <u>few</u>   <u>little</u>   <u>a little</u>

   a few periods   few clouds   little rain   a liitle snow
   a few thunderstorms few areas   little wind   a little sunshine
2. **Plural countable nouns** follow *a few* and *few*.
   Uncountable nouns follow *a little* and *little*.
3. *A few* and *a little* mean **not zero;** *few* and *little* mean **not a lot.**

CHECKING
1. Sydney will have **a little sunshine** in the morning, but the afternoon will be cloudy.
2. It was very windy in Vancouver today, with **a few gusts** of more than 60 kilometers per hour.
3. Tomorrow Paris will be mostly sunny, with only **a few clouds**.
4. This weekend, there is little rain in the forecast for New York; it will be clear and mild through Sunday.
5. It's not unusual for Washington, D.C., to receive **a little snow** in the winter.
6. The weather throughout Japan looks very good for the New Year's Day period; there should be **few** travel problems.
7. In Berlin, it will be sunny and warm for the rest of the afternoon, but tonight **a few thunderstorms** could pass through the area.
8. In the San Francisco Bay area, it will become increasingly cloudy this evening, and we may see **a little rain**.
9. Beijing will be cold and overcast, possibly with a few snow flurries.
10. Looking ahead to Thursday and Friday, Hong Kong will be warm and sunny, with **little wind**.

COMMON ERRORS (from the Grammar Explanation section)
1. Tomorrow there could be **a little** rain.
2. The last few days have been sunny, with only **a few** clouds from time to time.
3. The morning will be overcast, but by later this afternoon we may get **a little** clearing.

UNIT 23

ERROR BOX
Of all the animals, the cheetah is **the fastest**.
Mt. Everest is **taller** than Mt. Fuji.

LISTENING TO COMPREHEND
The heaviest animal in the world is the elephant. **F**
Mt. Fuji is the highest volcano in the world. **F**
The largest pyramid in the world is in Egypt. **F**

LISTENING TO NOTICE
Quiz-Show Host: Today's contestant, from Toronto, is Alison MacTavish. Welcome, Alison. Please say "True" or "False" after each statement I read to you. Remember, if you make three mistakes, the game is over, and you lose. Ready?
Alison: Yes.
Quiz-Show Host: All right. Number 1: (1) **The heaviest** animal in the world is the elephant.
Alison: True.
Quiz-Show Host: I'm sorry, that's not correct. Elephants are (2) **heavy**, but the blue whale is (3) **heavier** than the elephant. Let's try Number 2: Mt. Fuji is (4) **the highest** volcano in the world.
Alison: Yes, that's true.
Quiz-Show Host: Wrong again. Mt. Fuji is (5) **high**, but several volcanoes are (6) **higher** than Mt. Fuji. Here's Number 3: (7) **The largest** pyramid in the world is in Egypt.
Alison: True?
Quiz-Show Host: Oh, I'm sorry: Wrong again. The Great Pyramids of Egypt are (8) **large**. But the pyramid of Quetzalcoatl in Mexico is (9) **larger**. In fact, it's (10) **the largest** monument in the world. Better luck next time, Alison.

UNDERSTANDING THE GRAMMAR POINT
1.

adjective	adjective + -er	adjective + -est
heavy	heavier	heaviest
high	higher	highest
large	larger	largest

2. **We use the -er form of the adjective to compare two things.**
   We use the -est form of the adjective to compare three or more things.

CHECKING
1. What is the **fastest** elevator in the world?
2. The fastest elevator in the world travels over 40 kilometers per hour.
3. What is the **longest** snake ever found?
4. The **longest** snake ever found is over 10 meters long.
5. Mt. Fuji is not the **highest** volcano in the world.
6. I thought the Egyptian pyramids were **the** largest in the world.
7. Blue whales are much heavier than elephants.
8. Chicago is not bigger **than** New York.
9. New York **is** bigger than Chicago.
10. New York is the **biggest** city in the United States.

COMMON ERRORS
(from the Grammar Explanation section)
1. The blue whale is **heavier** than the elephant.
2. The cheetah is the **fastest** land animal in the world.
3. Mt. Everest is **the** tallest mountain in the world.
4. The pyramid of Quetzalcoatl is ~~more~~ **larger** than the pyramids of Giza in Egypt.

UNIT 24

ERROR BOX
He is **like** a lion.
He is as stubborn **as** a mule.

LISTENING TO COMPREHEND
tortoise - slow
fish - out of water
bull - in a china shop
chicken - head cut off
mule - stubborn
beaver - busy
clam - happy
ox - strong
fox - in a henhouse

LISTENING TO NOTICE
Welcome to "The Language Minute." I'm your host, Sara Glass. Our topic today is idioms. We will compare human characteristics with characteristics of animals.
Do you take a long time to get ready in the morning? We'll often say, "You're (1) **as slow as** a tortoise." Do you feel unhappy and uncomfortable in certain situations? We may say that you are "(2) **like a fish** out of water." We may describe someone who is very clumsy by saying he's "(3) **like a bull** in a china shop." And here's one of my favorites: saying that someone is so disorganized that she's running around "(4) **like a chicken** with its head cut off"!
Does someone refuse to see your point of view? We may want to say, "You're (5) **as stubborn as** a mule." How about someone who is always working? "(6) **As busy as** a beaver." And how about these: "(7) **as happy as** a clam"; "(8) **as strong as** an ox" ; "(9) **like a fox** in a henhouse." This last one describes someone who can't be trusted.
Well, that's all for today. Next time we'll look at how other languages use animals in idioms. Until then: See you later, alligator!

UNDERSTANDING THE GRAMMAR POINT
1.

as _____ as...	like a _____
as slow as a tortoise	like a fish out of water
as stubborn as a mule	like a bull in a china shop
as busy as a beaver	like a chicken with its head cut off
as happy as a clam	like a fox in a henhouse
as strong as an ox	

2. **Adjectives** are used with *as . . . as*. **Nouns** are used with *like*.

CHECKING
1. Tom and his brother look the same and act the same; they're **like two peas in a pod.**
2. My daughter is **as gentle as a lamb** with her baby brother.
3. When my husband goes into a sporting goods store, he's like a child in a candy shop.
4. He always keeps his promises; his word is **as good as gold**.
5. What did you put in this bookbag? It feels like a ton of bricks.
6. I often don't even know if Yoshi is in his room; he is as quiet as a mouse.
7. I thought they would be finished two hours ago! They're **as slow as molasses**.
8. She spends so much time washing her car; it's always as clean as a whistle.
9. They only met once; they were **like two ships passing in the night**.
10. Do you know that people used to compliment someone by saying he was **as healthy as a horse?**

COMMON ERRORS (from the Grammar Explanation section)
1. When my little brother goes into a toy store, he is **like** a bull in a china shop.
2. My sister really likes her new job. She is **as happy as** a clam.
3. My friend has been lifting weights. He is as strong **as** an ox.

UNIT 25

ERROR BOX
Compared with (**to**) Moscow, Rome is much older.
London is similar **to** Paris.

LISTENING TO COMPREHEND
Moscow and St. Petersburg are being compared. Moscow is more modern even though St. Petersburg is a newer city; St. Petersburg is more European; size, variety and complexity also differ.
Madrid and Barcelona are being compared. Madrid is far from the sea; Barcelona is on the sea; Madrid is the center of government; Barcelona has artistic spirit; Madrid is the nation's brain; Barcelona is the heart.

LISTENING TO NOTICE
Moscow and St. Petersburg: the two great cities of Russia. We Russians love to compare them. The two cities are very different (1) **from** each other. Compared (2) **with** Moscow, St. Petersburg is a fairly new city. But today Moscow has in many ways become the more modern city. And the cities are unlike (3) **0** each other in many other ways. For example, we say that in contrast (4) **to** St. Petersburg, which is a European city in Russia, Moscow is a truly *Russian* city: in its size, in its variety, in its complexity.
Madrid is different (5) **from** Barcelona in several ways. First, unlike (6) **0** Barcelona, which is a Mediterranean city, Madrid is deep in the interior of the country, far from the sea. Second, in contrast (7) **to** Barcelona, which is a city of great artistic spirit, Madrid is more dignified and stately — our center of government. No, Madrid is not like (8) **0** Barcelona; Madrid is our nation's brain, but Barcelona is its heart.

UNDERSTANDING THE GRAMMAR POINT
1.

Comparative term	Preposition
different	from
Compared	with
unlike	{0}
in contrast	to
like	{0}
not like	{0}

CHECKING
1. **Compared with** the normal winter in Minneapolis, winters in Washington are quite mild.
2. Boston differs from San Francisco in a number of ways.
3. Vancouver is **unlike** Seattle in some ways.
4. **Like Denver**, Atlanta has grown fast during the last 25 years.
5. Although they are both cosmopolitan cities, Montreal's atmosphere is different from Toronto's.
6. **Compared with** New York, Boston has the feel of a small city.
7. In contrast to Miami, San Diego gets very little rain.
8. Unlike Los Angeles, which is located on the Pacific Coast, Phoenix is hundreds of miles from water.

COMMON ERRORS (from the Grammar Explanation section)
1. Compared **with** (**to**) other capitals, Ottawa, the capital of Canada, is a small city.
2. Moscow is very different **from** St. Petersburg.
3. In my opinion, Buenos Aires is in many ways like ~~to~~ a European city.

UNIT 26

ERROR BOX
It is not far to the train station.
There is a bus stop at the corner.

LISTENING TO COMPREHEND

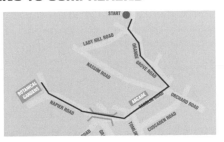

LISTENING TO NOTICE
You want to go jogging in the Botanical Gardens? That's one of my favorite places to go, especially when (1) **it's** sunny. No, (2) **it's** not too far from here. Turn left on Orange Grove Road and go all the way to Tanglin Road. If you're walking, (3) **it's** about five minutes. Go right on Tanglin Road. The road curves a little, and (4) **there's** a short arcade along the way. (5) **There's** a pedestrian bridge at a big intersection. Use it, because (6) **it's** dangerous to cross at the intersection. Actually, I think (7) **it's** illegal, also. From the corner of Orange Grove Road and Tanglin Road, (8) **it's** less than a kilometer. OK, take a right when you come down from the bridge. Walk for a few more minutes. You won't miss it. (9) **There's** a big ornate gate at the entrance, just what you'd expect. At this time of day, (10) **it's** pretty quiet in the Gardens.

UNDERSTANDING THE GRAMMAR POINT
1.

it's	there's
sunny	**a short arcade**
not too far	**a pedestrian bridge**
about five minutes	**a big ornate gate**
dangerous	
illegal	
less than a kilometer	
pretty quiet	

2. Use *it's* with distance, weather, time, conditions.
   Use *there's* with the existence of an object.

CHECKING
I'm going to give you directions to our house. Now, you have to take Highway 5 west out of the city. (1) **It's** 12 miles to the junction of Highway 5 and Silver Lake Road. (2) **It's** about fifteen or twenty minutes, a little more if (3) **there's** a lot of traffic. (4) **There's** a small shopping area on the left just before you get to Silver Lake Road. Turn right on Silver Lake Road and go about three miles. Silver Lake Road is narrow, and (5) **there's** one very steep hill, so drive carefully, especially if (6) **it's** raining or foggy. Our house is on the left. (7) **There's** a group of pine trees in the front just before our driveway. (8) **It's** very quiet out here in the country; you'll know you're not in the city.

COMMON ERRORS (from the Grammar Explanation section)
1. **It** is raining.
   There are four doors at the entrance; use the one on the far right.
2. **It** is not far to my office; we don't need to take a taxi.
3. **There** is a bookstore next to the north entrance to the train station.

UNIT 27

ERROR BOX
People with Alzheimer's disease **may** forget something.
People with Alzheimer's disease may **get** lost.

LISTENING TO COMPREHEND
People with Alzheimer's disease

may forget something and never remember it

may forget even very simple words
can get lost on their own street
may lose things all the time
can be calm one minute and angry the next

LISTENING TO NOTICE

Today I want to tell you how you can recognize when someone has Alzheimer's disease.

Most people forget things but they usually remember them later. People with Alzheimer's disease (1) **may** forget something and never remember it.

We all have trouble finding the right word sometimes. People with Alzheimer's disease (2) **may** forget even very simple words.

We all get lost sometime or other. People with Alzheimer's disease (3) **can** get lost on their own street!

We sometimes lose something like our wallet or our keys. People with Alzheimer's disease (4) **may** lose things all the time. For example, they (5) **might** put a wristwatch in the sugar bowl.

We are all moody sometimes. People with Alzheimer's disease (6) **can** be calm one minute and angry the next — for no reason. For example, they (7) **could** suddenly say you have stolen something from them.

Next, I'd like to talk about the treatment of Alzheimer's disease . . .

UNDERSTANDING THE GRAMMAR POINT

1. modal verbs   main verbs

may	forget
may	forget
can	get lost
may	lose
might	put
can	be
could	say

2. A modal verb is followed by **(c) a simple verb.**
3. The difference is that *Maria often forgets things* tells us about something that actually occurs now, while *She may forget her own name one day* tells us about something that will possibly happen in the future.

CHECKING

People with Alzheimer's disease (1) **forget** things. They (2) **may pre-pare** a meal and then forget they cooked it. We all (3) **say** strange things sometimes, but people with Alzheimer's disease (4) **may say** things that do not make any sense at all. Some people (5) **dress** in strange ways but people suffering from Alzheimer's disease (6) **may put on** several shirts or dresses at the same time. They also (7) **may do** some very odd things. For example, someone with Alzheimer's (8) **may put** an iron in a freezer. Everybody (9) **cries** sometimes but people with Alzheimer's disease (10) **may burst** into tears for no reason at all.

Note: You can use **might**, **can** or **could** instead of **may**.

COMMON ERRORS (from the Grammar Explanation section)

1. People with Alzheimer's disease may **forget** things.
   People with Alzheimer's disease may **forget** things.
   People with Alzheimer's disease may **forget** things.
2. People with Alzheimer's disease can ~~be able to~~ forget things.
3. People with Alzheimer's disease **may** forget things.
4. We thought she **might** (**could**) be suffering from Alzheimer's disease.

UNIT 28

ERROR BOX

You **have to** get a visa because it's required.
You should **use** bottled water.

LISTENING TO COMPREHEND

___ getting a passport
✔ getting a visa
___ bringing traveler's checks
✔ bringing gifts
___ buying souvenirs
✔ buying film
___ confirming hotel reservations
✔ confirming the return flight
✔ sightseeing
___ learning Russian

LISTENING TO NOTICE

Roberta: I'm planning a trip to Russia. I know you've been there several times. What do I need to do to get ready for my trip?

Boris: Well, first you (1) **have to** get a visa ahead of time. You can't enter the country without one, and you can't get one when you arrive. And when you arrive, you (2) **have to** fill out a currency declaration form. And don't lose it; you (3) **have to** turn it in at passport control when you leave. Oh, and you (4) **have to** reconfirm your return flight; if you don't, you'll lose your reservation. These are things you must do.

Roberta: Those are the rules? OK, I'll be sure to follow them. Do you have any advice about what I should bring or what I should do while I'm there?

Boris: Yeah, a few things. You (5) **should** use bottled water. And you (6) **should** bring plenty of film and extra batteries for your camera; film is very expensive in Russia, and you may have trouble replacing your camera battery. And you (7) **should** bring small gifts — souvenirs of the place you live are nice; it isn't necessary, of course, but it's a nice thing to do. And you (8) **should** try to see as much as you can; it's a fascinating country.

Roberta: Thanks for your help.

UNDERSTANDING THE GRAMMAR POINT

1. "You have to fill out a currency declaration form."
   It is necessary to fill out a currency declaration form.

   "You have to turn it in at passport control when you leave."
   It is necessary to turn it in at passport control when you leave.

   "You have to reconfirm your return flight."
   It is necessary to reconfirm your return flight.

   "You should use bottled water."
   It's a good idea to use bottled water.

   "And you should bring plenty of film and extra batteries for your camera."
   It's a good idea to bring plenty of film and extra batteries for your camera.

   "And you should bring small gifts."
   It's a good idea to bring small gifts.

   "And you should try to see as much as you can."
   And it's a good idea to try to see as much as you can.

2. The meaning of *have to* is **necessity.**
   The meaning of *should* is **recommnendation** or **advice.**

CHECKING

1. You **have to** show a photo I.D. at the check-in counter. This is a federal law.
2. You **should** bring plenty of film. Film is very expensive there.
3. You **have to** get a visa in advance. You cannot get one when you arrive.
4. You **have to** turn in your currency declaration form. You are required to turn it in when you leave.
5. It's not necessary, but you **should** bring flowers or a small gift if you are invited to someone's home.
6. At some airports, you **have to** pay an airport service fee or departure tax.
7. Instead of a large sum of cash, you **should** bring traveler's checks.
8. At the airport, you **have to** go through airport security.

Note: In numbers 1, 3, 4, 6 and 8 you can use either **have to** or **must**.

COMMON ERRORS (from the Grammar Explanation section)
1. I have **to** get a visa.
2. You should ~~to~~ bring plenty of film and extra batteries.
   You **must** reconfirm your return flight.
3. You **have to** (**must**) reconfirm your return flight. You will lose your
   reservation if you don't.

UNIT 29

ERROR BOX
He **has worked** here for five years.
He **has worked** here since 1989.

LISTENING TO COMPREHEND

Name	Place of Work	Job(s)
Maria Garcia	Bloomingdale's	• sales assistant • assistant manager
Julie England	The Essex Club	• receptionist • hostess • in charge of important customers
Mike Byson	Berlitz School	• teacher

LISTENING TO NOTICE
1. Maria Garcia (1) **has been** at Bloomingdale's since 1990. To begin with, she (2) **worked** in the cosmetics department as a sales assistant. For the last five years she (3) **has acted** as assistant manager in the women's apparel department. She (4) **has shown** herself dependable and highly professional. We will be sorry to see her leave.
2. Julie England (5) **has worked** as a hostess at the Essex Club since 1995. Initially, she (6) **acted** as a receptionist, greeting customers as they arrived. However, for the last 12 months she (7) **has taken** charge of some of the club's most important customers. Julie has a lot of personal charm and (8) **has been** extremely popular. We strongly recommend her.
3. Mike Byson (9) **has worked** at the Berlitz School since 1993. He (10) **came** to us with no teaching experience but since (11) **has developed** into a highly skillful teacher of English. He is now very popular with the students. For the last few months, however, Mr. Byson (12) **has chosen** to follow his own method of teaching English rather than the methods used by the school. For this reason we have asked him to find other employment.

UNDERSTANDING THE GRAMMAR POINT
1. The verbs in the simple past tense are: **worked, acted, came**
   The verbs in the present perfect tense are:
   has been, has acted, has shown, has
   worked, has taken, has been, has worked, has developed, has chosen
2. - Use the **simple past tense** to refer to actions that took place in the past and are now completed.
   - Use the **present perfect tense** to refer to an action that started in the past and is still continuing at the time of speaking.
3. The **present perfect tense** is used with *for* and *since*.
4. - Use **since** with the present perfect to refer to a time when an ongoing action first started.
     *She has been at Bloomingdale's **since** 1990.*
   - Use **for** with the present perfect to refer to a period of time an action has been going on.
     For the last five years she has worked as an assistant manager.

CHECKING
Rod Ellis was born in England. He (1) **has lived** overseas for most of his life. In 1967 he (2) **went** to Zambia where he (3) **lived** for 10 years. In 1978 he (4) **started** work in London. He (5) **worked** there from 1978 to 1989. In 1989 he (6) **left** London to work for Temple University in Japan and then in Philadelphia. He (7) **taught** at Temple for nine years. In July 1997 he (8) **moved** to Auckland in New Zealand where he (9) **has lived** since. He (10) **has enjoyed** working at the University of Auckland and

expects to stay there many more years.

COMMON ERRORS (from the Grammar Explanation section)
1. He **has worked** here since 1998.
   He **has worked** here for three years and does not want to leave.
2. He **has worked** here for three years.
3. He has worked here **for** two years.

UNIT 30

ERROR BOX
Every day Miss Leeson **went** out to work.

LISTENING TO COMPREHEND
1. **True** 2. **True** 3. **True** 4. **True** 5. **False**

LISTENING TO NOTICE
Miss Leeson (1) **found** a small room at the top of Mrs. Parker's guest house. It cost her only a few dollars.

Every day Miss Leeson (2) **left** the guest house early. She came back late. Sometimes she (3) **brought** back papers and copied them on her typewriter. Often, though, she (4) **had** no papers to copy. Then she just (5) **sat** with the other guests. They talked and laughed together.

One winter day Miss Leeson did not come down from her room. Clara, the maid, (6) **knocked** on her door but she did not answer. Clara forced the door open. Miss Leeson (7) **was lying** very still on her bed. She (8) **was still wearing** her outdoor clothes. She (9) **was hardly breathing**.

An ambulance (10) **came** and took Miss Leeson to the city hospital. When the doctor (11) **looked** at her he said that she (12) **was suffering** from starvation but that she would recover.

UNDERSTANDING THE GRAMMAR POINT
1. The verbs in the simple past tense are: **found, left, brought, had, sat, knocked, came, looked**
   The verbs in the past continuous are: **was lying, was still wearing, was hardly breathing, was suffering**
2. **c.** To refer to a past action that took place over a period of time.
3.

Past action completed at a definite point in the past	Past action happening several times
found	**left**
knocked	**brought**
came	**had**
looked	**sat**

4. **a** is correct: We use the simple past tense to refer to actions that happened often in the past.

CHECKING
Jimmy Spencer was a burglar. Every month he (1) **robbed** a different bank. Sometimes he (2) **got** a lot of money but he always (3) **spent** it quickly. Jimmy Spencer liked the good life.

One day he (4) **was visiting** a small town in Arkansas. He (5) **booked** into the local hotel and then (6) **walked** over to the bank. A beautiful young woman (7) **was going** into the bank.

"Who's she?" he asked a man.

"That's Polly Simpson. She's the bank manager's daughter," the man told him.

So Jimmy (8) **decided** not to rob the bank after all. Instead he (9) **stayed** on in the town and (10) **opened** a shoe shop. It was very successful. Jimmy (11) **started** a savings account at the bank.

Within a year he **married** Polly Simpson.

COMMON ERRORS (from the Grammar Explanation section)
1. Miss Leeson sometimes **typed** papers in her room.

REVIEW TESTS LEVEL 3

TEST A
1. have shown (Unit 29) 2. were suffering (Unit 30) 3. smarter (Unit 23) 4. to (Unit 25) 5. often (Unit 21) 6. few (Unit 22) 7. 0 (Unit 25) 8. as (Unit 24) 9. poorly (Unit 21) 10. will (Units 27) 11. there (Unit 26) 12. should (Unit 28)

TEST B
1. was working (Unit 30) 2. it is (Unit 26) 3. like (Units 24) 4. warmer (Unit 23) 5. unexpectedly (Unit 21) 6. a few (Unit 22) 7. little (Unit 22) 8. from (Unit 25) 9. have enjoyed (Unit 29) 10. there (Unit 26) 11. have to (Unit 28) 12. might (Unit 27)

UNIT 31

ERROR BOX
The airport is located in ~~the~~ Osaka Bay.
The international arrival lobby is on the third floor.

LISTENING TO COMPREHEND
✔ Osaka Bay
___ Italy
___ the ground floor
___ the shuttle trains
✔ the international departure lobby
✔ the international arrival lobby
✔ the domestic lobby
✔ McDonald's
✔ shops
___ the train station

LISTENING TO NOTICE
Welcome to (1) **0** Kansai International Airport, KIA. The airport is located on (2) **0** Airport Island in (3) **0** Osaka Bay.

KIA has (4) **the** world's largest passenger terminal. It was designed by (5) **0** Renzo Piano, (6) **the** famous Italian architect.

On arrival you will enter (7) **the** main terminal. You will find (8) **the** international arrival lobby on the first floor of the main terminal. (9) **The** international departure lobby is on the fourth floor. (10) **The** domestic lobby for both arrivals and departures is on the second floor.

There are 26 restaurants, including (11) **0** McDonald's, and 44 shops situated on the second and third floors.

Your departure gate will be in (12) **the** north or south wing. Shuttle trains leave the main terminal every two minutes.

UNDERSTANDING THE GRAMMAR POINT
1.
A no THE {0}	B THE
Kansai International Airport	the world's largest passenger terminal
Airport Island	the famous Italian architect
Osaka Bay	the main terminal
Renzo Piano	the international arrival lobby
McDonald's	the international departure lobby
	the domestic lobby
	the north or south wing

2. Do not use *the* before a proper noun like *McDonald's*.
   Use *the* before an ordinary noun when it refers to a person or a thing that is unique (there is only one in the particular context).

CHECKING
Trump Tower

Trump Tower was designed by Philip Johnson, one of (1) **the** leading architects in America. It overlooks (2) **0** Central Park in **the** heart of Manhattan.

At (3) **the** bottom of the tower is Trump International Hotel. Above this there are a number of luxury apartments. Some of (4) **the** apartments cost as much as 10 million U.S. dollars. Residents can use all the amenities of (5) **the** hotel, including (6) **the** gourmet restaurant, Jean-Georges, and (7) **the** fitness center.

In (8) **the** grand atrium of the tower you can find (9) **the** world's most exclusive shops. For example, in (10) **the** lobby you will find (11) **0** Cartier and Galeries Lafayette while on (12) **the** second floor there is (13) **0** Club Chagall.

You can be sure that in (14) **0** Trump Tower you will rub shoulders with some very rich and famous people.

COMMON ERRORS (from the Grammar Explanation section)
1. You can find ~~the~~ Japan Railways in the basement.
2. **The** arrivals lobby is on **the** first floor.
3. **The** arrivals lobby is on the first floor.

UNIT 32

ERROR BOX
A man stole ~~a~~ money from a diner.
He threatened the owner with **a** gun.

LISTENING TO COMPREHEND
1. They died after falling into a well.
2. Nothing. (He didn't steal anything.)

LISTENING TO NOTICE
1. (1) **An** accident occurred in rural Texas yesterday. The accident occurred when Jason B. Jones and his wife, Mary Ellen Jones, died from (2) **0** drowning. Apparently, (3) **a** chicken had fallen into (4) **a** well on their farm. Jason, known locally for (5) **0** stubbornness rather than (6) **0** intelligence, climbed in to rescue it. When he got stuck he called his wife, who lowered (7) **a** rope into the well. Jason grasped the rope and started to pull himself out. Unfortunately, he was too heavy for his wife, who toppled into the well. They both fell into the water at the bottom. Only the chicken survived.

2. (8) **An** unusual event took place in Ypsilanti, Michigan, yesterday. (9) **An** unemployed man tried to rob (10) **a** diner. He walked into the diner at 11:05 in the morning and threatened the owner with (11) **a** gun. However, the owner said he could not open the cash register unless the man ordered (12) **0** food. The man ordered (13) **0** bacon and eggs, but the owner told him breakfast finished at 11 o'clock. The man then asked for (14) **0** soup, but the owner told him it was not available. Full of (15) **0** frustration, the man walked away.

UNDERSTANDING THE GRAMMAR POINT
1. Story #1. Circle: **an unfortunate accident, 0 drowning, a chicken, a well, 0 stubbornness, 0 intelligence, a rope.** Story #2. Circle: **an unusual, an unemployed man, a diner, a gun, 0 food, 0 bacon and eggs, 0 soup, 0 frustration**

2.
Nouns with *a(n)*	Nouns without *a(n)*
an unfortunate accident	drowning
a chicken	stubborness
a well	intelligence
a rope	food
an unusual event	bacon and eggs
an unemployed man	soup
a diner	frustration
a gun	

3. We use *a* or *an* before a singular countable noun.
   We don't use *a* or *an* before uncountable nouns and abstract nouns.

CHECKING
A man in San Antonio, Texas, was arrested for stealing **a** cell phone and **a** money from a car. The owner of the car, feeling ~~an~~ anger, decided to trick the thief. He pretended that he was from **a** radio station. He called his cell phone number and the thief answered. He told the thief that he had won **a** $5,000 prize from the radio station and he had to come to the radio station to pick it up. When the thief arrived to pick up his prize, the

police were waiting. They arrested him for **a-** possession of stolen property.

COMMON ERRORS [from the Grammar Explanation section]
1. He shot himself in **a** hotel in New York.
2. He gave the beggar **a** half loaf of bread.
   She lost **a** hundred dollars.
3. He gave me **-a** good advice.
4. **A** Stubbornness can be very annoying.

UNIT 33

ERROR BOX
A tamagochi is a computerized toy. **The** tamagochi has become very popular.

LISTENING TO COMPREHEND
1. **A computerized toy**, 2. **push buttons to feed, play with, clean up and discipline the chick**, 3. **a live tamagochi (a live insect)**, 4. **because she spent so much time caring for her tamagochi.**

LISTENING TO NOTICE
(1) **A** tamagochi is a computerized toy invented in Japan. The name means a cute little egg. (2) **The** tamagochi has become very popular all around the world. The gadget hatches (3) **a** chick. (4) **The** chick makes a chirping noise every few minutes. (5) **An** owner has to push buttons to feed, play with, clean up and discipline the chick. If (6) **the** owner stops caring for the chick, it dies.

However, the electronic toy is expensive and many people cannot afford to buy one. (7) **A** street seller in China had a good idea. He decided to make a live tamagochi. He made (8) **a** small cage out of bamboo. Then he caught (9) **an** insect. He put (10) **the** insect inside (11) **the** cage. (12) **The** street seller was able to sell the tamagochi for three yuan (about 40 cents). Now he has become rich selling live tamagochis.

Some people think that the tamagochi is a bad thing. "I bought a tamagochi and spent a lot of time looking after it," explained Mariko Tada, a sales assistant in (13) **a** downtown Tokyo store. She spent so much time caring for her tamagochi that (14) **the** store fired her!

UNDERSTANDING THE GRAMMAR POINT

1.

a(n) + noun	the + noun
a tamagochi	**the tamagochi**
a chick	**the chick**
an owner	**the owner**
a street seller	**the street seller**
a small cage	**the cage**
an insect	**the insect**
a downtown Tokyo store	**the store**

2. *A* is used when a noun is first mentioned.
   The is used when the noun is mentioned again.

3. *A* is used with *computerized toy* because *toy* has not been mentioned before and it is not a particular toy.
   The is used with *gadget* because it refers to *tamagochi*, which has been mentioned once; it is a particular gadget, not just any gadget.

CHECKING
1. TUGGLES is (1) **a** cuddly pet with a leash. When you pull on (2) **the** leash the pet walks by itself. Kids love taking Tuggles for (3) **a** walk.
2. JOSEPHINA MONTOYA is (4) **a** realistic doll that looks Hispanic. It is accompanied by (5) **a** book. (6) **The** book tells you all about how to care for (7) **the** doll.
3. BULLDOG DOZER is (8) **a** construction set together with (9) **a** bulldozer. (10) **The** bulldozer keeps knocking down (11) **the** construction you are making. Kids will love it!

COMMON ERRORS [from the Grammar Explanation section]
1. A tamagochi is an electronic toy. **The** tamagochi has become very popular.
2. **The** streetseller who made live tamagochis has become rich.

UNIT 34

ERROR BOX
The other (**Another**) reason I like holidays is that I can visit my family.
Another (**The other**) thing I like about having sisters is that we can share clothes.

LISTENING TO COMPREHEND

	Amy	Bruce	Carla
Who has the largest family?	—	✔	—
Whose family has the most males?	✔	✔	—
Whose family has the most females?	✔	—	—
Who has the smallest family?	—	—	✔

LISTENING TO NOTICE
Amy: The person in my family I spend the most time with is my twin sister. I have two (1) **other** sisters, but one reason I spend so much time with my twin sister is that we understand each other perfectly. (2) **The other** reason is that we both love to cook.
Bruce: I come from a large family: There are four brothers. One of my brothers lives near Chicago, where we grew up; (4) **another** brother lives in Boston; and (5) **the other** brother lives in Miami. I love visiting him, especially in the winter! And then there are two sisters. Both of my sisters are in Chicago. One still lives at home; (6) **the other** sister lives only a few miles away.
Carla: I have two brothers. One lives in London; (7) **the other** brother lives in Sydney. Their lives are different in (8) **other** ways, too. One difference is that my brother in London has a big family, but my brother in Sydney is single. (9) **Another** difference is that my brother in London worries about everything, especially his career. My brother in Sydney never worries at all. (9) **The other** difference is that my brother in London has plenty of money, but my brother in Sydney is always broke.

UNDERSTANDING THE GRAMMAR POINT

A. - other sisters	B. - the other reason	C. - another reason
- other ways	- the other brother	- another brother
You must use **other.**	- the other sister	- another difference
	- the other brother	You must use **another**.
	- the other difference	
	You must use **the other**	

2. a. **the other**   b. **another**   c. **other**

CHECKING
1. My father's brother has two boys. One of them is much older than me; **the other** is about my age.
2. I know some of the people in Hiroko's family, but there are **other** members of her family I've never even met.
3. His sisters look alike and act alike. **Another** similarity is that they both love sports.
4. Some people think it would be nice to have a twin brother or sister; other people wouldn't like to have a twin.
5. I know you've met one of my brothers. Have you met **the other**?
6. Two of her four grandchildren are lawyers, and another is a doctor.
7. There are three children in my family; two of us are girls, and **the other** is a boy.
8. I have three sisters; two of them are older than me, but **the other** is five years younger.

COMMON ERRORS [from the Grammar Explanation section]
1. I have **another** cousin who lives in the same city I do.
2. There are **other** things my sister and I enjoy doing together.

3. Only one of my two sisters lives in Tokyo; **the other** lives in Vancouver.

UNIT 35

ERROR BOX
I enjoy **seeing** you every day.
I promise **to care** for you.

LISTENING TO COMPREHEND
1.

TO:	FROM:
1. Marcos	**Heart-throb**
2. Melisa	**Broken-hearted**
3. Yong-Jin	**True lover**
5. Grace	**Lost lover**

2. Broken-hearted — Melisa does not reply to his letters.
Lost lover — Grace will not talk to or see him.

LISTENING TO NOTICE
1. To Marcos
   My darling Marcos! I miss (1) **seeing** you every day. You are the nicest and kindest guy I have ever known. And you are so sexy. Please keep (2) **thinking** about me always!
   Your heartthrob
2. To Melisa
   I will never forget you even though you have forgotten me. You promised (3) **to write** to me but I have heard nothing. But I shall never stop (4) **thinking** of you.
   Broken-hearted
3. To Yong Jin
   I want (5) **to give** you a big kiss for Valentine's Day! I look forward to every day because I know I shall enjoy (6) **seeing** you.
   True lover
4. To Grace
   I think only of your face, your hair, your lips. But I know you avoid (7) **talking** to me and you can't stand (8) **looking** at me. Never mind. I refuse (9) **to give up** hope. You are the only woman for me! I swear never (10) **to forget** you.
   Lost lover

UNDERSTANDING THE GRAMMAR POINT
1. Circle: **miss, keep, promised, never stop, want, enjoy, avoid, can't stand, refuse, swear**

Verbs followed by an infinitive	Verbs followed by a gerund
promise	miss
want	keep
refuse	stop
swear	enjoy
	avoid
	stand (tolerate)

2. Verbs taking infinitive: **try, fail, agree, decide, prepare**
   Verbs taking gerund: **deny, suggest, finish, consider, delay**

CHECKING
1. I have enjoyed **spending** time with you.
2. I cannot avoid **seeing** you.
3. I promise never to forget you.
4. I miss **holding** you in my arms.
5. I keep **looking** at the photo of you.
6. I refuse to forget you!
7. Do not be so cruel! Why do you avoid **meeting** with me?
8. Please, never stop **thinking** of me!
9. I want to live my whole life with you!
10. I want to think of you every day of my life.
11. I fancy **holding** you in my arms.
12. Soon I shall risk **asking** you to be my lover.

COMMON ERRORS (from the Grammar Explanation section)
I have enjoyed **spending** time with you.
He suggested **sending** her a Valentine card.

UNIT 36

ERROR BOX
He **made** his daughter finish her homework before she could go out to play.

LISTENING TO COMPREHEND
1. Conversation 1: b   Conversation 2: b

LISTENING TO NOTICE
Conversation 1:
Teacher: This month you're going to read about current events.
Student 1: What topic will we be reading about?
Teacher: I'm going to (1) **let** you choose a topic. I'm not going to (2) **make** you all read about the same topic.
Student 2: You won't (3) **make** us read about politics?
Teacher: No, if you'd rather read about the environment, I'll (4) **let** you choose that topic.
Student 1: When do we have to decide on our topic?
Teacher: I'll (5) **let** you think about it until next week. Any other questions?
Conversation 2:
Secretary: Sorry I'm late. I was afraid Mr. Arroyo wouldn't even (6) **let** me leave for lunch.
Friend: What happened?
Secretary: There's a big proposal to finish, and Mr. Arroyo (7) **made** everyone stop whatever they were doing to work on it.
Friend: Was he angry?
Secretary: No, but he's afraid we won't meet the deadline. He'll (8) **make** us come in this weekend if we don't finish by the end of the week.
Friend: Well, enjoy your lunch. It sounds as if he's going to (9) **make** you work hard for the next few days.
Secretary: He's not going to (10) **let** us *breathe* until this proposal is done!

UNDERSTANDING THE GRAMMAR POINT
1. *Make* means *require* or *force* someone to do something.
   Let means *allow* someone to do something.
2. The verb following *let* and *make* is a simple infinitive form (e.g go); the verb following *allow* and *force* (and *require*) is to + infinitive (e.g. to go).
3. **Conversation 1**
   1. I'm going to <u>allow</u> you <u>to choose</u> a topic.
   2. I'm not going to <u>require (force)</u> you all <u>to read</u> about the same topic.
   3. You won't <u>require (force)</u> us <u>to read</u> about politics?
   4. I'll <u>allow</u> you <u>to choose</u> that topic.
   5. I'll <u>allow</u> you <u>to think</u> about it until next week.
   Conversation 2
   6. I was afraid Mr. Arroyo wouldn't <u>allow</u> me <u>to leave</u> for lunch.
   7. Mr. Arroyo <u>required (forced)</u> everyone <u>to stop</u> whatever they were doing to work on it.
   8. He'll <u>require (force) us to come</u> in this weekend…
   9. He's going to <u>force (require)</u> you <u>to work</u> hard for the next few days.
   10. He's not going to <u>allow us to breathe</u>…

CHECKING
1. He found so many errors in the report that he **made** his secretary retype it.
2. Our science teacher **lets** us use the laboratory after school if we want to do extra work.
3. Our office manager doesn't **let** us use our office telephones for personal calls.
4. Our company lets us ~~to~~ **leave** an hour early if we work through the lunch hour.
5. The plant manager **makes** everyone working in the factory wear safety glasses.

6. My English teacher **lets** us ask questions whenever we want.
7. Our supervisor **makes** us provide a receipt for even the smallest travel expense.
8. Because I had been sick, my teacher **let** me take the exam again.

COMMON ERRORS [from the Grammar Explanation section]
1. She **made** the staff stay until the report was finished.
2. If you finish your homework, I will **let** you watch television.
3. He made us ~~to~~ stop everything we were doing.
   I'll let you ~~to~~ choose the topic you want to read about.

UNIT 37

ERROR BOX
He is **always** quarreling.

LISTENING TO COMPREHEND
Answers will vary, as these are opinion questions.
Example answer for d: She should make him stop drinking.

LISTENING TO NOTICE
Dear Anne,
I am in a real quandary so I hope you can help me. I have been (1) **living** with Rick, my boyfriend, for over a year now and I love him very much. He is a very (2) **interesting** guy and sometimes he can be really (3) **amusing**. Most of the time he also is very (4) **caring**. However, he sometimes goes out (5) **drinking** with his friends and when he comes home, he starts (6) **quarreling** with me. He's always (7) **spending** all his money on alcohol and starts (8) **fighting** with me. Sometimes I find him really (9) **frightening**. Now he says we should get married. But I'm not so sure.
A very (10) **doubting** lover,
Angela

UNDERSTANDING THE GRAMMAR POINT
1. Verb -ing   Adjective -ing
   1. **living**   1. **interesting**
   2. **drinking**   2. **amusing**
   3. **quarreling**   3. **caring**
   4. **spending**   4. **frightening**
   5. **arguing**   5. **doubting**
2. a. Words that go with verbs: **always, sometimes**
   b. Words that go with adjectives: **very, really**

CHECKING
1. Rick is **always** quarreling with Angela.
2. He is a very interesting guy.
3. He is also really amusing sometimes.
4. Sometimes he is really caring.
5. But he is **always** drinking with his friends.
6. Angela is a very loving person.
7. He is **always** spending his money on alcohol.
8. He is **always** fighting with Angela.
9. He can be really frightening.
10. Now Angela is **always** doubting (that) she loves him.

COMMON ERRORS [from the Grammar Explanation section]
1. He is **sweating**. (He is a **sweaty** person.OR (He is **sweating** a lot today.)
2. She is very **argumentative**. or She **argues a lot**.

UNIT 38

ERROR BOX
They **will carry** out repairs to Mir soon.

LISTENING TO COMPREHEND
1. August 12th: Two new cosmonauts blast off
   August 14th: **Two Russian cosmonauts return to earth**
   September 15th: **Leakey returns to earth**
2. **They will carry out repairs to Spiv.**

LISTENING TO NOTICE
Two new cosmonauts (1) **blast** off August 12th. They (2) **relieve** Russian crew members on the Spiv space station.
Cosmonauts Markov Zhlinksi and Boris Petrogrov (3) **depart** at 1536 GMT Tuesday from the space center in Kazakhstan. They (4) **join** two other Russians and Brad Leaky, a U.S. astronaut, on Spiv. The Russian cosmonauts (5) **return** to earth on August 14th. Leaky, however,(6) **stays** until September 15th when another American astronaut (7) **replaces** him.
The cosmonauts (8) **will carry** out repairs to the damaged energy systems on Spiv. The two Russians (9) **will work** inside a darkened space module. They (10) **will attach** electric cables to the solar panels in the module. Their work (11) **will be** risky. Leaky, the American, however, (12) **will wait** in the Spivlet space vehicle.
Zhlinksi, a veteran cosmonaut, said, "I expect everything (13) **will go** according to plan. We (14) **will finish** the repairs in a few days."

UNDERSTANDING THE GRAMMAR POINT
1. **a.** (will happen)
2.

Simple Present Tense	Future Tense
blast	will carry
relieve	will work
depart	will attach
join	will be
return	will wait
stays	will go
replaces	will finish

3. a. This usage is not correct for referring to a prediction.
   b. This usage is i**correct**; it refers to an action that is part of a planned journey.
   c. This usage is generally not correct, unless it refers to a planned series of actions.

CHECKING
Shuttle Discovery and its crew of six **blast** off from the Kennedy Space Center in Florida at 10.41 a. m. Thursday. The shuttle **will release** a German satellite which **will study** the earth's upper atmosphere. It **will provide** scientists with very useful information.
The cosmonauts **will carry** out a number of space walks. They **will test** a Japanese robot.
The shuttle **returns** after 11 days.

COMMON ERRORS [from the Grammar Explanation section]
The astronauts **will work** inside the darkened space module.

UNIT 39

ERROR BOX
If I knew how to solve the problem, I **would** tell you.
If I **had** enough money, I would take a long vacation. OR
If I have (=get) enough money, I **will** take a long vacation.

LISTENING TO COMPREHEND
1. What does Sara want to do? **get a part-time job**
2. Why does Sara need money? **to go to diving school**
3. What does Jim like to do most? **spend time with his freinds**
4. How would Jim spend any money he had? **buy a big-screen TV**

LISTENING TO NOTICE
Sara: I'm going to get a part-time job.
Jim: Why? If you (1) **need** some money, Mom or Dad (2) **will** lend you some.

Sara: I know, but I want to earn my own money. If I (3) **start** working at a part-time job now, I (4) **will** earn a lot of money by the beginning of summer.

Jim: If I (5) **took** a part-time job, I (6) **wouldn't** have time to spend with my friends.

Sara: That's true.

Jim: If I (7) **had** to choose between working and spending time with my friends, I (8) **would** rather spend time with my friends.

Sara: Well, me too, but if I (9) **earn** two thousand dollars, I (10) **will** be able to spend a month at Waikiki Diving Camp in Hawaii.

Jim: If I (11) **had** two thousand dollars, I (12) **would** buy a big-screen TV.

Sara: Yeah, I could buy something, but if I (13) **go** to that diving school, I (14) **will** become a certified diving instructor by the end of the summer.

Jim: Wow, you're so ambitious!

UNDERSTANDING THE GRAMMAR POINT

1. **Column 1:** IF + simple present tense + will + verb
- If you need some money, Mom or Dad will lend you some.
- If I start working at a part-time job now, I will earn a lot of money...
- ...if I earn $2,000, I will be able to spend a month at Waikiki Diving Camp in Hawaii.
- ...if I go to that diving school, I will become a certified diving instructor...

Column 2: IF + simple past tense + would + verb
- If I took a part-time job, I wouldn't have time to spend with my friends.
- If I had to choose..., I would rather spend time with my friends.
- If I had $2,000, I would buy a big-screen TV.

2. **Column 1** sentences show a greater possibility that the action will take place. **Column 2** sentences show that the action probably will not take place; the action is hypothetical.

3. Sara uses the conditional in **column 1**; she is more certain that the action will happen. Jim uses the conditional in **column 2**; he is not certain that these actions will ever happen; they are hypothetical to him.

CHECKING

1. If she doesn't get the promotion, she **will** look for another job.
2. If we won the lottery, we **would** buy an apartment in Paris.
3. I doubt that I'll be assigned to our office in Buenos Aires. If I had the opportunity to go there, I would accept it in a minute.
4. If my husband loses his job, he will start a new career.
5. If I had a daughter studying English, I would encourage her to go on a homestay program.
6. If we buy a new car, we'll probably get a sport utility vehicle.
7. He said he's going to call in a few minutes. If we have to cancel our vacation plans, I **will** be disappointed.
8. If we went to live in another country, I **would** try to learn the language of that country right away.

COMMON ERRORS (from the Grammar Explanation section)

1. - If I earn enough money, I **will** move to a larger apartment. (If I **earned** enough money, I would move to a larger apartment.)
   - If I had enough money to buy a vacation home, I **would** look for a place in Hawaii.
   (If I **have** enough money to buy a vacation home, I will look for a place in Hawaii.)
2. It's not going to happen, of course, but if I **became** the head of state of my country, I **would make** many changes.
3. I didn't get the promotion. If I **had gotten** the promotion, I **would be** very happy. (If I **had gotten** the promotion, I **would have been** very happy.)

UNIT 40

ERROR BOX

If I **lost** my job at the bank, I would become a gardener.

If I **had had** a family, it would have been more difficult to change careers.

LISTENING TO COMPREHEND

Speaker:	What the speaker is:	What the speaker would like to be:
Cynthia	banker	garden designer
Lynn	forester	forester
Lance	salesman	accountant

LISTENING TO NOTICE

Cynthia: I work for a large bank. About three years ago, I started to do gardening. If I (1) **changed** careers now, I (2) **would become** a garden designer. I took up gardening only because we moved from an apartment into a house. If we (3) **had stayed** in that apartment, I (4) **would never have become** interested in gardening.

Lynn: I've worked for the Forest Service all my adult life. Twenty years ago, if you (5) **had asked** me about my future plans, I (6) **would have answered**, "Working outside, taking care of the forests!" I'm very happy with my work. If I (7) **had spent** the last 20 years working in a city office, I (8) **would have been** very unhappy.

Lance: I have wanted to get out of sales work for many years. If I (9) **had had** more courage, I (10) **would have done** it a long time ago. Of course, if I (11) **had studied** harder, I (12) **would have gone** to a university, to become an accountant. If I (13) **decided** to start a new career now, I (14) **would become** an accountant.

UNDERSTANDING THE GRAMMAR POINT

1. **If I** [past tense], **I would** + verb
- **If I changed careers now, I would become a garden designer.**
- **If I decided to start a new career now, I would become an accountant.**

If I had + past participle, **I would have** + past participle
- **If we had stayed in that apartment, I would never have become interested in gardening.**
- **if you had asked me about my future plans, I would have answered, "Working outside...**
- **If I had spent the last twenty years working in a city office, I would have been very unhappy.**
- **If I had had more courage, I would have done it a long time ago.**
- **If I had studied harder, I would have gotten into university...**

2. **If I** [past tense], **I would** + **verb** describes hypothetical situations. **I had** + past participle, **I would have** + **past participle** describes unreal situations.

CHECKING

1. If I hadn't had a family to support, I would have quit my job to go back to school. **unreal**
2. If she had wanted to travel, she would have applied to one of the overseas posts in her company. **unreal**
3. She has said that if she ever stopped teaching, she would become a counselor. **hypothetical**
4. If I had known how interesting gardening is, I would have started doing it years ago. **unreal**
5. If we had a child now, our lifestyle would change drastically. **hypothetical**
6. If we lost our possessions in a fire or some other disaster, we would stay right here and rebuild our lives. **hypothetical**
7. If I had the chance to spend a year working in Japan, I would do it. **hypothetical**
8. If Mr. Lee had been in better health, he would not have retired. **unreal**

COMMON ERRORS (from the Grammar Explanation section)

1. If I changed jobs, **I would have to move**.
2. If he **had been** unhappy in his job, he **would have left**.

LEVEL 4 REVIEW TESTS

TEST A

1. a (Unit 32) 2. the (Unit 31) 3. solve (Unit 35) 4. one (Unit 34) 5. the other (Unit 34) 6. interesting (Unit 37) 7. the (Unit 31) 8. another (Unit 34) 9. a (Unit 32) 10. travel (Unit 38) 11. 0 (Unit 31) 12. will (Unit 39)

TEST B

1. 0 (Unit 31) 2. worried (Unit 37) 3. surprised (Unit 37) 4. to eat (Unit 35) 5. other (Unit 34) 6. a (Unit 32) 7. made (Unit 36) 8. the (Unit 33) 9. would have (Unit 40) 10. living (Unit 35) 11. start (Unit 38) 12. worrying (Unit 35)

UNIT 41

ERROR BOX

She is a **difficult** person.
He does not have a **healthy** diet.

LISTENING TO COMPREHEND

Answers will vary, as these are opinions.

LISTENING TO NOTICE

1. I think **wealthy** people shouldn't have to pay a lot of tax.
2. I don't think we should bother about having a **healthy** diet.
3. I think an **efficient** government is more important than a **democratic** government.
4. I think old people shouldn't wear **sexy** clothes.
5. I think teachers should never give **difficult** tests.
6. I think children should never be punished, even if they are **naughty**.
7. I think it is more important to have cheap cars than **safe** cars.
8. I think it is best to let **angry** people have their own way.
9. I think there are no **honest** politicians.
10. I think hard-working people should earn more money than **creative** people.

UNDERSTANDING THE GRAMMAR POINT

2.

	Adjective	Noun
1.	wealthy	wealth
2.	healthy	health
3.	efficient	efficiency
4.	democratic	democracy
5.	sexy	sex
6.	difficult	difficulty
7.	naughty	naughtiness
8.	safe	safety
9.	angry	anger
10.	honest	honesty
11.	creative	creativity

3. **c**. If a word ends in a -y it can be an adjective or a noun.

CHECKING

1. Michael Jackson is a very **creative** person.
2. Some countries do not have democratic governments.
3. Rap musicians sometimes seem to be very angry people.
4. Japanese cars are recognized as very **safe** cars.
5. Vegetarians have a very **healthy** diet.
6. Famous film actors and actresses are very wealthy people.
7. Pop singers generally wear sexy clothes.
8. My country faces a lot of **difficult** problems.
9. Children are often not punished for their naughty behavior.
10. I have never met a completely **honest** person.

COMMON ERRORS (from the Grammar Explanation section)

1. She is a **difficult** person.
2. I don't like to talk about **sex**.

UNIT 42

ERROR BOX

By the time he arrived, we **had** already made several calls trying to locate him.

LISTENING TO COMPREHEND

1.
1959 — Dien is born.
1971 — Dien has lost his parents. (His parents have died.)
1979 — Dien has arrived in the U.S.
1984 — Dien has saved enough money to bring his relatives to the U.S.
         Dien has bought a florist shop.
1994 — Dien has expanded his business to six stores.

LISTENING TO NOTICE

Dien Tranh

My neighbor Dien Tranh was born in 1959 in Vietnam, in the city of Hue. By the time he was 12, he (1) **had lost** both his parents. Somehow he cared for himself and his younger sister. By the time he was 20 he (2) **had arrived** in the United States as a refugee, and he (3) **had begun** working two and sometimes three jobs at a time. Within five years, he (4) **had already saved** enough money to help bring many of his relatives to the United States, and he (5) **had bought** a small florist shop. By 1994 — 10 years after he bought that small shop — Tranh (6) **had expanded** his business to include six stores and more than 30 employees.

UNDERSTANDING THE GRAMMAR POINT

1.

	Time 1 (Past Perfect)
DIEN TRANH:	
By the time Dien was 12	**his parents had died**
By the time he was 20	**he had arrived in the U.S.**
By the time he was 20	**he had begun working...**
Within 5 years	**he had saved enough money to...**
Within 5 years	**he had bought a small florist shop**
By 1994	**he had expanded his business...**

2. We use the past perfect to contrast two past events. We use the past perfect to show the more distant past time. We use the simple past to show the more recent past time.

CHECKING

1. Before she came to the United States, Cecilia Sanchez **had** never traveled more than 100 miles from Mexico City.
2. When she came to the United States with her family, she **had had** very little education.
3. Within a few years, however, Cecilia had learned English.
4. When she entered junior high school, her physical education teachers **noticed** Cecilia's natural ability as a runner.
5. She **had** joined her school's track team a few weeks later.
6. Even before she began her last year of high school, several universities **offered** her an athletic scholarship.
7. After graduating from college, Cecilia **became** a track coach.
8. By her 40th birthday, Cecilia had received mumerous awards for her work in the community.

COMMON ERRORS (from the Grammar Explanation section)

1. Last year she **started** a new career.
2. While Mr. and Mrs. Sato were traveling in Southeast Asia, Mrs. Sato's sister **stayed** in their apartment.

ERROR BOX

A damp cloth **is used** to clean it.
A computer should **be kept** in a cool room.
Computers must **be cared for** properly.

LISTENING TO COMPREHEND

1.

What should you do?	Right	Wrong
1. Keep it in a cool place.	✔	
2. Keep it away from sunlight.	✔	
3. Keep drinks away from it.	✔	
4. Clean it with chemical cleaner.		✔
5. Turn it off and on quickly.		✔

LISTENING TO NOTICE

Today we are going to learn about computer care. Ready?

Now a computer (1) **should be kept** in a cool room — not too hot and not too cold and not too humid and not too dry.

Also, a computer (2) **should be put** in a place that is free of dust.

Bright sunlight (3) **should be avoided**.

Liquids like coffee or Coke (4) **must never be consumed** near a computer.

And if some liquid (5) **is spilled** onto your computer, the power (6) must **be switched** off immediately. It must be completely dry before it (7) **is turned** on again.

A computer (8) **should be cleaned** regularly. A slightly damp cloth is best. No chemical cleaners. All right? But a glass cleaner (9) **can be sprayed** onto the monitor screen to clean it.

And one last thing. When a computer (10) **is switched** off it (11) **should not be turned** on again right away.

Now, can you remember all this?

UNDERSTANDING THE GRAMMAR POINT

1. **Passive**
2.

Active verb	Passive verb
1. should keep	**should be kept**
2. should put	**should be put**
3. should avoid	**should be avoided**
4. must never consume	**must never be consumed**
5. spill	**is spilled**
6. must switch	**must be switched**
7. turn	**is turned**
8. should clean	**should be cleaned**
9. can spray	**can be sprayed**
10. switch	**is switched**
11. should not turn	**should not be turned**

3. The passive of the present simple tense consists of:

modal verb + be + past partiple
should   be   kept

If there is no modal verb it consists of:

is/are + past participle
is   spilled

4. The speaker used the passive in the lecture because he did not want to mention who does each action (the agent).

CHECKING

1. The overall life of the car can be **increased** if it is **serviced** regularly.
2. The oil in your car should **be checked** frequently.
3. The oil must **be changed** after 10 thousand kilometers.
4. The tires must **be** checked for wear.
5. The tires should **be rotated** from time to time.
6. The spare wheel must **be inspected** occasionally.
7. The brakes must **be replaced** after 30 thousand kilometers.
8. The car should be **washed** every week.
9. It is best if the car is **kept** in a garage.
10. Above all, a car should be **driven** carefully.

COMMON ERRORS (from the Grammar Explanation section)

1. A damp cloth **is used** to clean it.
2. A computer should **be kept** in a cool place.
3. Computers must **be cared for** properly.

UNIT 44

ERROR BOX

The man **died** suddenly.
It consists of chocolate ~~the cake~~. OR **The cake** consists of chocolate.

LISTENING TO COMPREHEND

Brad	Sook
✔ a swim suit	✔ dentist
___ father	___ mother
✔ a cake	✔ a car
✔ mother	✔ a ball
___ a window	✔ father
✔ an orchestra	✔ a forest

LISTENING TO NOTICE

Brad's dreams

I often dream about my mother. Sometimes I dream that she is dying. You see, my mother (1) **died** when I was still a small child. Sometimes I dream I am outside a house and the door (2) **opens**. I can see my mother standing there but somehow I can't go in to join her. Then after a while she (3) **disappears**. Sometimes, though, I have nice dreams about my mother. Once I dreamed it was my birthday and my mother had given me a big cake which (4) **consisted** entirely of ice cream. And once something really funny (5) **occurred** in a dream. My mother was dressed in a swim suit conducting an orchestra.

Sook's dreams

I often have nightmares about my father. Once I dreamed I was at the dentist and the dentist (1) **changed** into my father. Another time I dreamed my father was driving a car that was trying to hit me. I ran and ran and just as the car was about to hit me it (2) **stopped**. Then there was the time I dreamed I was in a dark forest and a tree (3) **fell** on me. Except it wasn't a tree — it was my father! The other night something really strange (4) **happened** in my dream. My father threw a ball to me. The ball (5) **increased** in size until it was bigger than me.

UNDERSTANDING THE GRAMMAR POINT

1. The verbs in these sentences are in the PASSIVE but they should be in the ACTIVE

   1. My mother **died**.
   2. My mother **disappeared**.
   3. A strange thing **happened**.
   4. A funny thing **occurred**.
   5. A tree **fell** on me.
   6. The cake **consisted** of ice cream.

Some verbs such as *die* and *disappear* describe events that have no known cause. They can be used only in the **ACTIVE** voice. They cannot be used in the **PASSIVE** voice.

2. The **(a)** sentences refer to events that take place without any known cause and so use the active voice. The **(b)** sentences refer to events where the speaker knows the cause (*who* did the action) but does not want to say what it is and so uses the passive voice.

3. Verbs that can be used only in the active:

   become, continue, fall in love, decline, rise, disappear

   Verbs that can be used in the active and passive:

   decrease, hurt, break, sink, dry, develop, close

CHECKING

1. Last year my father **died** suddenly.
2. **A strange thing happened** to me.
3. The window opened by itself.
4. My head suddenly **increased** in size a lot.

5. **A strange thing occurred** the other day.
6. **The evening grew very dark.**
7. A slate from the roof **fell** on me.
8. **The cake consisted of chocolate and icing**.
9. The weather sudddenly **changed** for the better.
10. **The rain stopped suddenly**.

COMMON ERRORS (from the Grammar Explanation section)
1. A very strange thing ~~was~~ happened.
2. A very strange thing **happened**.
3. The wet clothes ~~were~~ dried quickly in the sun.

UNIT 45

ERROR BOX
A: I don't want to take a cruise.
B: Me neither. (Neither do I.)

LISTENING TO COMPREHEND
1.

place	still considering?		If not, why not?
	Yes	No	
Hawaii	__	✔	**They've been there before.**
Venice	__	✔	**Too many tourists in the summer.**
The Rocky Mountains	✔	__	

LISTENING TO NOTICE
Paula: OK, where should we go during the holidays? How about Hawaii? I've always had a good time there.
Alonzo: (1) **I have, too.** And I love those beaches!
Paula: (2) **So do I.** But I don't want to keep going back to the same place every year.
Alonzo: (3) **I don't, either.** All right, let's go someplace else this year.
Paula: We've never been to Venice. I'd love to see Venice.
Alonzo: (4) **I would, too.** But the crowds are terrible in the summer. And I don't want to find myself surrounded by so many other tourists.
Paula: Well, (5) **neither do I.** But I don't think it's as nice there during the winter.
Alonzo: (6) **I don't, either.**
Paula:What about the Rockies? I wouldn't mind having a vacation closer to home.
Alonzo: (7) **I wouldn't, either.** Since we have only a week, I don't want to deal with jet lag.
Paula: (8) **Neither do I.** And I think it would be nice to do a lot of hiking and bicycling.
Alonzo: (9) **I do, too.** I'll ask people I know about nice hotels and places to visit.
Paula: (10) **So will I.**

UNDERSTANDING THE GRAMMAR POINT
1. Positive
You can use ...*too*:
•I have, too.
•I would, too.
•I do, too
You can use *So* ....
•So do I.
•So will I.

Negative
You can use ...*either*:
•I don't either.
•I don't either.
•I wouldn't, either.
You can use *Neither*...
•Neither do I.
•Neither do I.

2. *I do, too.* vs. *So do I.*
    The word order is inverted (the subject goes last) with *so.*
I don't, either. vs. *Neither do I.*
    The word order is inverted and the auxiliary verb becomes affirmative with *neither.*

CHECKING
1. A:•Northwest Arilines flies from Tokyo to Beijing.
    B: **So does** Japan Airlines. (OR Japan Airlines does, too.)
2. A: Hawaii is a very popular vacation spot.
    B: Florida is, too.

3. A: Trains to my town are not very frequent.
    B: Buses **aren't, either**. (**Neither are** buses.)
4. A: Sydney is a fascinating city to visit.
    B: Melbourne **is**, too.
5. A: I enjoyed our holiday in Thailand.
    B: So **did** the rest of my family.

COMMON ERRORS (from the Grammar Explanation section)
1. **I don't, either.** or **Neither do I.**
2. **I do, too.** or **So do I.**
3. So **does he.**
    Neither **can they**.

UNIT 46

ERROR BOX
The doorway is **too** narrow to get the sofa through.
He is **strong enough** to carry those boxes.

LISTENING TO COMPREHEND
1. Where is this conversation taking place?
    In a new apartment
2. Why isn't the piano in the room where they had planned to put it?
    The doorway was too narrow./The piano was too big to get through the door.
3. How are they going to spend the rest of the day?
    Going out to dinner

LISTENING TO NOTICE
Mike: Well, I think that's (1) **enough** work for one day!
Toni: Why didn't you put that big piano in the extra bedroom?
Mike: The doorway is (2) **too narrow**. It's not (3) **wide enough** to get the piano through.
Toni: Did you try?
Mike: No, I know the opening isn't (4) **big enough**. Anyway, it's (5) **too heavy** to move, especially since neither of us is an Olympic weightlifter.
Toni: Never mind. Right now I'm (6) **too tired** to care.
Mike: I hope you're (7) **awake enough** to celebrate the big move. I made a dinner reservation for 7:30. We have (8) **enough time** to wash up and change clothes.
Toni: Well, I certainly have (9) **enough energy** to go out for a nice meal. But not at that Thai restaurant we went to last time, I hope. The food was (10) **too spicy** to eat.

UNDERSTANDING THE GRAMMAR POINT
1.

TOO	ENOUGH (with nouns)	ENOUGH (with adjectives)
too narrow	enough work	wide enough
too heavy	enough time	big enough
too tired	enough energy	awake enough
too spicy		

2. **Adjectives** always follow **too**.
    Enough **precedes the noun.**
    Enough follows an adjective.
    The *to* form of the verb (*to go*) follows *too* and *enough.*
3. A. The doorway is too narrow.
        We can't get the piano through the doorway.
    B. That's enough work for one day.
        We don't need to do any more work.
4.- We use the word **too** to express the idea of *excessive.*. This has a negative meaning.
    - We use the word **enough** to express the idea of *sufficient.* This has a positive meaning.

167

CHECKING

1. The table was **too heavy** for one person to lift.
2. It's too late to start moving our things; we'll begin tomorrow morning.
3. Are you **too tired** to move anything else?
4. These boxes aren't heavy; they're light enough for me to carry.
5. The closet is **big enough** to store all our sports equipment.
6. The door was **wide enough** to get the sofa through. (or **too narrow**)
7. This apartment is **too expensive**; we'll have to find a cheaper one.
8. I am **strong enough** to lift this chair by myself.

COMMON ERRORS (from the Grammar Explanation section)

1. The doorway is **too** narrow to get the sofa through.
2. The doorway is **too** narrow to get the sofa through.
3. She is **strong enough** to lift the table by herself.
4. We already have **enough furniture** in that room.

UNIT 47

ERROR BOX

I don't know where ~~do~~ I want to go.

LISTENING TO COMPREHEND

1. __ free hotel rooms
   ✔ the cheapest fares
   ✔ vacation planning
   __ free travel once a year
   __ homestay programs for teenagers
   ✔ discounts at restaurants and shops
   __ special services for senior citizens
   __ free membership for the first year

LISTENING TO NOTICE

How (1) **can you get** more value for your travel dollar? If this is a question you've been asking, then you should find out what (2) **the All-Continent Travel Club has** for you.
All-Continent Travel Club is a full-service club. Where (3) **do you want** to go? We'll help you find the cheapest fares. What (4) **would you like** to do? We'll help you plan your ideal vacation. We'll tell you how (5) **you can enjoy** discounts at hotels, restaurants and shops at your favorite destinations. (6) How much **do all these benefits cost**? Only $50 a year. If you think about how much (7) **you can save** the very first time you use our service, it's like having a free membership.
Call us now at 1-888-543-6936. You'll soon learn why (8) **the All-Continent Travel Club is** the traveler's best friend.

UNDERSTANDING THE GRAMMAR POINT

1.

Sentence starts with WH question
1. How can you get more value for your travel dollar?
2. Where do you want to go?
3. What would you like to do?
4. How much do all these benefits cost?

WH question is embedded
1. You should find out what the All-Continent Travel Club has for you.
2. We'll tell you how you can enjoy discounts at hotels, restaurants and shops at your favorite destinations.
3. If you think about how much you can save the very first time you use our service, it's like having a free membership.
4. You'll soon learn why the All-Continent Travel Club is the traveler's best friend.

2. The auxiliary verb **do/does** or **did** in a direct question is deleted in an embedded question. The tense marking goes to the main verb.

When does he arrive? > I don't know when ~~does~~ he arrive__s__.
When did he arrive? > I don't know when ~~did~~ he arrive__d__.
Other auxiliary verbs (**is/are, was/were, can**) are inverted in an embedded question.
When is he arriving? > I don't know when he **is** arriving.
When can we leave? > I don't know when we **can** leave.
3. He wanted to know what country I am visiting.
The *be* auxiliary verb was not correctly inverted.

CHECKING

1. Do you know when **the flight arrives**?
2. Masako is not sure **how long she can be away.**
3. I wonder how long **the ship takes to reach Shanghai.**
4. Tell me where you want to go in Italy.
5. I don't know **how much a membership costs.**
6. The travel agent asked me what kind of vacation I want to take.
7. I wonder **how the weather in Ireland is at this time of year.**
8. My friend Antonio asked **me when we would visit him in Costa Rica.**

COMMON ERRORS (from the Grammar Explanation section)

1. The travel agent wants to know when **you are** going to pick up the ticket.
   I don't know how **I can** make reservations for that sightseeing tour.
2. My wife wants to know if (**whether**) **she will** have time to shop each day.
   I will ask them **if** (**whether**) this tour **includes** all meals.
3. She was wondering **if** (**whether**) she could stay an extra day or two in Capetown.

UNIT 48

ERROR BOX

Chirashi consists of raw fish which the chef arranges ~~it~~ over a bowl of rice.
Maki-sushi consists of a long roll of rice **that** (**which**) is covered with seaweed.

LISTENING TO COMPREHEND

top picture: nigiri-sushi
second from top: chirashi-sushi
third from top: maki-sushi
bottom: sashimi

LISTENING TO NOTICE

Hi, my name is Michiko. I want to tell you about my favorite food — sushi! Mmmm!
Do you know what sushi is? Well, it consists of pieces of raw fish (1) **which the chef serves with** chunks of rice. There are many different kinds of sushi. I hope you'll try them all.
Maki-sushi consists of a long roll of rice (2) **that is covered with** seaweed. To make it the chef uses a bamboo mat (3) **which he covers with** seaweed, rice and strips of tuna.
Nigiri-sushi consists of pieces of fish (4) **which the chef places** on top of fingers of rice.
Sashimi is an assortment of raw fish (5) **that the chef serves** with shredded radish, often as an appetizer.
Chirashi consists of sashimi and chopped vegetables (6) **which the chef arranges** over a bowl of rice.
Sushi is usually eaten with soy sauce and wasabi (green horseradish) (7) **that you mix together** in a small bowl.
Now, why don't you try some sushi? You'll love it!

UNDERSTANDING THE GRAMMAR POINT

Sentence 1	Sentence 2
1. Sushi consists of pieces of raw fish.	The chef serves the raw fish with chunks of rice.
2. Maki-sushi consists of a long roll of rice.	The rice is covered with seaweed.
3. To make it the chef uses a bamboo mat.	He covers the bamboo mat with seaweed, rice and strips of tuna.

4. Nigiri-sushi consists of pieces of fish. | The chef places the pieces of fish on top of fingers of rice.

5. Sashimi is an assortment of raw fish. | The chef serves the assortment of raw fish with shredded radish.

6. Chirashi consists of sashimi and chopped vegetables. | The chef serves the sashimi and chopped vegetables over a bowl of rice.

7. Sushi is usually eaten with soy sauce and wasabi. | You mix the soy sauce and wasabi together in a small bowl.

2.

1. It consists of pieces of raw fish < which the chef serves with chunks of rice.

2. Maki-sushi consists of a long roll of rice < that is covered with seaweed.

3. To make it the chef uses a bamboo mat < which he covers with seaweed, rice and strips of tuna.

4. Nigiri-sushi consist of pieces of raw fish < that the chef places on top of fingers of rice.

5. Sashimi is an assortment of raw fish < that the chef serves with shredded radish, often as an appetizer.

6. Chirashi consists of sashimi and chopped vegetables < which the chef arranges over a bowl of rice.

7. Sushi is usually eaten with soy sauce and wasabi < that you mix together in a small bowl.

CHECKING

1. Tempura is a Japanese dish. It consists of seafood and vegetables **that** (or **which**) have been lightly fried in batter.

2. Chapati is an Indian food. It is a kind of bread that the cook makes ~~it~~ with wholemeal flour.

3. Paella is a Spanish dish. It is made with rice **that** (or **which**) the chef cooks with seafood.

4. Mtedza is a Malawian dish. It is a meat stew which the cook makes ~~it~~ with minced groundnuts.

5. Spaghetti bolognese is an Italian dish. It consists of a rich meat sauce **that** (or **which**) the chef serves over spaghetti.

6. A Cornish pasty is an English food. It is a small pie **which** (or **that**) the chef fills with potatoes and meat.

COMMON ERRORS (from the Grammar Explanation section)

1. Sushi consists of raw fish that ~~it~~ is served with rice.
   Sushi consists of raw fish which you eat ~~it~~ with rice.

2. Paella is made with rice **which** (that) the chef cooks with seafood.

3. Sushi consists of raw fish **which** (that) is eaten with rice.

4. Sushi consists of raw fish **which** (that) is eaten with rice.

UNIT 49

ERROR BOX

Hawaii is a place where thousands of people get married ~~there~~ every year.
Hawaii is a place where **there** are many chapels.

LISTENING TO COMPREHEND

1. The five places mentioned are:
   1. **a zoological garden**
   2. **a volcanic crater**
   3. **a tennis court**
   4. **underwater in a submarine**
   5. **in the sky**

2. The three times are:
   1. **at dawn**
   2. **at midday**
   3. **in the evening**

LISTENING TO NOTICE

Are you about to get married? Are you looking for a wedding with a difference? How about Hawaii?

Hawaii is a place (1) **where** thousands of couples say or renew their vows every year.

You can get married in a zoological garden, (2) **where** there is a chapel by the sea.

Or you can choose a volcanic crater, (3) **where** the service is held in a helicopter.

Or you can do it on a tennis court (4) **where** the minister calls out "Love-all."

Or you can choose underwater in a submarine, (5) **where** you are surrounded by tropical fish.

Or you can get married in the sky, (6) **where** the service is held with everyone in parachutes.

And there are also different times (7) **when** you can get married. You can get married at dawn, (8) **when** the sun rises over the mountains, or at midday, (9) **when** the sun beats down on the beaches, or in the evening (10) **when** the sun sets over the ocean.

Hawaii offers you a wedding that you will never forget. A wedding made in paradise. Call the Hawaii Visitors Bureau at (808) 923-1811.

UNDERSTANDING THE GRAMMAR POINT

1.

WHERE	WHEN
place	times
zoological garden	dawn
volcanic crater	midday
tennis court	evening
submarine	
sky	

- Use *where* to refer to a place. Use *when* to refer to a time.

2.

Sentence 1	Sentence 2
1. Hawaii is a place.	Thousands of couples say or renew their vows there every year.
2. You can choose a zoological garden.	There is a chapel by the sea there.
3. Or you can choose a volcanic crater.	The service is held in a helicopter there.
4. Or you can do it on a tennis court.	The minister calls out "Love-all" there.
5. Or you can choose underwater in a submarine.	You are surrounded by tropical fish there.
6. Or you can get married in the sky.	The service is held with everyone in parachutes there.
7. There are also different times.	You can get married then.
8. You can get married at dawn.	The sun rises over the mountains then.
9. Or you can get married at midday.	The sun beats down on the beaches then.
10. Or you can get married in the evening.	The sun sets over the ocean then.

3. Hawaii is a place where thousands of couples say or renew their vows ~~there~~ every year.

The error is the use of **there** in the relative clause. This has the same reference as the relative pronoun **where** and should not be included.

CHECKING

1. Wolfgang and Maria got married last year ~~that~~ **when** they were on holiday ~~then~~ in Hawaii.

2. The service was held in an old church where the minister began

the service ~~there~~ with a traditional Hawaiian song.

3. They were married early in the morning when **it** was cool and the birds were singing ~~then~~.

4. They stayed in a hotel ~~and~~ where newlyweds are especially welcome.

5. "That was a time when we were ~~then~~ perfectly happy," they said.

COMMON ERRORS (from the Grammar Explanation section)

1. They got married in a zoological garden **where** there is a chapel by the sea.
   They got married in the evening **when** it was cool.

2. They got married in a zoological garden where **there** is a chapel by the sea.
   They got married in the evening when **it** was cool.

3. Hawaii is a place where many people get married ~~there~~.
   They got married in the evening when it is cool ~~then~~.

4. They stayed in a hotel **which** (**that**) caters especially to newlyweds.
   "That was an experience **which** (**that**) we will never forget," they said.

UNIT 50

ERROR BOX

The novel is about a girl whose ~~her~~ parents die in a plane crash.
The novel is about a girl **whose** parents die in a plane crash.

LISTENING TO COMPREHEND

Book	Main Character
The Color Purple	**an African American woman**
The Day of the Jackal	**an assassin**
The Invisible Man	**an African American traveler**
The Remains of the Day	**an English butler**
The Ginger Tree	**a young Scottish woman**
The Passion	**Henri, Napoleon's cook**

LISTENING TO NOTICE

The Color Purple by Alice Walker
This novel is in the form of letters written by <u>an African American woman</u> (1) **whose life** is made miserable by her cruel husband.

The Day of the Jackal by Frederick Forsyth
This thriller tells the story of <u>an assassin</u> (2) **whose attempt** to shoot the French president, Charles de Gaulle, nearly succeeds.

The Invisible Man by Ralph Ellison
This novel tells the story of <u>an African American man</u> (3) **whose journey** through America reveals the chronic racism of that country.

The Remains of the Day by Kazuo Ishiguro
This is the strange story of <u>an English butler</u> (4) **whose life** is governed by his complete loyalty to his master.

The Ginger Tree by Oswald Wynd
This novel tells the story of <u>a young Scottish woman</u> (5) **whose marriage** to a young English officer in China is a failure.

The Passion by Jeanette Winterson
This historical romance tell the story of <u>Henri, Napoleon's cook</u> (6) **whose love** is happily accepted by Villanelle, the daughter of a Venetian boatman.

UNDERSTANDING THE GRAMMAR POINT

1. *The Color Purple*
   This novel is in the form of letters written by <u>an African American woman</u>.
   Her life was made miserable by her cruel husband.

   The Day of the Jackal
   This thriller tells the story of <u>an assassin</u>.
   His attempt to shoot the French president, Charles de Gaulle,

nearly succeeds.

The Invisible Man
This novel tells the story of <u>an African American man</u>.
His journey through America reveals the chronic racism of that country.

The Remains of the Day
This is a strange story of <u>an English butler</u>.
His life is governed by his complete loyalty to his master.

The Ginger Tree
This novel tells the story of <u>a young Scottish woman</u>.
Her marriage to a young English officer in China is a failure.

The Passion
This historical romance tells the story of <u>Henri, Napoleon's cook</u>.
His love is happily accepted by Villanelle, the daughter of a Venetian boatman.

2.

1. This novel is in the form of letters written by <u>an African American woman</u> > <u>whose</u> life is made...
2. This thriller tells the story of <u>an assassin</u> > <u>whose</u> attempt to shoot the French president,...
3. This novel tells the story of <u>an African American man</u> > <u>whose</u> journey through America...
4. This is the strange story of <u>an English butler</u> > <u>whose</u> life is governed...
5. This novel tells the story of <u>a young Scottish woman</u> > <u>whose</u> marriage to a young...
6. This historical romance tells the story of <u>Henri</u>, Napoleon's cook, > <u>whose</u> love is happily...

CHECKING

The Murder by Grant Nelson
This is a story of a man **whose** murder leads to the resignation of the president of the United States.

Funeral Service by Colin Coffin
In this short novel we follow the story of a man **whose** ~~his~~ life is changed by the death of his father.

Sad Ending by Marilyn Hornchurch
This bittersweet comedy tells the story of two teenagers **whose** parents try to destroy their marriage.

Broken Glass by Stephanie Bottle
This exciting thriller is about a woman **whose** ~~the~~ government imprisons her husband as a spy.

COMMON ERRORS (from the Grammar Explanation section)

1. We helped the woman **whose** purse was stolen.
2. We helped the woman whose ~~her~~ purse was stolen.
   We helped the boy whose ~~the~~ father is ill.

LEVEL 5 REVIEW TESTS

TEST A

1. allowed (Unit 43) 2. had (Unit 42) 3. which (Unit 48) 4. enough (Unit 46) 5. dirty (Unit 41) 6. are (Unit 43) 7. she kept (Unit 47) 8. do (Unit 45) 9. too (Unit 46) 10. where (Unit 49) 11. whose (Unit 50) 12. increasing (Unit 44)

TEST B

1. where (Unit 49) 2. had (Unit 42) 3. does (Unit 45) 4. which (Unit 48) 5. she worked (Unit 47) 6. whose (Unit 50) 7. consists (Unit 44) 8. too (Unit 46) 9. is (Unit 43) 10. changes (Unit 44) 11. efficient (Unit 41) 12. fun (Unit 41)

a few 9, 22
a little 9, 22
a lot (of) 9
a / an 32, 33
adjectives 6, 15, 23, 37, 41
adjectives (-ing) 37
adverb position 15, 21
adverbials 4
adverbial clauses 42
adverbs 15, 21
adverbs of manner 15, 21
agentless passives 43
agreement (*too, so, either, neither*) 45
agreement (subject-verb) 18
already 42
always 37
another 34
any 9
articles 31, 32, 33
as 24, 25
at 13, 14
auxiliary verbs 4, 5, 11, 19, 29, 30, 37, 42
be 3, 10
by 42, 43
can 27
causative verbs 36
comparatives 22, 23, 24, 25
complements 35
conditional statements 39, 40
contractions 1, 2, 26
contrast 23, 24, 25
could 27
countable nouns 7, 8, 9, 22, 32
definite article *the* 31, 33
determiners 9, 22
did 16
do 5
does 5
either 45
embedded questions 47
enough 46
expressions of similarity 24
few 22
for 29
from 25
future 38, 39
gerunds 35
have 3
have to 28
he 1
how 20, 47
how much 20, 47

hypothetical conditional 39, 40
if 39, 40
in 13, 14
indefinite articles 32
indefinite past 19
infinitives 35
-ing in adjectives 37
intonation in questions 10
intransitive process verbs 44
intransitive verbs 17, 37, 44
inversion in *wh-* questions 20
inversion in *yes/no* questions 10
irregular verbs 12
it 1
it is 26
let 36
like 24
little 22
location, prepositions of 14
make 36
many 9
mass nouns 8, 9, 22, 32
may 27
might 27, 28
modal verbs 27, 28
modals of obligation 28
modals of possibility 27
much 9
must 28
negatives 6
neither 45
no 6
not 6
not...either 45
noncount nouns 8, 9, 32
non-referential subject (*there is*) 2, 26
non-referential subject (*it is*) 26
nouns
    countable 7, 8, 9, 22, 31, 33
    definite article *the* 31, 33
    indefinite article *a/an* 32
    irregular 7
    mass vs. plural 8
    noncount 8, 9, 22, 32
    nouns ending in *-y* 41
    plural 2, 7, 8
    plural and singular determiners 9
    proper 31
    singular 2, 7, 8
    uncountable 8, 9, 32
omission of indefinite article *a /an* 32, 33
omission of definite article *the* 31, 33

on 13, 14
other 34
participial adjectives 37
passive voice 43
past tense 12, 16, 29, 30
past continuous 30
past perfect 42
place, expressions of 49
plural nouns 2, 7, 9
possession, expressions of 3, 50
possible conditional 39
prepositions 13, 14, 25
prepositional phrases 13, 14
prepositions in comparisons 25
prepositions in expressions of time 13
prepositions of location and direction 14
present continuous 4, 11, 37
present perfect 19, 29
proforms 45
pronouns 1
questions 5, 10, 16, 20, 47
really 37
relative clauses with *where* and *when* 49
relative clauses with *which* and *that* 48
relative clauses with *whose* 50
relative pronouns 48, 49, 50
several 9
she 1
should 28
simple past 12, 16, 30
simple past (vs. present perfect) 29
simple present 4, 11, 18, 38
since 29
singular nouns 2
so 45
some 9
sometimes 37
stative verbs with simple present 11
subject-verb agreement 18
superlatives 23
than 25
that 48
the 9, 31, 33
the other 34
there are 2, 26
there is 2, 26
third-person singular pronouns 1
time, expressions of 13, 49
to 14, 25
too 45, 46
transitive verbs 17, 37, 44
uncountable nouns 8, 9, 32
unique reference
    with and without *the* 31

unreal conditional 40
verb complements 35
verbs (-ing) 37
verbs (modal) 27, 28
verb tense:
    future 38
    past continuous 30
    past perfect 42
    present continuous 4, 11, 37
    present perfect 19, 29
    simple past 12, 16, 30
    simple past (vs. present perfect) 29
    simple present 4, 11, 18, 38
very 37
wh- questions 20
what 20, 47
when 20, 49
where 20, 47, 49
which 48
who 20
whose 50
why 20, 47
with 25
yes/no questions with *be* 10, 16
yes/no questions with *do/does* 5
yes/no questions with
    simple past tense 16